THE UNITED STATES AND CANADA

PEARSON

Prentice
Hall

Needham, Massachusetts
Upper Saddle River, New Jersey

Program Consultants

Heidi Hayes Jacobs

Heidi Hayes Jacobs has served as an educational consultant to more than 1,000 schools across the nation and abroad. Dr. Jacobs served as an adjunct professor in the Department of Curriculum on Teaching at Teachers College, Columbia University. She has written a best-selling book and numerous articles on curriculum reform. She completed her undergraduate studies at the University of Utah in her hometown of Salt Lake City. She received an M.A. from the University of Massachusetts, Amherst, and completed her doctoral work at Columbia University's Teachers College in 1981.

The backbone of Dr. Jacobs' experience comes from her years as a teacher of high school, middle school, and elementary school students. As an educational consultant, she works with K–12 schools and districts on curriculum reform and strategic planning.

Brenda Randolph

Brenda Randolph is the former Director of the Outreach Resource Center at the African Studies Program at Howard University, Washington, D.C. She is the Founder and Director of Africa Access, a bibliographic service on Africa for schools. She received her B.A. in history with high honors from North Carolina Central University, Durham, and her M.A. in African studies with honors from Howard University. She completed further graduate studies at the University of Maryland, College Park, where she was awarded a Graduate Fellowship.

Brenda Randolph has published numerous articles in professional journals and bulletins. She currently serves as library media specialist in Montgomery County Public Schools, Maryland.

Michal L. LeVasseur

Michal LeVasseur is an educational consultant in the field of geography. She is an adjunct professor of geography at the University of Alabama, Birmingham, and serves with the Alabama Geographic Alliance. Her undergraduate and graduate work is in the fields of anthropology (B.A.), geography (M.A.), and science education (Ph.D.).

Dr. LeVasseur's specialization has moved increasingly into the area of geography education. In 1996, she served as Director of the National Geographic Society's Summer Geography Workshop. As an educational consultant, she has worked with the National Geographic Society as well as with schools to develop programs and curricula for geography.

Special Program Consultant

Yvonne S. Gentzler, Ph.D.
Iowa State University
College of Family and Consumer Sciences
Ames, Iowa

ISBN 0-13-062976-6

2 3 4 5 6 7 8 9 10   07 06 05 04 03

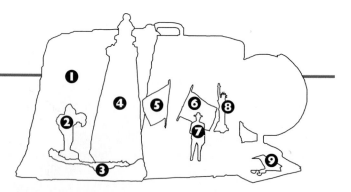

On the Cover

1 Quilt
2 Kachina
3 Native American corn necklace
4 Folk art lighthouse
5 American flag
6 Canadian flag
7 Canadian Mountie figure
8 Statue of Liberty figure
9 Canadian money

Content Consultants for the World Explorer Program

Africa
Barbara Brown
African Studies Center
Boston University
Boston, Massachusetts

Ancient World
Maud Gleason
Department of Classics
Stanford University
Stanford, California

East Asia
Leslie Swartz
Vice President for Program
    Development and Harvard East
    Asian Outreach Program at The
    Children's Museum, Boston
Boston, Massachusetts

Latin America
Daniel Mugan
Center for Latin American Studies
University of Florida
Gainesville, Florida

Middle East
Elizabeth Barlow
Center for Middle Eastern and
    North African Studies
University of Michigan
Ann Arbor, Michigan

North Africa
Laurence Michalak
Center for Middle East Studies
University of California
Berkeley, California

Religion
Michael Sells
Department of Religion
Haverford College
Haverford, Pennsylvania

Russia, Eastern Europe,
Central Asia
Janet Vaillant
Davis Center for Russian Studies
Harvard University
Cambridge, Massachusetts

South Asia
Robert Young
Department of History
West Chester University
West Chester, Pennsylvania

Western Europe
Ruth Mitchell-Pitts
Center for West European Studies
University of North Carolina
Chapel Hill, North Carolina

Teacher Advisory Board

Jerome Balin
Lincoln Junior High School
Naperville, Illinois

Elizabeth Barrett
Tates Creek Middle School
Lexington, Kentucky

Tricia Creasey
Brown Middle School
Thomasville, North Carolina

Patricia H. Guillory
Fulton County Schools
Atlanta, Georgia

Stephanie Hawkins
Oklahoma City Public Schools
Oklahoma City, Oklahoma

Fred Hitz
Wilson Middle School
Muncie, Indiana

Kristi Karis
West Ottawa Public Schools
Holland, Michigan

Peggy Lehman
Carmel Junior High/Carmel-Clay
    Schools
Carmel, Indiana

Peggy McCarthy
Beulah School
Beulah, Colorado

Cindy McCurdy
Hefner Middle School
Oklahoma City, Oklahoma

Deborah J. Miller
Detroit Public Schools
Detroit, Michigan

Lawrence Peglow
Pittsburgh Public Schools
Pittsburgh, Pennsylvania

Paula Rardin
Riverview Gardens Schools
St. Louis, Missouri

Kent E. Riley
Perry Meridian Middle School
Indianapolis, Indiana

Christy Sarver
Brown Middle School
Thomasville, North Carolina

Lyn Shiver
Northwestern Middle School
Alpharetta, Georgia

Mark Stahl
Longfellow Middle School
Norman, Oklahoma

TABLE OF CONTENTS

THE UNITED STATES AND CANADA   1

	ACTIVITY ATLAS	2
CHAPTER 1	The United States and Canada: Physical Geography	8
	1 Land and Water	9
	2 Climate and Vegetation	15
	3 Natural Resources	21
	Skills Activity Using Distribution Maps	26
	Chapter 1 Review and Activities	28
	Activity Shop Lab Making a Model River	30
CHAPTER 2	The United States and Canada: Shaped by History	32
	1 The First Americans and the Arrival of the Europeans	33
	2 Growth, Settlement, and Civil War in the United States	38
	3 The United States Becomes a World Power	44
	4 Growth, Settlement, and Independence in Canada	50
	5 Partners and Friends: The United States and Canada Today	56
	Skills Activity Interpreting Diagrams	62
	Chapter 2 Review and Activities	64
	Activity Shop Interdisciplinary Transportation	66
CHAPTER 3	Cultures of the United States and Canada	68
	1 The United States: A Nation of Immigrants	69
	2 Canada: A Mosaic	75
	Skills Activity Organizing Information	80
	Chapter 3 Review and Activities	82
	Literature Western Wagons by Steven Vincent Benét	84

CHAPTER 4 **Exploring the United States**   **86**

  1 Culture The Northeast: Land of Big Cities   87
  2 Economics The South: A Changing Landscape   93
  3 Economics The Midwest: Moving From the Farm   99
  4 Economics The West: Using Resources Wisely   105
     Skills Activity Understanding Circle Graphs   110
     Chapter 4 Review and Activities   112
     Literature From *Childtimes* by Eloise
        Greenfield *et al.*   114

CHAPTER 5 **Exploring Canada**   **118**

  1 Culture Ontario and Quebec: Connecting Two Cultures   119
  2 Culture The Canadian Plains: Canada's Breadbasket   127
  3 Culture British Columbia: Ties to the Pacific Rim   132
  4 Economics The Atlantic Provinces: United by the Seas   138
  5 Geography The Northern Territories: New Frontiers   142
     Skills Activity Writing for a Purpose   146
     Chapter 5 Review and Activities   148

     PROJECT POSSIBILITIES   **150**

     REFERENCE   **152**
     Map and Globe Handbook   153
     Regional Database   170
     Atlas   192
     Glossary of Geographic Terms   208
     Gazetteer   210
     Glossary   212
     Index   216
     Acknowledgments   226

OF SPECIAL INTEREST

Maps and charts providing a closer look at countries, regions, and provinces.

The Northeast	88
The South	94
The Midwest	100
The West	106
Ontario	121
Quebec	124
Prairie Provinces	128
British Columbia	133
Atlantic Provinces	139
Northern Territories	143

ACTIVITY SHOP

Step-by-step activities for exploring important topics in the United States and Canada

Lab: Making a Model River	30
Interdisciplinary: Transportation	66

CITIZEN HEROES

Profiles of people who made a difference in their country

Clara Barton	42
Louis Riel	53
Terry Fox	79
Cesar Chavez	109

REGIONAL DATABASE

Maps and statistics for every state and province in the U.S. and Canada

United States	170
Canada	186

SKILLS ACTIVITY

A hands-on approach to learning and applying social studies skills

Using Distribution Maps	26
Interpreting Diagrams	62
Organizing Information	80
Understanding Circle Graphs	110
Writing for a Purpose	146

LITERATURE

Literature selections by authors from the United States and Canada

Western Wagons by Stephen Vincent Benét	84
From *Childtimes* by Eloise Greenfield *et al.*	114

EXPLORING TECHNOLOGY

Detailed drawings show how the use of technology makes a country unique

A Southwestern Pueblo	34
The Brooklyn Bridge	90

STUDENT ART

A view of a country through the eyes of a student artist

Toronto and the CN Tower	54
Here's the Pitch	74

MAPS

United States and Canada:
Relative Location 2
United States and Canada: Relative Size 2
United States and Canada: Political 3
United States and Canada: Physical 4
United States and Canada: Land Use 5
United States and Canada: Climate 6
Tornadoes in the United States 17
United States and Canada: Vegetation 18
United States and Canada:
Natural Resources 23
Canada: Population Distribution 27
United States and Canada: Place Location 29
European Influence on North America 32
North America in 1783 36
Indian Removal During the 1830s 39
Growth of the United States From 1783 41
The Underground Railroad 42
Dates Provinces and Territories Joined Canada 55
Wind Patterns and Air Pollution 58
Canada: Place Location 65
Native Americans and Europeans, 1753 70
Native American Groups: Place Location 83
Regions of the United States 86
The Northeast: Population Density 88
An Urban Megalopolis 89
Crops in the South 94
The Midwest: Land Use 100
United States: Railroad Routes of the Late 1800s 103
The West: Natural Resources 106
United States: Place Location 113
Canada: Political 118
Ontario: Population Density 121
Quebec: Population Density 124
Prairie Provinces: Land Use 128
British Columbia: Natural Resources 133
Trade Routes Across the Pacific Ocean 136
Atlantic Provinces: Natural Resources 139

European Land Claims in
the United States and Canada, 1682 140
European Land Claims in
the United States and Canada, 1763 140
Northern Territories: Native American Groups 143
Canada: Place Location 149
Mercator Projection 160
Equal-Area Projection 161
Robinson Projection 161
Azimuthal Projection 161
West Africa: Population Density 162
Russia: Political 164
Hawaii: Physical 165
North Africa and the Middle East:
Oil Production 166
Regional Database 170
The United States: Political 170
The Northeast (U.S.): Political 172
The South (U.S.): Political 174
The Midwest (U.S.): Political 178
The West (U.S.): Political 182
Canada: Political 186
Atlas 192
The World: Political 192
The World: Physical 194
United States: Political 196
North and South America: Political 198
North and South America: Physical 199
Europe: Political 200
Europe: Physical 201
Africa: Political 202
Africa: Physical 203
Asia: Political 204
Asia: Physical 205
Australia, New Zealand, and the Pacific
Islands: Physical-Political 206
The Arctic and Antarctica 207

CHARTS, GRAPHS, AND TABLES

Immigration to the United States and Canada 7
Time Line: United States From the
1860s to 1990s 48
The Great Lakes–St. Lawrence Seaway 60
How a Locomotive Works 63
New York to St. Louis 67
Immigration to the United States, 1951–1998 71
Canada: Ethnic Groups 76
The Northeast: Population 88
The South: Land Use and Climate 94
The Midwest: Land Use 100
United States Farms, 1965–1999 101

The West: Energy and Resources 106
Average Yearly Precipitation 111
Ontario: Population 121
Quebec: Population 124
Prairie Provinces: Land Use and Climate 128
British Columbia: Natural Resources 133
Atlantic Provinces: Resources 139
Northern Territories: Ethnic Groups
and Population 143
Earth's Revolution and the Seasons 156
Climate Regions 168
Natural Vegetation Regions 169

READ ACTIVELY

How can I get the most out of my social studies book? How does my reading relate to my world? Answering questions like these means that you are an active reader, an involved reader. As an active reader, you are in charge of the reading situation!

The following strategies tell how to think and read as an active reader. You don't need to use all of these strategies all the time. Feel free to choose the ones that work best in each reading situation. You might use several at a time, or you might go back and forth among them. They can be used in any order.

BEFORE YOU READ

Give yourself a purpose

The sections in this book begin with a list called "Questions to Explore." These questions focus on key ideas presented in the section. They give you a purpose for reading. You can create your own purpose by asking questions like these: How does the topic relate to my life? How might I use what I learn at school or at home?

Preview

To preview a reading selection, first read its title. Then look at the pictures and read the captions. Also read any headings in the selection. Then ask yourself: What is the reading selection about? What do the pictures and headings tell about the selection?

Reach into your background

What do you already know about the topic of the selection? How can you use what you know to help you understand what you are going to read?

WHILE YOU READ

Ask questions

Suppose you are reading about the continent of South America. Some questions you might ask are: Where is South America? What countries are found there? Why are some of the countries large and others small? Asking questions like these can help you gather evidence and gain knowledge.

Predict

As you read, make a prediction about what will happen and why. Or predict how one fact might affect another fact. Suppose you are reading about South America's climate. You might make a prediction about how the climate affects where people live. You can change your mind as you gain new information.

Connect

Connect your reading to your own life. Are the people discussed in the selection like you or someone you know? What would you do in similar situations? Connect your reading to something you have already read. Suppose you have already read about the ancient Greeks. Now you are reading about the ancient Romans. How are they alike? How are they different?

Visualize

What would places, people, and events look like in a movie or a picture? As you read about India, you could visualize the country's heavy rains. What do they look like? How do they sound? As you read about geography, you could visualize a volcanic eruption.

AFTER YOU READ

Respond

Talk about what you have read. What did you think? Share your ideas with your classmates.

Assess yourself

What did you find out? Were your predictions on target? Did you find answers to your questions?

Follow up

Show what you know. Use what you have learned to do a project. When you do projects, you continue to learn.

THE UNITED STATES AND CANADA

Spreading "from sea to shining sea," the United States and Canada take up nearly seven-eighths of North America. In this book, you'll see how the United States and Canada are working to create a good life for every citizen in these vast countries.

GUIDING QUESTIONS

The readings and activities in this book will help you discover answers to these Guiding Questions.

1 GEOGRAPHY How has physical geography affected the cultures of the United States and Canada?

2 HISTORY How have historical events affected the cultures of the United States and Canada?

3 CULTURE How has the variety of people in the United States and Canada benefited and challenged the two nations?

4 GOVERNMENT How do the governments of the United States and Canada differ? How are they alike?

5 ECONOMICS How did the United States and Canada become two of the wealthiest nations in the world?

PROJECT PREVIEW

You can also discover answers to the Guiding Questions by working on projects. You can find several project possibilities on pages 150–151 at the back of this book.

1 How has physical geography affected the cultures of the United States and Canada?

2 How have historical events affected the cultures of the United States and Canada?

3 How has the variety of people in the United States and Canada benefited and challenged the two nations?

5 How did the United States and Canada become two of the wealthiest nations in the world?

4 How do the governments of the United States and Canada differ? How are they alike?

A journal can be your personal book of discovery. As you explore the United States and Canada, you can use your journal to keep track of things you learn and do. You can also record thoughts about your journey. For your first entry, write your thoughts on where in the United States and Canada you would like to go and what you would want to see there.

EXPLORER'S · JOURNAL

The United States and Canada

Learning about Canada and the United States means being an explorer and a geographer. No explorer would start out without first checking some facts. Begin by exploring the maps of the United States and Canada on the following pages.

Relative Location

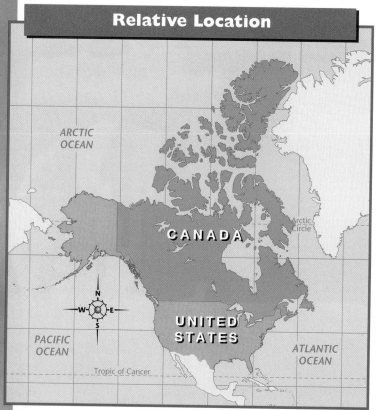

LOCATION

1. **Explore the Location of the United States and Canada** Look at the map at left. In this book you will read about the United States, which is colored orange on the map, and Canada, which is green. Which country extends farther north? If you were on the east coast of the United States, which direction would you travel to get to the Pacific Ocean? Why do Canadians think of the United States as their neighbor to the south?

Relative Size

REGIONS

2. **Compare the Sizes of the United States and Canada** Look at the map to the right. Compare it to the map above. Notice that not all of the United States is shown on the map at right. Which country do you think is bigger, the United States mainland or Canada? Check your estimate by looking up both of the countries in the Regional Database at the back of this book.

3. Explore the United States and Canada

The United States and Canada together take up most of the continent of North America. Look at the map. What other country is on the same continent? What countries border the United States? Name the cities that are the national capitals of the United States and Canada. Which two of the 50 United States do not share a border with any other state? Which states share a border with Canada? Which Canadian province reaches the farthest north?

4. Locate Bodies of Water Important to the United States and Canada

What three oceans surround the United States and Canada? Find the Great Lakes on the map. How many are there? Which one lies entirely within the United States? What river connects the Great Lakes to the Atlantic Ocean? The largest bay in the world is located in Canada. What is its name? Would you enter the bay from the Pacific Ocean or from the Atlantic Ocean?

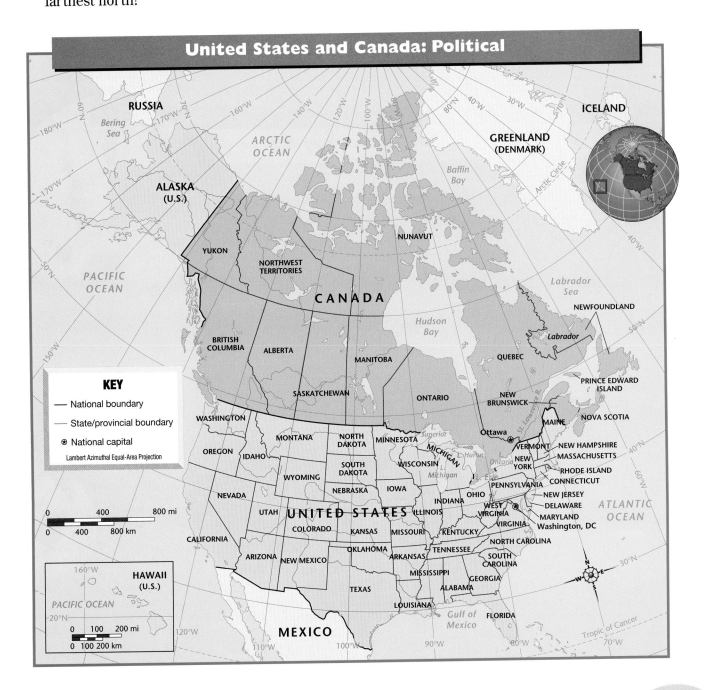

United States and Canada: Political

KEY
— National boundary
-- State/provincial boundary
⊛ National capital
Lambert Azimuthal Equal-Area Projection

PLACE

5. Find Geo Cleo   Geo Cleo is traveling through the United States and Canada. Use her clues and the map below to answer her questions about where she has been on her tour of the United States and Canada.

A. Whew! I've been hiking through the Rocky Mountains! Right now I'm heading south. I just crossed the Colorado River. What country am I in?

B. Today, I crossed the border of the United States, and I'm flying to Victoria Island in Canada. Which direction am I going?

C. Now I'm on a ship. We're heading from the Gulf of St. Lawrence to the Great Lakes. What river will we travel on?

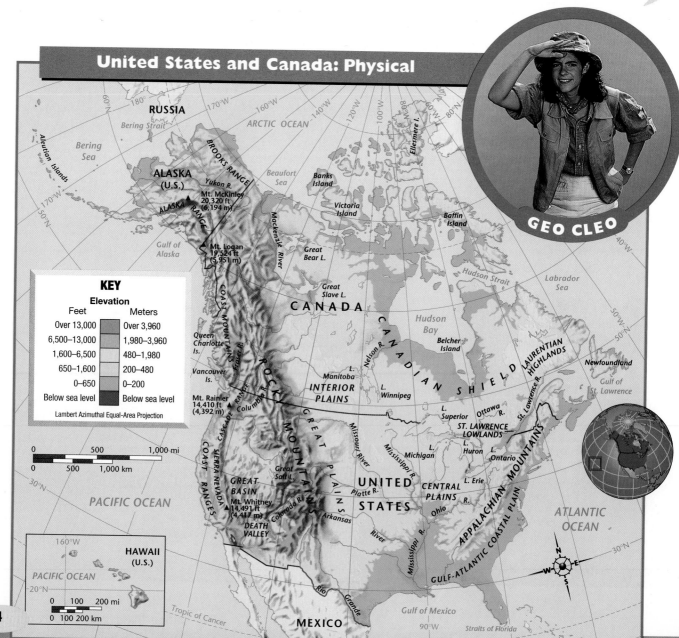

United States and Canada: Physical

GEO CLEO

KEY

Elevation

Feet	Meters
Over 13,000	Over 3,960
6,500–13,000	1,980–3,960
1,600–6,500	480–1,980
650–1,600	200–480
0–650	0–200
Below sea level	Below sea level

Lambert Azimuthal Equal-Area Projection

0   500   1,000 mi
0   500   1,000 km

HAWAII (U.S.)

PACIFIC OCEAN

0   100   200 mi
0   100 200 km

6. Investigate Land Use in the United States and Canada   The use of land is one of the main features of a place. How many different types of land use are identified on the map? Which is the most common use of the land in Canada? In the United States? Compare the use of land in the eastern half of the United States to that in the western half. What are the main differences?

7. Compare Land Use to Physical Features   Look at the physical map on the opposite page. Compare it to the land use map on this page. What relationship do you see between physical features and the way people use the land? How do people use the land in mountainous regions? What type of land seems to be good for farming? Look at the manufacturing areas. What physical feature is close to most of them?

United States and Canada: Land Use

RUSSIA

ICELAND

GREENLAND (DENMARK)

Bering Sea

ARCTIC OCEAN

ALASKA (U.S.)

Baffin Bay

Arctic Circle

Labrador Sea

KEY

- Nomadic herding
- Hunting and gathering
- Forestry
- Livestock raising
- Commercial farming
- Subsistence farming
- Manufacturing and trade
- Commercial fishing
- Little or no activity

Lambert Azimuthal Equal-Area Projection

Hudson Bay

C A N A D A

Great Lakes

U N I T E D   S T A T E S

PACIFIC OCEAN

ATLANTIC OCEAN

HAWAII (U.S.)

PACIFIC OCEAN

0   100   200 mi
0   100 200 km

0   400   800 mi
0   400   800 km

MEXICO

Gulf of Mexico

Tropic of Cancer

REGIONS

8. Investigate the Climates of the United States and Canada You already know that climate affects the way people live. For example, you don't find snowplows on the beach or skis in the desert! Look at the map below. How many different types of climate regions are there in the United States and Canada? Do the climates seem to change more from east to west or from north to south? Which of the two countries has a region of humid subtropical climate? Which has the biggest area of subarctic climate?

INTERACTION

9. Investigate How Climate Affects the Way People Live Look at the climate map below. What city fits each of these descriptions?

• In this area of marine west coast climate, winds blowing from the ocean help keep the climate very damp. People in this Canadian city are used to a climate with lots of rain.

• People who live here are in a tropical wet and dry climate. They do not own winter coats or boots, and many have never seen snow.

• The humid continental climate region includes some major cities of both countries. People here usually need clothes for all four seasons. Their houses must have good heating systems. Many are also air conditioned in the summer. This city is on Lake Michigan.

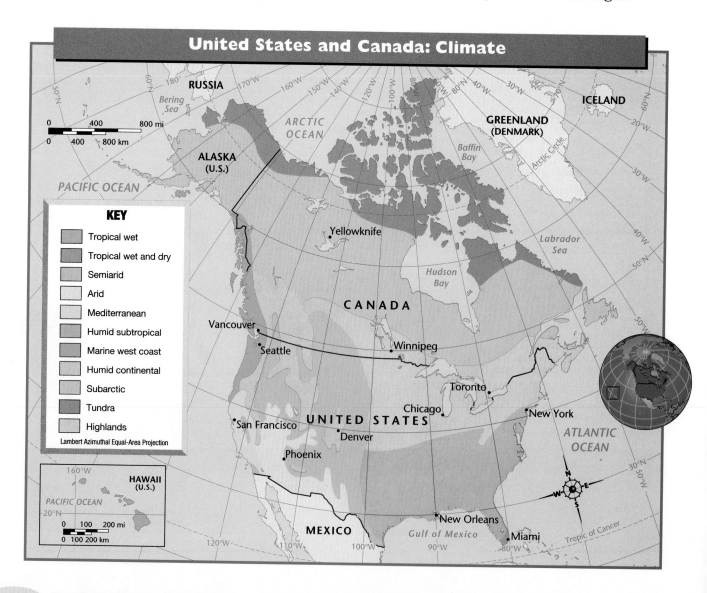

United States and Canada: Climate

KEY

- Tropical wet
- Tropical wet and dry
- Semiarid
- Arid
- Mediterranean
- Humid subtropical
- Marine west coast
- Humid continental
- Subarctic
- Tundra
- Highlands

Lambert Azimuthal Equal-Area Projection

MOVEMENT

10. Analyze Immigration to the United States and Canada The United States and Canada are often referred to as "countries of immigrants." Through the years, people from all over the world have moved to both of these countries. The graphs below show the origins of immigrants in the United States and Canada and the total amount of immigrants who came to the two countries over a period of time. Where do the most immigrants in the United States come from? In Canada? What trends do you see in immigration to both countries from 1950 to 1998?

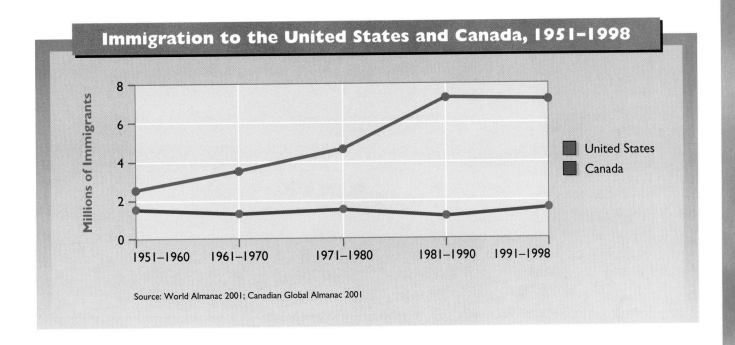

Immigration to the United States and Canada, 1951–1998

Source: World Almanac 2001; Canadian Global Almanac 2001

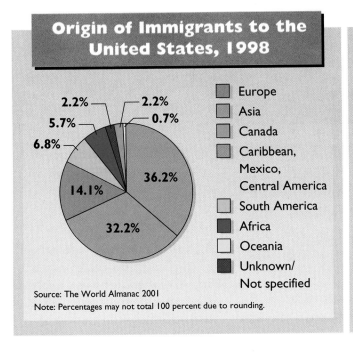

Origin of Immigrants to the United States, 1998

- Europe
- Asia
- Canada
- Caribbean, Mexico, Central America
- South America
- Africa
- Oceania
- Unknown/ Not specified

36.2%
32.2%
14.1%
6.8%
5.7%
2.2%
2.2%
0.7%

Source: The World Almanac 2001
Note: Percentages may not total 100 percent due to rounding.

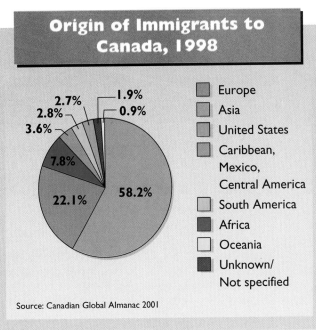

Origin of Immigrants to Canada, 1998

- Europe
- Asia
- United States
- Caribbean, Mexico, Central America
- South America
- Africa
- Oceania
- Unknown/ Not specified

58.2%
22.1%
7.8%
3.6%
2.8%
2.7%
1.9%
0.9%

Source: Canadian Global Almanac 2001

THE UNITED STATES AND CANADA

Physical Geography

SECTION 1
Land and Water

SECTION 2
Climate and Vegetation

SECTION 3
Natural Resources

PICTURE ACTIVITIES

These scenic peaks are part of a huge mountain system called the Rocky Mountains. They stretch across parts of the United States and Canada. To get to know this mountain system, do the following activities.

Study the picture
What do you think the weather is like in the Rocky Mountains? Based on what you see in the photograph, what kind of vegetation probably grows here?

Tour the Rockies
Why do you think tourists visit national parks in the Rocky Mountains? What sports or other activities might they enjoy in the parks? What effect do you think tourism has on the economies of the Rocky Mountain states and provinces?

Land and Water

BEFORE YOU READ

Reach Into Your Background

Have you ever climbed a hill or mountain—or been to the top of a skyscraper? What could you see from such a high place that you could not see from the ground? You probably saw the landscape and how places related to each other. Keep that idea in mind as you read this section.

Questions to Explore

1. What are the main physical features of the United States and Canada?
2. How do the physical environments of the United States and Canada affect the way people live?

Key Terms

glacier
tributary
Continental Divide

Key Places

Rocky Mountains
Appalachian Mountains
Death Valley
Great Lakes
St. Lawrence River
Mississippi River

Alaska's Mount McKinley is the highest mountain in North America and attracts thousands of visitors every year. In 1992, Ruth Kocour joined a team of climbers to scale the 20,320-foot (6,194-m) peak. After the team had set up camp at 9,500 feet (2,896 m), the first storm arrived. The team quickly built walls of packed snow to shield their tents from the wind. They dug a snow cave to house their kitchen and waited for the storm to blow itself out. Kocour recalls, "Someone on another team went outside for a few minutes, came back, and had a hot drink. His teeth cracked."

Maybe camping in the cold mountains is not for you. Perhaps you would prefer the sunny beaches of Florida or the giant forests of the Northwest. Maybe you would like to see the Arizona desert or the vast plains of central Canada. The landscape of the United States and Canada varies greatly.

▼ Dressed for warmth and carrying heavy backpacks, hikers stride across Mount McKinley's Kahiltna Glacier.

Where in the World Are We?

The United States and Canada are located in North America. To the east is the Atlantic Ocean, to the west, the Pacific. To the north, Canada borders the Arctic Ocean, while to the south, the United States borders Mexico and the Gulf of Mexico. The United States also includes Alaska and Hawaii.

Which is bigger, the United States or Canada? Canada has more land—it is the second-largest country in the world. The United States is the fourth largest. But the United States has more people—almost 10 times more people—than Canada. The United States has the third-largest population in the world, after China and India.

Landforms of the United States and Canada

From outer space, the United States and Canada appear as one landmass, with mountain ranges and vast plains running from north to south. Locate these mountains and plains on the physical map in the Activity Atlas at the front of your textbook.

Extending about 3,000 miles (4,830 km) along the western section of the continent, the Rocky Mountains are the largest mountain system in North America. In the east, the Appalachian (ap uh LAY chun) Mountains are the second largest. They stretch about 1,600 miles (2,570 km). In Canada, the Appalachians meet the Laurentian (loh REN shun) Highlands. Tourists visit these mountain ranges year round.

Predict What are the major landforms of the United States and Canada?

▼ White-water rafters splash their way down a mountain stream in the Appalachians in West Virginia.

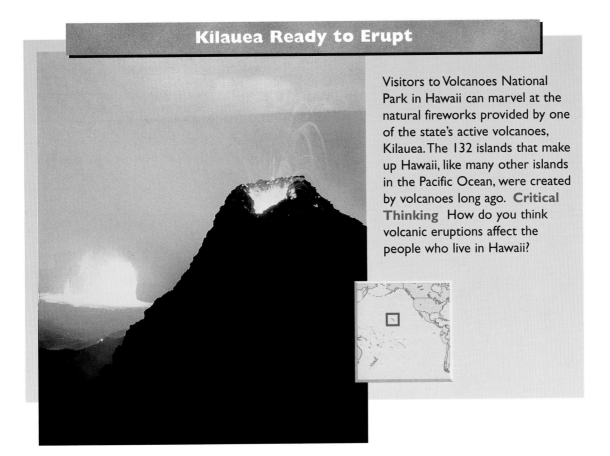

Visitors to Volcanoes National Park in Hawaii can marvel at the natural fireworks provided by one of the state's active volcanoes, Kilauea. The 132 islands that make up Hawaii, like many other islands in the Pacific Ocean, were created by volcanoes long ago. **Critical Thinking** How do you think volcanic eruptions affect the people who live in Hawaii?

Between the Rockies and the Appalachians lies a huge plains area. In Canada, these lowlands are called the Interior Plains. In the United States, they are called the Great Plains and the Central Plains. Much of this region has rich soil. In the wetter eastern area, farmers grow crops like corn and soybeans. In the drier western area, farmers grow wheat, and ranchers raise livestock.

Special Features of the United States The United States has several unique features. A plains area runs along its eastern and southern coasts. In the Northeast, this plain is narrow; it broadens as it spreads south and west. Flat, fertile land and access to the sea attracted many settlers to this area. Large cities developed here.

West of the Rockies lies a region of plateaus and basins. Perhaps the most notable feature of this area is the Great Basin. In the northeast section of this bowl-shaped valley is the Great Salt Lake. Death Valley is in the southwest section. Much of Death Valley lies below sea level. It is also the hottest place in North America. Summer temperatures here regularly climb to 120°F (50°C).

To the west of this region of plateaus and basins lie two more mountain ranges. These are the Sierra Nevada in California and the Cascades in Washington and Oregon. The Cascades were formed by volcanoes. One of these volcanoes—Mount St. Helens—erupted in 1980. People over 1,000 miles (1,609 km) away, in Denver, had to scrape volcanic ash from the eruption off of their cars.

LINKS TO SCIENCE

The Next Hawaiian Island Loihi, off the southern tip of Hawaii, is the world's most active volcano. But no one has seen it erupt. Its peak is 3,000 feet (914 m) below the ocean's surface. Years of continuous eruption have produced layer after layer of molten lava. Scientists predict that in 100,000 years or fewer Loihi will rise above the surface of the ocean and become the next Hawaiian Island.

Far to the north, snow and ice cover Alaska's many mountains. **Glaciers,** huge, slow-moving sheets of ice, fill many of the valleys between these mountains. Most of Alaska's people live along the warmer southern coast.

Special Features of Canada Canada, too, has a number of unique features. East of Alaska lies the Yukon (YOO kahn) Territory of Canada. Mount Logan, Canada's highest peak, is here. It is part of the Coast Mountains, which stretch south along the Pacific almost to the United States border.

Further east, beyond the Interior Plains, lies the Canadian Shield. This huge region of ancient rock covers about half of Canada. The land on the shield is rugged. As a result, few people live here.

Southeast of the shield are the St. Lawrence Lowlands. Located along the St. Lawrence River, these lowlands are Canada's smallest land region. However, they are home to more than half of the country's population. The region is also Canada's manufacturing center. And because the lowlands have fertile soil, farmers in this region produce about one third of the country's crops.

Major Bodies of Water

Both the United States and Canada have important lakes and rivers. People use these bodies of water for transportation, recreation, and industry. Many American and Canadian cities developed near these bodies of water. As you read, find these water bodies on the physical map in the Activity Atlas.

▶ French Canadians own this farmland in Canada's fertile St. Lawrence Lowlands. Unlike English Canadian farmers, who favor square fields, French Canadians prefer farming long strips of land.

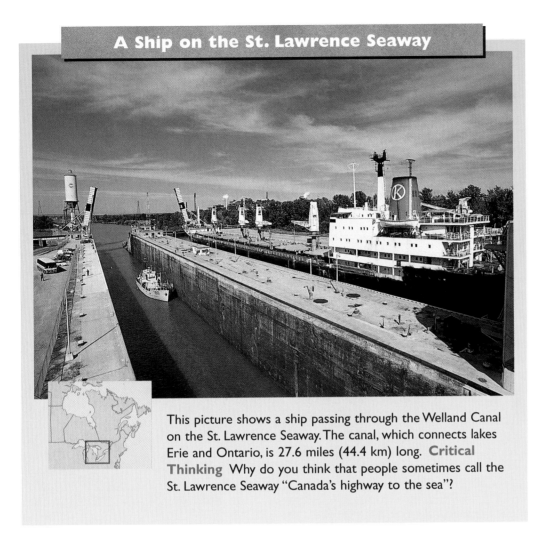

A Ship on the St. Lawrence Seaway

This picture shows a ship passing through the Welland Canal on the St. Lawrence Seaway. The canal, which connects lakes Erie and Ontario, is 27.6 miles (44.4 km) long. **Critical Thinking** Why do you think that people sometimes call the St. Lawrence Seaway "Canada's highway to the sea"?

The Great Lakes Lakes Superior, Michigan, Huron, Erie, and Ontario make up the Great Lakes, the world's largest group of fresh-water lakes. Of the five, only Lake Michigan lies entirely in the United States. The other four lakes are part of the border between the United States and Canada.

During an ice age long ago, glaciers formed the Great Lakes. As the glaciers moved, they dug deep trenches in the land. Water from the melting glaciers filled these trenches to produce the Great Lakes and many other lakes. Today, the Great Lakes are important waterways in both the United States and Canada. Shipping on the Great Lakes helped industry to develop in the two countries.

Mighty Rivers Canada has two major rivers. The Mackenzie River, the country's longest, forms in the Rockies and flows north into the Arctic Ocean. The St. Lawrence River connects the Great Lakes to the Atlantic Ocean. A system of locks and canals enables large ships to navigate the river. As a result, the St. Lawrence is one of North America's most important transportation routes.

In Canada, the St. Lawrence is called the "Mother of Canada." In the United States, America's largest river has an equally grand title.

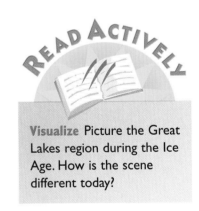

READ ACTIVELY

Visualize Picture the Great Lakes region during the Ice Age. How is the scene different today?

As the Mississippi River flows into the Gulf of Mexico, it dumps silt, forming a huge triangular plain called a delta. This satellite image shows the shape of the delta. The waters of the Mississippi are shown as light blue, the land is shown in shades of black.

Native Americans call the Mississippi River the "Father of Waters." It has its headwaters, or starting point, in Minnesota. From here, the river flows through the Central Plains to the Gulf of Mexico. Two other major rivers, the Ohio and the Missouri, are tributaries of the Mississippi. A **tributary** (TRIB yoo ter ee) is a stream or river that flows into a larger river.

Look again at the physical map in the Activity Atlas and find the Rocky Mountains. Notice that the Fraser, Columbia, and Colorado rivers form in the Rockies and flow west. Now find the Platte and Missouri rivers. They flow east from the Rockies. This is because the Rockies form the **Continental Divide,** the boundary that separates rivers flowing toward opposite sides of the continent.

SECTION 1 REVIEW

1. **Define** (a) glacier, (b) tributary, (c) Continental Divide.

2. **Identify** (a) Rocky Mountains, (b) Appalachian Mountains, (c) Death Valley, (d) Great Lakes, (e) St. Lawrence River, (f) Mississippi River.

3. (a) Which lakes lie on the border between the United States and Canada? (b) Why are these bodies of water important?

4. Give two examples of ways in which physical features have affected life in the United States and Canada.

Critical Thinking

5. **Drawing Conclusions** Hundreds of years ago, many people coming to the United States and Canada settled along coastal plains and rivers. Why do you think these areas attracted settlers?

Activity

6. **Writing to Learn** Suppose that you are planning a vacation. If you had your choice, what physical features of the United States and Canada would you like to see? Write a paragraph describing the places you would like to visit and why.

Climate and Vegetation

SECTION 2

BEFORE YOU READ

Reach Into Your Background
Would you like to go snow skiing in summer? Or how about taking a dip in an open-air pool at the height of winter? The climates of the United States and Canada are so varied that you can do these things!

Questions to Explore
1. What kinds of climates and vegetation do the United States and Canada have?
2. How do climate and vegetation affect where and how the people of the United States and Canada live?

Key Terms
rain shadow
tropics
tundra
permafrost
prairie
province

Key Places
Vancouver
Winnipeg

▼ Whatever the weather outside, it is always pleasant in climate-controlled Eaton Centre, a shopping mall in Toronto, Ontario.

On a hot and sunny February morning, a reporter left his home in Miami Beach, Florida, and headed for the airport. Wearing lightweight pants and a short-sleeved shirt, he boarded a plane to snowy Toronto. Was he forgetting something? Surely he knew that the temperature would be below freezing in Toronto.

He did, indeed, know all about the bitter cold that would greet him when he got off the plane. But he was going to research an article on Toronto's tunnels and underground malls. He wanted to find out whether people could really visit hotels, restaurants, and shops without having to go outside and brave the harsh Canadian winter.

Climate Zones

As the reporter well knew, Toronto and Miami Beach have very different climates. Climate zones in the United States and Canada range from the polar climate of the northern reaches of Canada to the desert climate of the southwestern United States. What accounts for this great variety in climates? The size of the region, first of all. Also, such factors as latitude, mountains, and oceans affect the kinds of climates found in the region.

15

Predict How do you think the ocean affects Canada's climate?

Canada's Climates—Braving the Cold Generally, the farther a location is from the Equator, the colder its climate. Look at the climate regions map in the Activity Atlas at the front of your textbook. Notice that much of Canada lies well to the north of the 40° line of latitude, a long way from the Equator. Therefore, much of Canada is very cold!

The ocean affects Canada's climates, too. Water heats up and cools down more slowly than land. Winds blowing across water tend to warm the land in winter and cool the land in summer. Therefore, areas that are near an ocean generally have fairly mild climates year round. Also, winds blowing across the ocean pick up moisture. When these winds blow over land, they drop the moisture in the form of rain or snow.

The climate regions map shows how oceans influence climate. Notice that much of the northwestern coast of Canada has a marine west coast climate. The waters of the Pacific Ocean help make the climate mild all year. And moisture-carrying winds blowing from the Pacific make the northwestern coast rainy, especially during winter. If you are planning a vacation in the west coast city of Vancouver, take an umbrella and a raincoat. It rains year round.

Being a great distance from the ocean also affects climate. Inland areas often have climate extremes. Find Winnipeg, in Canada's Interior Plains, on the map. Winter temperatures here are very cold, averaging around 0°F (–18°C). Yet summer temperatures run between 70°F and 90°F (20°C and 32°C).

One final factor—mountains—influences climate, especially rainfall. Winds blowing from the Pacific Ocean rise as they meet the various mountain ranges in the west. As they rise, they cool and drop their moisture. The air is dry by the time it reaches the other side of the

▼ In Canada's humid continental climate zone, moist air and hot summer temperatures can combine to produce heavy rainstorms. People in Winnipeg (below) shelter under the first thing at hand—garbage bags. In winter, temperatures can be so cold that rivers and canals freeze. People in Ottawa, Ontario (below right), skate on a frozen canal.

mountains. The area on the side of the mountains away from the wind is in a rain shadow. A **rain shadow** is an area on the dry, sheltered side of a mountain that receives little rainfall.

Climates of the United States   Latitude also influences climate in the United States. On the climate map in the Activity Atlas, you will see that Alaska lies north of the 60°N line of latitude. Far from the Equator, Alaska is cold for a good part of the year. Now find the southern tip of Florida and Hawaii. They lie near or within the **tropics,** the area between the $23\frac{1}{2}$°N and $23\frac{1}{2}$°S lines of latitude. Here, it is almost always hot.

The Pacific Ocean and mountains affect climate in the western United States. Wet winds from the ocean drop their moisture before they cross the mountains. As a result, the eastern sections of California, Nevada, and Arizona are semiarid or desert. Death Valley, which is located here, has the lowest average rainfall in the country—about 2 inches (5 cm) a year.

East of the Great Plains, the country has continental climates. In the north, summers are warm and winters are cold and snowy. In the south, summers tend to be long and hot, while winters are mild. The coastal regions of these areas sometimes experience violent weather. In

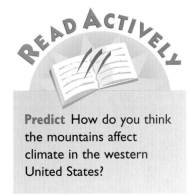

Predict How do you think the mountains affect climate in the western United States?

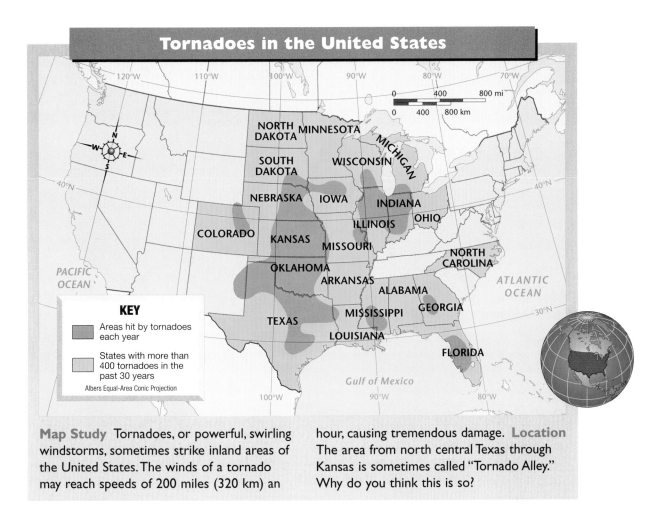

Tornadoes in the United States

KEY

Areas hit by tornadoes each year

States with more than 400 tornadoes in the past 30 years

Albers Equal-Area Conic Projection

Map Study Tornadoes, or powerful, swirling windstorms, sometimes strike inland areas of the United States. The winds of a tornado may reach speeds of 200 miles (320 km) an hour, causing tremendous damage. **Location** The area from north central Texas through Kansas is sometimes called "Tornado Alley." Why do you think this is so?

summer and fall, hurricanes and tropical storms develop in the Atlantic Ocean. These storms sometimes hit the coasts of the southeastern and eastern United States. Bringing winds of more than 74 miles (119 km) per hour, the storms can do incredible damage.

Natural Vegetation Zones

Climate in the United States and Canada helps produce four major kinds of natural vegetation or plant life. As you can see on the map below, these are tundra, grassland, desert scrub, and forest.

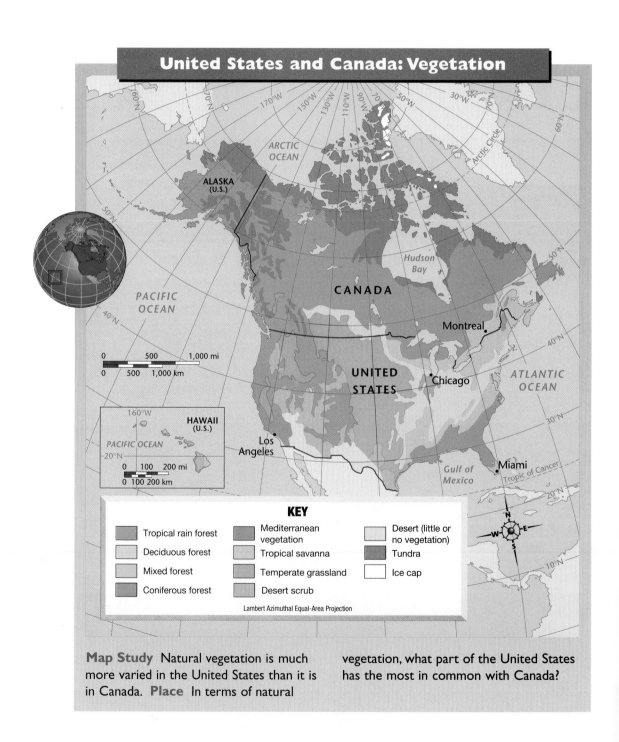

United States and Canada: Vegetation

KEY

- Tropical rain forest
- Deciduous forest
- Mixed forest
- Coniferous forest
- Mediterranean vegetation
- Tropical savanna
- Temperate grassland
- Desert scrub
- Desert (little or no vegetation)
- Tundra
- Ice cap

Lambert Azimuthal Equal-Area Projection

Map Study Natural vegetation is much more varied in the United States than it is in Canada. **Place** In terms of natural vegetation, what part of the United States has the most in common with Canada?

Cattle Raising in the West

Many people in the plains and other lowland areas of western North America make a living by raising cattle. These cowhands in California are rounding up cattle and bringing them into a fenced area. **Critical Thinking** Why do you think that areas of flat or rolling land are better for raising cattle than mountainous areas?

Northern Tundras   The tundra is found in the far north. It is a cold, dry region that is covered with snow for more than half the year. The Arctic tundra contains permafrost, or permanently frozen soil. During the short, cool summer, the surface of the permafrost thaws. Mosses, grasses, and bright wildflowers grow. Few people live in the tundra. However, some Inuits (IN oo wits), a native people of Canada and Alaska, live here. They make a living by fishing and hunting.

Prairies   Prairies are regions of flat or rolling land covered with grasses. They are located in areas that have humid climates. The world's largest prairie lies in the plains of North America. It covers much of the American central states and stretches into the Canadian provinces of Alberta, Saskatchewan (suh SKACH uh wun), and Manitoba. These three provinces are sometimes called the Prairie Provinces. A province is a political division of Canada, much like our states. Look at the physical map in the Activity Atlas to locate the prairies, or plains areas, of the United States and Canada.

When pioneers first saw the prairies of the Midwest, they described the land as "a sea of grass." Today, farmers grow fields of corn and soybeans here. Further west, the Great Plains receive less rainfall. Therefore, only short grasses will grow. These grasses are ideal for grazing cattle. And the land is suitable for growing wheat. The Prairie Provinces, too, have many wheat farms and cattle ranches.

LINKS ACROSS TIME

Hundreds of Years of Storms Between 1493 and 1870, 400 hurricanes struck the Gulf of Mexico and Florida. Residents suffered because they did not know that the storms were coming. Things improved when sailing became more common and radios were invented. Sailors, therefore, could warn that storms were coming. Today, high-tech weather satellites provide the warning people on land require.

► The forests of the United States and Canada are ideal places for many kinds of outdoor activities. These people are bird watching in the forests of Quebec (kwih BEK) province, Canada.

Desert Scrub   With little rainfall, desert and semiarid regions have few plants. The Great Basin is a large, very dry region between the Rocky Mountains and the Sierras in the United States. The land cannot support large numbers of people, but many sheep graze on the area's short grasses and shrubs.

Forests   Forests cover nearly one third of the United States and almost one half of Canada. The mild climate of the northern Pacific Coast encourages great forests of coniferous (koh NIF ur us) trees, such as fir and spruce. Coniferous trees have cones that carry and protect their seeds. The Rockies and the Appalachians, too, are blanketed with coniferous forests. From the Great Lakes across southeastern Canada and New England and down to the southeastern United States, you will find forests of coniferous trees mixed with deciduous (dee SIJ oo us) trees. The latter shed their leaves in the fall.

SECTION 2 REVIEW

1. **Define**   (a) rain shadow, (b) tropics, (c) tundra, (d) permafrost, (e) prairie, (f) province.

2. **Identify**   (a) Vancouver, (b) Winnipeg.

3. (a) Describe the climate and vegetation of the American prairie. (b) What are the climate and vegetation of Canada's Pacific Coast?

4. What geographic features might lead someone to settle in Vancouver, rather than in Winnipeg?

Critical Thinking
5. **Making Comparisons** Contrast the climate and vegetation of the tundra with the climate and vegetation of the area around the Great Lakes.

Activity
6. **Writing to Learn**   You are taking a journey from northwestern Canada to the southeastern United States. Describe some of the climate zones you pass through.

Natural Resources

Reach Into Your Background

Jot down four or five activities that you do in a typical day— take a shower, eat lunch, ride the bus to school, and so on. As you read this section, think about how natural resources play a part in these activities.

Questions to Explore
1. What are the major resources of the United States and Canada?
2. How do these resources affect the economies of these countries?

Key Terms
alluvial
agribusiness
hydroelectricity

Key Places
Imperial Valley
Grand Coulee Dam
St. Lawrence Lowlands

Surrounded by redwood forests, Carlotta, California, has little more than a gas station and a general store. Yet on one day in September 1996, police arrested more than 1,000 people here. Was Carlotta filled with outlaws like some old Wild West town? No, but it was the scene of a showdown. A logging company wanted to cut down some of the oldest redwood trees in the world. Protesters wanted to preserve the forest and the animals that live there. Both sides believed in the importance of natural resources. But they disagreed strongly about how to use them.

As in Carlotta, people all over North America use their natural resources for recreation, industry, and energy. In this section, you will read about the natural resources of the United States and Canada. You will also learn how people use them.

Natural Resources of the United States

Native Americans, pioneers, and explorers in North America knew it was a land of plenty. Fertile soil, water, forests, and minerals were abundant. These resources helped to build two of the leading economies in the world.

▼ These redwood trees are part of Muir Woods National Monument, a national park just northwest of San Francisco, California.

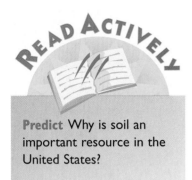

Predict Why is soil an important resource in the United States?

Soil   The United States has vast expanses of fertile soil. Two soil types are especially important. The Midwest and the South have rich, dark soils. Along the Mississippi and other river valleys are **alluvial** (uh LOO vee ul) soils. These are deposited by water; they are the fertile topsoil left by rivers after a flood. Areas that have good soil are suitable for farming. Until the 1900s, most American farms were owned by families. Since then, large companies have bought more and more family farms across the country. For example, southern California's Imperial Valley has vast vegetable fields operated by **agribusinesses.** These are large companies that run huge farms.

Water   Water is a vital resource all over the United States. People need water to drink. And they need it to grow crops. Factories rely on water for many industrial processes, including cooling moving parts. And both industry and farmers transport goods on rivers. Canada's St. Lawrence and Mackenzie rivers serve as shipping routes. The same is true of the Mississippi, Ohio, and Missouri rivers in the United States.

A Modern Irrigation System

Where rainfall averages less than 10 inches (25 cm) a year, as in the southwestern United States, irrigation supplies the water that crops need to thrive. However, the Southwest's limited supply of river water must be carefully rationed. This photograph shows a high-technology irrigation system watering several fields on a California farm. **Critical Thinking** Look back at the photograph of French-Canadian farmland in Section 1. How do the shapes of fields in that photograph compare with the shapes of fields here?

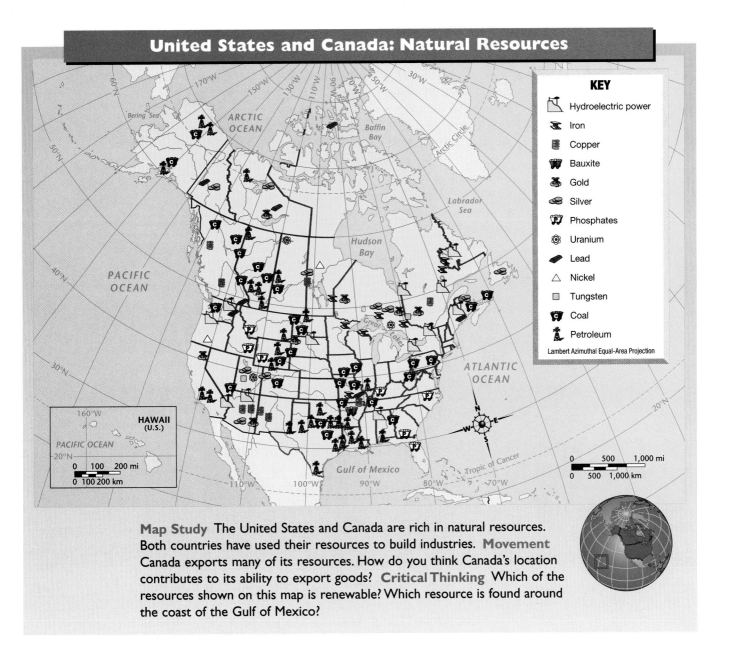

KEY

- Hydroelectric power
- Iron
- Copper
- Bauxite
- Gold
- Silver
- Phosphates
- Uranium
- Lead
- Nickel
- Tungsten
- Coal
- Petroleum

Lambert Azimuthal Equal-Area Projection

Map Study The United States and Canada are rich in natural resources. Both countries have used their resources to build industries. **Movement** Canada exports many of its resources. How do you think Canada's location contributes to its ability to export goods? **Critical Thinking** Which of the resources shown on this map is renewable? Which resource is found around the coast of the Gulf of Mexico?

Water is used for other purposes, too. Dams along many rivers generate **hydroelectricity** (hy dro ee lek TRIS ih tee), or power generated by moving water. The Grand Coulee (KOO lee) Dam on the Columbia River in the state of Washington produces more hydroelectricity than any other dam in the United States.

Abundant Energy and Mineral Resources The United States is the second-largest producer of coal, petroleum, and natural gas in the world. North America's biggest oil reserves are along the northern coast of Alaska. A pipeline carries crude oil south from the wells to the port of Valdez. From here, giant tankers carry the oil to the south to be refined. Abundant energy resources have fueled industrial expansion. They have also helped to provide Americans with one of the world's highest standards of living.

The World's First Oil Well

The modern oil industry began almost 150 years ago on a farm near Titusville, Pennsylvania. On August 27, 1859, a retired railroad conductor named Edwin L. Drake (on the left in this picture) struck oil almost 70 feet (21 m) underground. At first, the oil fetched $20 a barrel. After Drake showed neighbors how to drill their own wells, however, oil prices plunged to 10 cents a barrel. **Critical Thinking** Why do you think oil prices fell after Drake shared his knowledge with neighbors?

The United States also has valuable deposits of copper, gold, granite, iron ore, and lead. Mining accounts for a small percentage of the country's economy and employs about 1 percent of its workers. But these minerals are very important to other industries.

A Wealth of Trees People once claimed that a squirrel could leap from one tree to another all the way from the Atlantic Coast to the Mississippi River. That is no longer true, but America's forests are still an important resource. In the Pacific Northwest, the South, the Appalachians, and areas around the Great Lakes, forests produce lumber, wood pulp for paper, and fine hardwoods for furniture.

Natural Resources of Canada

Canada's first European settlers earned their living as fur trappers, loggers, fishers, and farmers. Today, the economic picture has changed. Less than 5 percent of Canada's workers earn their living in these ways.

Farmland About 9 percent of Canada's land is suitable for farming. Most is located in the Prairie Provinces. This region produces most of Canada's wheat and beef. The St. Lawrence Lowlands are another major agricultural region. This area produces grains, milk, vegetables, and fruits.

READ ACTIVELY

Predict What resources do the United States and Canada share?

◄ Powerful tugboats tow huge booms of logs harvested from Canada's forests.

Minerals and Energy Resources The Canadian Shield contains much of Canada's mineral wealth. About 85 percent of the nation's iron ore comes from mines near the Quebec-Newfoundland border. The region also has large deposits of gold, silver, zinc, copper, and uranium. The Prairie Provinces, particularly Alberta, have large oil and natural gas deposits.

Canada harnesses the rivers of Quebec Province to make hydro-electricity. These rivers generate enough hydroelectric power that some can be exported to the northeastern United States.

Forests With almost half its land covered in forests, Canada is a leading producer of timber products. These products include lumber, paper, plywood, and wood pulp. The major timber-producing provinces include British Columbia, Quebec, and Ontario.

SECTION 3 REVIEW

1. **Define** (a) alluvial, (b) agribusiness, (c) hydroelectricity.

2. **Identify** (a) Imperial Valley, (b) Grand Coulee Dam, (c) St. Lawrence Lowlands.

3. Describe the major natural resources in the United States and Canada.

4. Why is water an important resource? Give two examples of how it is used in the United States and Canada.

Critical Thinking

5. **Making Comparisons** Based on what you know about the physical geography of the two countries, why do you think their resources are similar?

Activity

6. **Writing to Learn** What do you think is the most important resource in the United States and Canada? Write a paragraph explaining your choice.

Using Distribution Maps

Your weekend adventure includes hiking alone in a deep, dark forest. You carry everything you need—tent, sleeping bag, stove, food, and water—in a backpack. Tree branches creak in the wind, and a hawk calls in the distance. You hear the rustle of a small animal scurrying through the leaves.

You soon realize there are sounds you do not hear—the sounds of people. You do not hear traffic, or the hum of a washing machine, or anyone talking.

Where can you go to have such a wonderful experience? There are many wilderness areas in the United States and Canada. Some are forested, others are desert areas, and still others are in mountain regions. What they all have in common, however, is that few people live there.

You can find these places by looking at a special kind of map called a population distribution map. Such a map will also show you a lot more about people and where they live.

Get Ready

A population distribution map is a map that shows the areas in which people live as well as the areas in which people do not live.

You can use a population distribution map to better understand a country or region you are learning about. But a population distribution map also provides clues to why people live where they do. This information is basic to understanding human life on the Earth.

Try It Out

Knowing how population distribution maps are made will help you understand how to use one. Make a population distribution map of your school. A model of such a map is shown below.

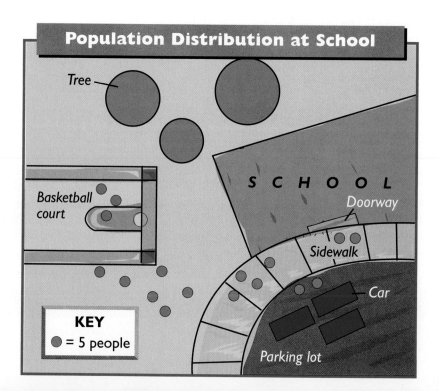

Population Distribution at School

Tree

Basketball court

SCHOOL

Doorway

Sidewalk

Car

Parking lot

KEY
● = 5 people

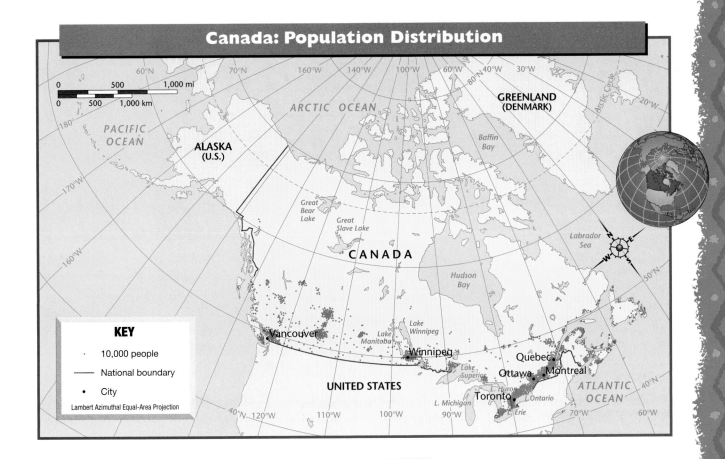

Canada: Population Distribution

KEY

· 10,000 people

— National boundary

• City

Lambert Azimuthal Equal-Area Projection

A. Draw a map of your schoolyard or playground. It does not have to be perfect, but it should show the area around the school, the entrances to the school and the sidewalks leading to the school's doorways, and the school parking lot.

B. Make a key for your map. Have each dot represent five people.

C. Add dots to your map to represent how the population of your school is distributed. Choose a specific time of day, such as 11:00 A.M. Place the dots in the places where people are at 11:00 A.M. on an average day. Remember to draw the right number of dots to show how many people are in the area around the school.

D. Give your map a title. Now study your population distribution map. Your map answers the same two questions that any population distribution map answers: Where are the people? How many people are in each place? Your map also provides clues about another question: Why is the population distributed in the way that it is?

Apply the Skill

Now you know how population distribution maps are made and what questions they answer. Try looking at one that shows a whole country. Use the map to follow the steps below.

1 Familiarize yourself with the map. Look it over to get a sense of what it is about. What country is shown? How is population represented? How many people does each dot stand for?

2 Answer the "where" and "how many" questions that population distribution maps address.
- Where do the people of Canada live?
- Where do *most* of the people live?

3 Answer the "why" question that this population distribution map addresses. Write a paragraph to answer this question.
- Why do you think the population of Canada is distributed the way it is? Consider geographic reasons such as climate and landforms.

Review and Activities

Reviewing Main Ideas

1. List two major geographic features of the United States and Canada and describe their importance.
2. Why do relatively few people live in the deserts of the United States or in the Canadian Shield region in Canada?
3. How does the climate in the Great Basin affect the area's vegetation?
4. (a) What is Canada's smallest land region? (b) Why do most Canadians live there?
5. Of which three energy sources is the United States the world's second-largest producer?
6. Which natural resources help support the economy of Canada's Prairie Provinces?

Reviewing Key Terms

Match the definitions in Column I with the key terms in Column II.

Column I

1. an area on the dry, sheltered side of a mountain that receives little rainfall
2. a region of flat or hilly land covered with tall grasses
3. a large mass of ice that flows slowly over land
4. relating to soil deposited by a river or stream
5. a stream that flows into a larger river
6. a cold, dry region that is covered with snow for more than half the year

Column II

a. tributary
b. glacier
c. rain shadow
d. tundra
e. prairie
f. alluvial

Critical Thinking

1. **Drawing Conclusions** If you were going to build a new city in the United States or Canada, where would you locate it? What geographic features would influence your decision?
2. **Recognizing Cause and Effect** How does climate affect the growth of vegetation in the United States and Canada? Give two examples.

Graphic Organizer

Copy this web on a sheet of paper and complete it. You may choose any region in the United States or Canada.

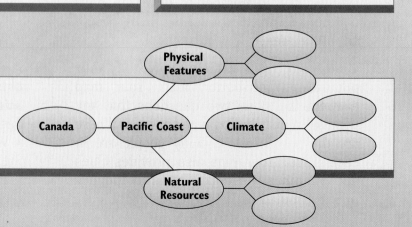

Map Activity

United States and Canada

For each place listed below, write the letter from the map that shows its location. Use the maps in the **Activity Atlas** to help you.

1. Canadian Shield
2. Great Basin
3. Great Plains
4. Rocky Mountains
5. Appalachian Mountains
6. Pacific Ocean
7. Atlantic Ocean
8. Great Lakes

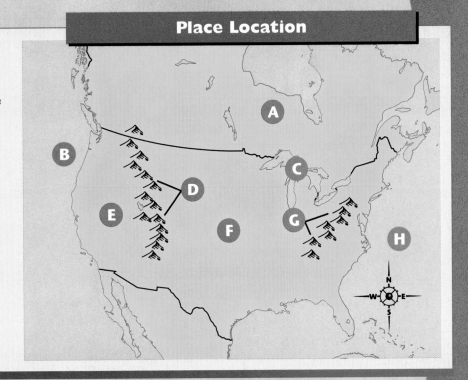

Place Location

Writing Activity

Write a Poem

Write a poem describing some aspect of the geography of the region where you live. Choose from landforms, bodies of water, climate, vegetation, or other natural resources.

Take It to the NET

Activity View interactive natural resource maps of Canada and use the menus and tools to change the features each map shows. For help in completing this activity, visit www.phschool.com.

Chapter 1 Self-Test To review what you have learned, take the Chapter 1 Self-Test and get instant feedback on your answers. Go to www.phschool.com to take the test.

Skills Review

Turn to the Skills Activity. Review the parts of a population distribution map. Then list the three questions a distribution map answers.

How Am I Doing?

Answer these questions to help you check your progress.

1. Can I describe the main physical features of the United States and Canada?

2. Do I understand how geography and climate affect the way people live in the United States and Canada?

3. Can I identify some of the natural resources of the United States and Canada?

4. What information from this chapter can I include in my journal?

Making a Model River

Charles Kuralt, a famous traveler and journalist, knew how important rivers are. "I started out thinking of America as highways and state lines," he wrote. "As I got to know it better, I began to think of it as rivers. . . . It wouldn't be much of a country without the rivers, and the people who have figured out a way to make a living beside them. . . . America is a great story, and there is a river on every page of it."

People of both the United States and Canada have long depended on their rivers. Native Americans and immigrants alike built their villages and towns on the banks of rivers, where they could fish and hunt and water their crops. These natural highways have carried boats through rugged land from the earliest times. Recently, they have become sources of hydroelectric power. Even today, most major cities stand on riverbanks.

Purpose

Rivers have an important place in both the geography and history of the United States and Canada. This activity will help you understand the growth and behavior of rivers.

Materials

- a plastic or flexible 12-by-9-inch aluminum tray with sides at least 4 inches high
- sand
- scissors
- a bucket or pan
- a pitcher of water
- a ruler
- duct tape
- a plastic or rubber hose about 3 feet long
- a brick or square object
- a funnel small enough to fit inside the hose

◄ The Chenoga River meanders through eastern New York state.

Procedure

STEP ONE

Predict how your river will flow. You will make the model river in a box of sand. What do you think it will look like? Will it flow in a straight line, or will it wind back and forth? Will the channel of the river be shallow or deep? Will the channel be the same along the whole length of the river, or will it change? Draw a sketch of how you think your river will look.

STEP TWO

Construct a river box. First, fill the tray with sand, leaving 1 inch at the top of the tray. Then use the scissors to cut a 1-inch V-shaped notch into the center of one end of the tray. This notch will allow the "river" water to drain away. Arrange the tray so that the water will drain into a pan or a bucket.

STEP THREE

Create a landscape for the river's flow. With a pitcher of water, wet the sand evenly until it is damp and packed, but not soupy. With the scissors, poke a small hole below the notch to drain excess water from the sand. Drag the ruler across the sand to make it level. Use duct tape to secure the hose at the end of the tray opposite the notch. Prop the tray up on the brick so that the landscape slopes toward the notch.

STEP FOUR

Let the river run! Put the funnel into the end of the hose. Use the pitcher to slowly pour a stream of water into the funnel. The water will start to make a river in the landscape. Then watch. You'll see a river form before your very eyes!

Observations

1. How did the shape and size of your river compare with the way you predicted it would look in Step One?

2. What happened to the sand in the river's channel?

3. Sediment is material picked up, carried, and deposited by a river. Describe the shape made in the sand as your river deposited its sediment near the drainage notch.

ANALYSIS AND CONCLUSION

1. What factors influenced the form your river took?

2. Increase the flow of water in your river. How does this affect the size and shape of your river?

3. Explain why knowledge of how rivers behave is important to each of the following groups of people: city planners, farmers, people who live near rivers, and boaters.

THE UNITED STATES AND CANADA
Shaped by History

SECTION I
The First Americans and the Arrival of the Europeans

SECTION 2
Growth, Settlement, and Civil War in the United States

SECTION 3
The United States Becomes a World Power

SECTION 4
Growth, Settlement, and Independence in Canada

SECTION 5
Partners and Friends
THE UNITED STATES AND CANADA TODAY

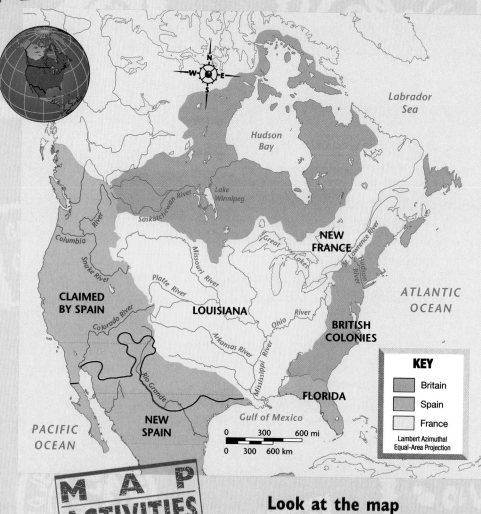

Labrador Sea

Hudson Bay

Saskatchewan River

Lake Winnipeg

Columbia River

Snake River

Platte River

Missouri River

Great Lakes

NEW FRANCE

St. Lawrence River

Hudson River

ATLANTIC OCEAN

CLAIMED BY SPAIN

Colorado River

LOUISIANA

Ohio River

Arkansas River

Mississippi River

BRITISH COLONIES

FLORIDA

Rio Grande

PACIFIC OCEAN

NEW SPAIN

Gulf of Mexico

0   300   600 mi

0   300   600 km

KEY
Britain
Spain
France
Lambert Azimuthal Equal-Area Projection

MAP ACTIVITIES

As you can see, three different European countries influenced North America in the 1700s. To help you identify which country influenced which areas, do the following activities.

Look at the map
Find the area in which you live. In 1753, what country controlled that area?

Compare and contrast
Which European country held the largest territory? Which European country had the territory farthest north?

The First Americans and the Arrival of the Europeans

Reach Into Your Background

Suppose you go on a world trip. You land on an isolated island and meet the inhabitants. How do you react? Are you suspicious and frightened because the inhabitants'

culture and yours are so different? Or are you excited and eager to learn from them and teach them about your culture?

Questions to Explore

1. Who were the first Americans?
2. What effect did the arrival of Europeans have on Native Americans?
3. How did the United States win its independence from Great Britain?

Key Terms

indigenous
missionary
indentured servant
plantation
boycott
Revolutionary War

Key People and Places

Christopher Columbus
Jamestown
William Penn
Pennsylvania Colony
Thomas Jefferson
George Washington

Perhaps as early as 30,000 years ago, small family groups of hunters and food gatherers reached North America from Asia. This migration took place during the last ice age. At that time, so much water froze into thick ice sheets that the sea level dropped. As a result, a land bridge was exposed between Siberia and Alaska. Hunters followed herds of bison and mammoths across this land bridge. Other migrating people may have paddled small boats and fished along the coasts.

Over time, the first Americans spread throughout North and South America. They developed different ways of life to suit the environment of the places where they settled.

▼ These bone tools were found near the area where scientists think a land bridge once connected Asia and North America.

A Southwestern Pueblo

Some Native American groups in the Southwest—the modern-day states of New Mexico, Arizona, Utah, and Colorado—used very distinctive building styles. Around A.D. 700, they began building their villages into the sides of steep cliffs or on top of flat-topped hills called mesas. These villages, or pueblos, were as big as our high-rise apartment buildings. As many as 1,200 people might live in one village. Below is a diagram of a room in a pueblo.

The thick (4–6 in, or 10–15 cm) walls were made of adobe, a clay mixture. It was poured into special molds to make bricks, which dried in the sun. After a wall was built, it was coated with a layer of adobe similar to paint.

Pueblos were also designed for defense. In case of an attack, someone could pull away the ladder from the rooftop "door." This made it hard for intruders to enter the house.

In one corner of the room were the *metates*, specially shaped stones for grinding corn for cooking.

Who Were the First Americans?

Louise Erdrich is an American writer. She is also part Native American. In her novel *The Crown of Columbus,* she describes the variety of Native American cultures before the Europeans arrived:

> "[T]hey] had hundreds of societies, millions of people, whose experience had told them that the world was a pretty diverse place. Walk for a day in any direction and what do you find: A tribe with a whole new set of gods, a language as distinct from your own as Tibetan is from Dutch—very little, in fact, that's even slightly familiar."

The Europeans Arrive

Many scientists think that Native Americans migrated from Asia. Many Native Americans disagree, believing they always lived in the Americas. In any case, all people consider Native Americans **indigenous** (in DIJ uh nus) people, meaning they belong to and are native to this place. Their ways of life began to change after 1492. That year, Christopher Columbus, a sea captain sailing from Spain, explored islands in the Caribbean Sea.

Spanish and French Claims to the Americas Spanish settlers spread out across the Americas. Some went to today's southwestern United States and Mexico. Others went to Florida and the Caribbean islands. Still others went to South America. These colonists often enslaved Native Americans. The colonists forced Native Americans to work in mines or on farms. Working conditions were so harsh that thousands died. Spanish missionaries tried to make Native Americans more like Europeans, often by force. **Missionaries** are religious people who want to convert others to their religion.

Spain gained great wealth from its American colonies. Seeing this, other countries soon also wanted colonies in the Americas. French explorers claimed land along the St. Lawrence and Mississippi rivers. Unlike the Spanish, the French were more interested in furs than gold. French traders and missionaries often lived among the Native Americans and learned their ways. The French did not take over Native American land.

The English Colonists Grow Powerful English settlers established 13 colonies along the Atlantic Coast. These settlers came to start a new life. Some wanted to be free from debt. Others wanted to own land or practice their religions in their own ways. Some came as **indentured servants,** or people who had to work for a period of years to gain freedom.

LINKS TO SCIENCE

Migrating Plants When Columbus returned from the Americas to Spain, he brought gold. But he carried something else that may have been even more valuable—corn. In the next hundred years, European travelers brought back beans, squash, potatoes, peppers, and tomatoes. These foods changed European diets forever.

▼ Explorers used compasses like this one, which dates from 1580, to help them find their way to the Americas.

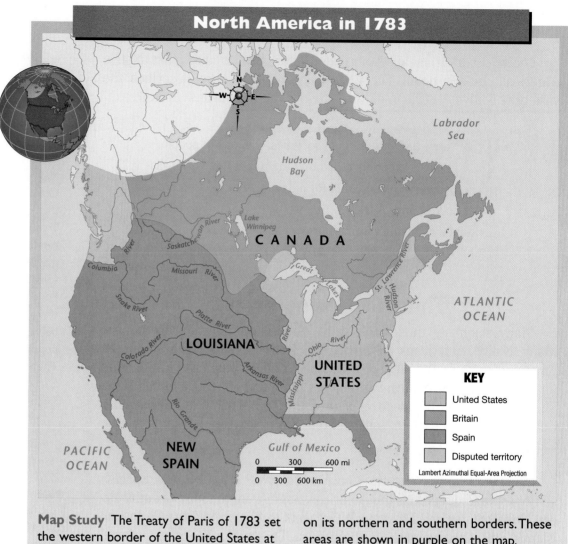

North America in 1783

Labrador Sea

Hudson Bay

CANADA

Lake Winnipeg

Saskatchewan River

Columbia River

Missouri River

Snake River

Platte River

Colorado River

Arkansas River

Rio Grande

Mississippi

Ohio River

Red River

Great Lakes

St. Lawrence River

Hudson River

LOUISIANA

UNITED STATES

NEW SPAIN

Gulf of Mexico

ATLANTIC OCEAN

PACIFIC OCEAN

KEY

United States
Britain
Spain
Disputed territory

Lambert Azimuthal Equal-Area Projection

0 300 600 mi
0 300 600 km

Map Study The Treaty of Paris of 1783 set the western border of the United States at the Mississippi River. The United States claimed, but did not have possession of, areas on its northern and southern borders. These areas are shown in purple on the map. **Location** With which countries did the United States have disputes over territory?

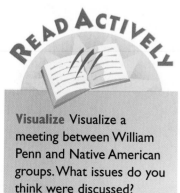

Visualize Visualize a meeting between William Penn and Native American groups. What issues do you think were discussed?

The first permanent English settlement was Jamestown, Virginia, founded in 1607. By 1619, it had the beginnings of self-government. In the same year, the first Africans arrived here as indentured servants. Later, about 1640, Africans were brought as slaves. Many were forced to work on the **plantations.** These were large farms in the South.

In 1620, the Pilgrims arrived in Massachusetts from England. They wanted to worship God in their own way and to govern themselves. They named their settlement Plymouth. About 60 years later, William Penn founded the Pennsylvania Colony. He wanted a place where all people, regardless of race or religion, were treated fairly. Penn was unusual because he paid Native Americans for their land. Before Penn— and after—most settlers took land, then fought Native Americans to control it.

In 1754, Britain and France went to war over land in North America. Americans call this war the French and Indian War. (At this time, Native

Americans were called "Indians," because early European explorers thought that they had found India.) With the colonists' help, the British were victorious.

The Break With Britain

The war with France had been very expensive. And, despite the victory over France, the British felt they needed an army in North America to protect the colonists. The British thought the colonists should help pay for the war and for their defense. Therefore, the British put taxes on many goods the colonists bought from Britain. No one represented the colonists in the British Parliament. The colonists demanded, "no taxation without representation." They also **boycotted,** or refused to buy, British goods.

Patriots such as Samuel Adams, Thomas Paine, and Patrick Henry encouraged colonists to rebel against British rule. The **Revolutionary War** began in 1775. In July 1776, representatives from each colony voted for independence. Thomas Jefferson wrote the Declaration of Independence. His powerful words *liberty, equality,* and *justice* inspired many colonists to fight. George Washington led the American forces to victory in 1781. The Treaty of Paris, signed in 1783, made American independence official.

In 1777, the 13 new states agreed to work together. They agreed on a plan of government called the Articles of Confederation. But the Articles did not provide for a strong central government. For example, Congress was not given the power to tax. To form a stronger government, representatives from each state except Rhode Island met in Philadelphia in 1787. They wrote the Constitution, which set up the framework for our federal government. The Constitution, approved in 1788, is still the highest law of the United States.

▲ Great Britain imposed several different kinds of taxes on the colonies. Many colonists especially hated the tax which required them to buy stamps, like this one, for legal documents and almost every other type of printed matter.

SECTION 1 REVIEW

1. **Define** (a) indigenous, (b) missionary, (c) indentured servant, (d) plantation, (e) boycott, (f) Revolutionary War.

2. **Identify** (a) Christopher Columbus, (b) Jamestown, (c) William Penn, (d) Pennsylvania Colony, (e) Thomas Jefferson, (f) George Washington.

3. Where do many scientists think the first Americans came from?

4. What was a major conflict between Native Americans and the European colonists?

Critical Thinking

5. **Recognizing Cause and Effect** Why did the colonists object to the taxes placed on them by the British?

Activity

6. **Writing to Learn** How were Native Americans involved with the people who arrived from Europe? Do some research about one Native American group. Write a report telling what happened as its people met the Europeans.

SECTION 2

Growth, Settlement, and Civil War in the United States

BEFORE YOU READ

Reach Into Your Background

Have you ever gone camping? As you lay in your sleeping bag surrounded by trees and stars, what thoughts did you have about the wilderness? Did you think of keeping it just the way it was, or did you picture it as it might look if people lived there?

Questions to Explore

1. What were the effects of westward movement in the United States?
2. What were the causes and effects of the United States Civil War?

Key Terms

Louisiana Purchase
Manifest Destiny

immigrant
Industrial Revolution
abolitionist
Civil War
Reconstruction
segregate

Key People

Meriwether Lewis
William Clark
Thomas Jefferson
Andrew Jackson
Harriet Beecher Stowe
Abraham Lincoln
Andrew Johnson

▼ It took Meriwether Lewis (left) and William Clark (right) three years to complete their exploration of the lands west of the Mississippi River.

In 1803, President Thomas Jefferson sent Meriwether Lewis and William Clark to explore land west of the Mississippi River. They traveled all the way to the Pacific Coast. As they journeyed up the Missouri River, Lewis and Clark found plants and animals completely new to them. They also created accurate, highly valuable maps of the region. Much of the information was new. Lewis and Clark also met Native American groups along the way. During these meetings, the two men tried to learn about the region and set up trading alliances. Few of those Native Americans had any idea how the visit would change their way of life.

A Growing Nation

In 1803, President Jefferson had a great piece of luck. France offered to sell to the United States all the land between the Mississippi River and the eastern slopes of the Rocky Mountains—for only $15 million. This sale of land, called the Louisiana Purchase, doubled the size of the United States.

Before this new land could be settled, the United States faced another challenge from Great Britain. The War of 1812 lasted two years. Though the war ended in a draw, the United States experienced peace and prosperity in the following years.

The Nation Prospers

As the country grew, so did the meaning of democracy. In the 13 original states, only white males who owned property could vote. New states passed laws giving the vote to all white men 21 years old or older, whether they owned property or not. Soon, all states gave every adult white male the right to vote. Women and African Americans, however, could not vote.

In 1828, voters elected Andrew Jackson as President. He looked after the interests of poor farmers, laborers, and settlers who wanted Native American lands in the Southeast. In 1830, President Jackson persuaded Congress to pass the Indian Removal Act. It required the

▲ In the 1820s, a Cherokee leader named Sequoyah developed a system of writing that enabled his people to read and write in their own language.

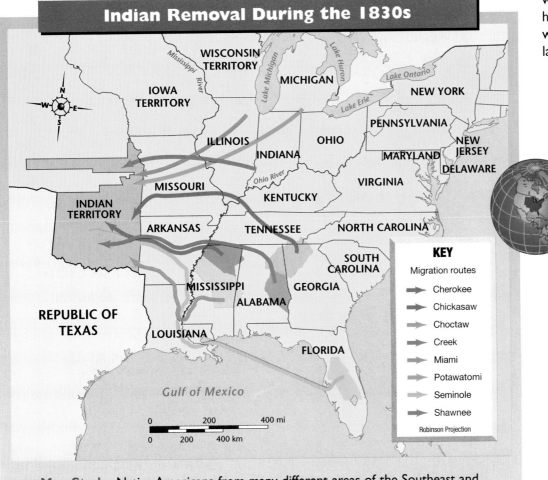

Indian Removal During the 1830s

KEY
Migration routes
➡ Cherokee
➡ Chickasaw
➡ Choctaw
➡ Creek
➡ Miami
➡ Potawatomi
➡ Seminole
➡ Shawnee

Robinson Projection

Map Study Native Americans from many different areas of the Southeast and Midwest were forced to leave their lands. **Movement** Which Native Americans crossed the Gulf of Mexico on their journey west?

Cherokee and other Native Americans in the area to leave their homelands. They were sent to live on new land in Oklahoma. So many Cherokee died on the journey that the route they followed is known as the Trail of Tears.

More Room to Grow   The United States continued to gain land. In 1836, American settlers in the Mexican territory of Texas rebelled against Mexican rule. The Texans then set up the Lone Star Republic. In 1845, Texas became part of the United States. Only a year later, the United States went to war with Mexico. The U.S. won the war and gained from Mexico much of what is now the Southwest region.

Many Americans believed that it was the United States' **Manifest Destiny** to "own" all the land from the Atlantic to the Pacific. By this they meant the United States had a right to it. They also meant that it was America's fate to rule it. In the 1840s, American wagon trains began to cross the continent heading for the West.

The Industrial Revolution   At the same time, thousands of people were pouring into cities in the Northeast. Some had left farms to work in factories. Others were **immigrants,** or people who move from one country to another. These people came from Europe in search of jobs in the United States. This movement was spurred by the **Industrial Revolution,** or the change from making goods by hand to making them by machine.

The first industry to change was clothmaking, or textiles. New spinning machines and power looms enabled people to make cloth more quickly than they could by hand. Other inventions, such as the steam engine, made travel easier and faster. Steamboats and steam locomotives moved people and goods rapidly. By 1860, railroads linked most major Northeastern and Southeastern cities.

READ ACTIVELY

Predict How did the cotton gin and new lands affect slavery in the United States?

▼ Settlers heading west moved their belongings in covered wagons like this one. Some people called the wagon a *prairie schooner* because, from a distance, its white canvas cover looked like a ship's sail.

The Civil War and Reconstruction

In 1793, an important new invention set off a chain of events that deeply divided the young nation. The machine, called the cotton gin, quickly removed seeds from cotton, which made the crop more profitable. But growing cotton still required many laborers for planting and harvesting. This is one reason why slaves were an important part of plantation life. Cotton wore out the soil, though. Plantation owners wanted to expand into new western lands. But that meant that slavery would spread into the new territories. Some people did not want this. The debate began. Should the states or the federal government decide about slavery in the new territories?

Causes of Conflict   Until 1850, there were equal numbers of slave and free states in the United States. Then California asked to be admitted to the union as a free state. After a heated debate, Congress granted the request. The Southern states were not pleased. To gain their support, Congress also passed the Fugitive Slave Act. It said people anywhere in the country must return runaway slaves to their owners. This action only increased the argument over slavery. In 1852, Harriet Beecher Stowe published *Uncle Tom's Cabin,* a novel about the evils of slavery.

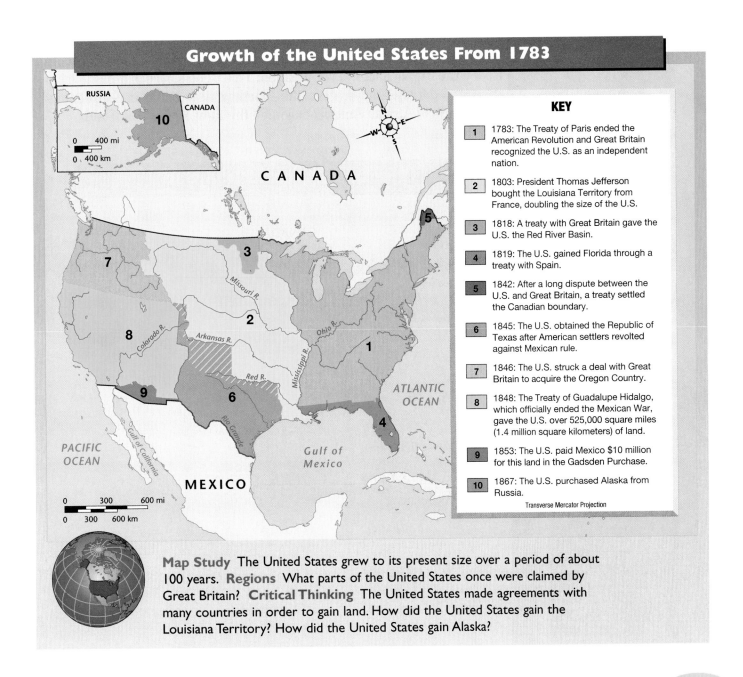

Growth of the United States From 1783

RUSSIA
CANADA
10
0   400 mi
0   400 km

CANADA

3

7

Missouri R.

2

8
Colorado R.
Arkansas R.

Ohio R.

1

9
Red R.
6

Mississippi R.

ATLANTIC OCEAN

4

Rio Grande

Gulf of California

PACIFIC OCEAN

Gulf of Mexico

MEXICO

0   300   600 mi
0   300   600 km

KEY

| 1 | 1783: The Treaty of Paris ended the American Revolution and Great Britain recognized the U.S. as an independent nation. |

| 2 | 1803: President Thomas Jefferson bought the Louisiana Territory from France, doubling the size of the U.S. |

| 3 | 1818: A treaty with Great Britain gave the U.S. the Red River Basin. |

| 4 | 1819: The U.S. gained Florida through a treaty with Spain. |

| 5 | 1842: After a long dispute between the U.S. and Great Britain, a treaty settled the Canadian boundary. |

| 6 | 1845: The U.S. obtained the Republic of Texas after American settlers revolted against Mexican rule. |

| 7 | 1846: The U.S. struck a deal with Great Britain to acquire the Oregon Country. |

| 8 | 1848: The Treaty of Guadalupe Hidalgo, which officially ended the Mexican War, gave the U.S. over 525,000 square miles (1.4 million square kilometers) of land. |

| 9 | 1853: The U.S. paid Mexico $10 million for this land in the Gadsden Purchase. |

| 10 | 1867: The U.S. purchased Alaska from Russia. |

Transverse Mercator Projection

Map Study The United States grew to its present size over a period of about 100 years. **Regions** What parts of the United States once were claimed by Great Britain? **Critical Thinking** The United States made agreements with many countries in order to gain land. How did the United States gain the Louisiana Territory? How did the United States gain Alaska?

After reading this book, thousands of Northerners became abolitionists (ab uh LISH un ists). These people wanted to end slavery. Many helped slaves escape to Canada. There, slavery was illegal. Most Southerners, however, felt that abolitionists were robbing them of their property.

The debate over slavery raged. When Abraham Lincoln, a Northerner, was elected President in 1860, many Southerners feared they would have little say in the government. As a result, some Southern states seceded, or withdrew, from the United States. They founded a new country—the Confederate States of America, or the Confederacy.

Conflict Erupts Into War   In 1861, the Civil War between the Northern states and the Confederacy erupted. It lasted four years. The North, known as the Union, had more industry, wealth, and soldiers. The Confederacy had experienced military officers. They also had cotton. Many foreign countries bought southern cotton. Southerners hoped that they would help supply the Confederacy.

Despite the North's advantages, the war dragged on. In 1863, Lincoln issued the Emancipation Proclamation. This freed slaves in areas loyal to the Confederacy. And it gave the North a new battle cry—freedom! Thousands of African Americans joined the fight against the South.

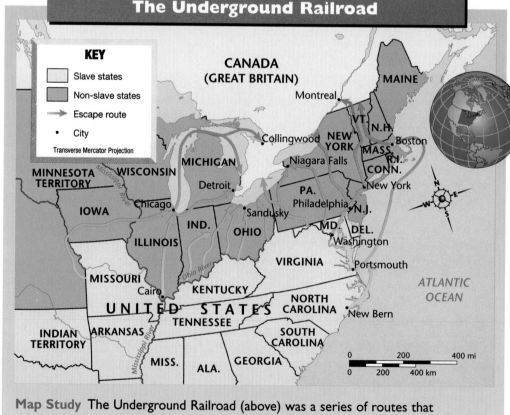

Map Study The Underground Railroad (above) was a series of routes that escaped slaves used to travel secretly to the North or to Canada. Slaves relied on "conductors," like Harriet Tubman (left), to guide them on their journey.
Location What slave states bordered nonslave states?

The picture to the left shows African American soldiers outside their barracks at Fort Lincoln, Washington, D.C., in early 1865. Twenty-one African Americans received the Congressional Medal of Honor (below), the country's highest award for bravery. **Critical Thinking** Why do you think African Americans were willing to fight for the Union?

The Civil War ended in 1865. Lincoln wanted the Southern states to return willingly to the Union. This was the first step in his plan for the **Reconstruction,** or rebuilding, of the nation.

Reconstructing the Union   Less than a week after the end of the war, Lincoln was killed. Vice President Andrew Johnson tried to carry out Lincoln's plan. But Congress resisted his efforts. Finally, Congress took complete control of Reconstruction. The Union Army governed the South until new state officials were elected.

In 1877, the Union Army withdrew. But Southern lawmakers soon voted to **segregate,** or separate, blacks from whites. Segregation affected all aspects of life. The difficult struggle to preserve the United States had succeeded. But the long struggle to guarantee equality to all Americans still lay ahead.

SECTION 2 REVIEW

1. **Define**   (a) Louisiana Purchase, (b) Manifest Destiny, (c) immigrant, (d) Industrial Revolution, (e) abolitionist, (f) Civil War, (g) Reconstruction, (h) segregate.

2. **Identify**   (a) Meriwether Lewis, (b) William Clark, (c) Thomas Jefferson, (d) Andrew Jackson, (e) Harriet Beecher Stowe, (f) Abraham Lincoln, (g) Andrew Johnson.

3. (a) What was the Indian Removal Act? (b) How did it affect Native Americans?

4. How did the Industrial Revolution affect the United States?

5. Why did the Southern states withdraw from the Union?

Critical Thinking

6. **Expressing Problems Clearly**   How did the issue of slavery become a cause of the Civil War?

Activity

7. **Writing to Learn**   Write an entry that Lincoln might have made in his diary on his plan for Reconstruction.

SECTION 3

The United States Becomes a World Power

BEFORE YOU READ

Reach Into Your Background

Have you ever wondered about the contrast between rich and poor neighborhoods in a city? Such contrasts have always been part of city life, where rich, middle-class, and poor people live near each other but live very different lives.

Questions to Explore

1. How did the United States become a world power?
2. How did the citizens of the United States gain more equality from the 1950s to the present?

Key Terms

labor force
settlement house
Homestead Act
communism
Cold War
civil rights movement

Key People

Jacob Riis
Jane Addams
Woodrow Wilson
Franklin D. Roosevelt
Harry S. Truman
Martin Luther King, Jr.

▼ Jacob Riis argued that tenements like these in New York City, which crowded as many as 10 people to a room, bred misery, disease, and crime.

Jacob Riis was an angry man. In his book *How the Other Half Lives,* he took his readers on tours of slum life in the late 1800s. He wanted other people to be angry, too—angry enough to change things.

"**C**ome over here. Step carefully over this baby—it is a baby, in spite of its rags and dirt—under these iron bridges called fire escapes, but loaded down . . . with broken household goods, with washtubs and barrels, over which no man could climb from a fire. . . . That baby's parents live in the rear tenement [slum] here. . . . There are plenty of houses with half a hundred such in."

The United States From 1865 to 1914

The Industrial Revolution made life easier for the rich and the middle class. By the late 1800s, a handful of people had made millions of dollars in industry. But life did not improve for the poor. City slums were crowded with poor immigrants. Many could not speak English. These newcomers were a huge **labor force,** or supply of workers. Employers paid them very little. Even small children had to work so that families could make ends meet.

Reformers like Jacob Riis began to protest such poverty. In Chicago, Jane Addams set up a **settlement house,** or community center, for poor immigrants. Mary Harris Jones helped miners organize for better wages. Because of her work to end child labor, people called her "Mother Jones."

One way for people to leave poverty behind was to move to the open plains and prairies of the Midwest. To attract settlers to this region, the United States government passed the **Homestead Act** in 1862. It gave 160 acres (65 hectares) of land to any adult willing to farm it and live on it for five years. Life on the plains was not easy. Trees and water were in short supply. And settlers faced swarms of insects, wild prairie fires, and temperatures that were very hot in summer and cold in winter. Still, most homesteaders held on for the five years. Railroads helped connect the East Coast with the West, which speeded up settlement.

READ ACTIVELY

Visualize Visualize life on a homestead farm on the prairie.

Life in the West, 1900s

New technology helped settlers turn vast areas of the West into productive farmland. Above, a huge combine harvester cuts wheat on a farm in Washington State. Shown at right is a settler's suitcase packed with treasured belongings for the trip to the West. **Critical Thinking** Why was the development of new farming technology important to the settling of the Plains region?

The United States Expands Beyond Its Shores The United States also expanded beyond its continental borders. Russia owned the territory of Alaska. In 1867, Secretary of State William Seward arranged for the United States to buy it. In 1898, the United States took control of Hawaii, another territory. The same year, the United States fought and won the Spanish-American War. The victory gave the United States control of the Spanish lands of Puerto Rico, Guam, and the Philippines. America had a strong economy, military might, and overseas territory.

The World at War

Now the United States was a player in world affairs. As a result, the country was drawn into international conflicts. In 1914, World War I broke out in Europe. President Woodrow Wilson did not want America to take part. But when Germany began sinking American ships, Wilson had no choice. He declared war. The United States joined the Allied Powers of Great Britain and France. They fought against the Central Powers, which included Germany, Austria-Hungary, and Turkey. In 1917, thousands of American soldiers sailed to Europe. With this added strength, the Allies won the war in 1918. The terms of peace in the Treaty of Versailles punished Germany severely. Its harshness led to another worldwide conflict 20 years later.

BUY WAR BONDS

▲ During World War I, the United States government paid for the war effort by selling bonds. These were certificates that included a promise to pay back the face amount plus interest. Posters like this one urged Americans to buy bonds to win the war.

Fighting World War I

American troops in World War I and World War II served with great bravery. Here, a United States Army soldier in World War I rests during a pause in the shooting. More than 4 million Americans served in World War I. About 15 million Americans served in World War II.

Charles Lindbergh, a 25-year-old stunt flier and airmail pilot from Minnesota, made the world's first nonstop flight between the Americas and Europe in 1927. His flight from New York to Paris took 33½ hours. Lindbergh and his plane, *Spirit of St. Louis,* became a symbol of a daring, adventuresome spirit.

In the United States, during the 10 years after World War I, the economy boomed. Women enjoyed new freedoms and the hard-won right to vote. More and more people bought cars, refrigerators, radios, and other modern marvels.

In 1929, however, the world was grabbed by an economic disaster called the Great Depression. In America, factories closed, people lost their jobs, and farmers lost their farms. Many banks closed, and people lost their life's savings. By 1933, people were losing hope. But that year, President Franklin D. Roosevelt took office. He created a plan called the New Deal. This was a series of government programs to help people get jobs and to restore the economy. Some of these programs, like Social Security, are still in place today. Social Security provides income to people who are retired or disabled.

The Great Depression was very hard on Germany. Its people also lost hope. In 1933, they responded by turning to Adolf Hitler. Soon he had become dictator of Germany. Hitler convinced Germans that their nation would become wealthy and powerful by taking over other countries. Also, he claimed that Germans were a superior ethnic group—and should lead Europe. In 1939, Hitler's armies invaded Poland. This started World War II.

By the end of the war in 1945, Europe was in ruins. People around the world learned that Hitler had forced countless Jews, Gypsies, Slavs, and others into brutal prison camps. Millions of people, including some six million Jews, were murdered in these camps. This horrible mass murder is called the Holocaust (HAHL uh kawst).

READ ACTIVELY

Connect Why is it important that women, as well as men, can vote?

A New Home During the Cold War, the United States built underground "silos" for missiles. As new missiles were built, the Air Force removed the old ones and sold the silos. Some were used to store crops and other materials. One Kansas county turned a silo into a school. In 1984, a family bought a silo and built a home inside. The family paid $40,000 for the silo. Originally, it had cost the American people $4 million to build.

As with World War I, the United States tried to stay out of the conflict. But in 1941, Japan attacked the United States naval base at Pearl Harbor, Hawaii. The United States declared war on Japan. Germany, who was allied with Japan, then declared war on the United States. The United States sent armed forces to fight in Europe and in the Pacific. President Roosevelt, who led the nation in war, did not live to see peace. He died in April 1945. Vice President Harry S. Truman became President.

In May, the Allies defeated the Germans. During the summer, President Truman decided to drop two atomic bombs on Japan. That convinced Japan to give up. Finally, World War II was over.

Postwar Responsibilities

After World War II, the United States took on new international responsibilities. In 1922, the Soviet Union had been created. It adopted a form of government called **communism.** Under this system, the state owns all property, such as farms and factories, on behalf of its citizens. After World War II, the communist Soviet Union took control of many Eastern European countries. The United States feared that the Soviets were trying to spread communism throughout the world. As a result, the United States and the Soviet Union entered the **Cold War.** This was a period of great tension, although the two countries never faced each other in an actual war. Two wars grew out of this tension. One was the Korean War, and the other was the Vietnam War. The Cold War lasted more than 40 years.

The economy of the United States boomed after World War II. But not all citizens shared in the benefits. In the South, segregation was a way of life. Many people began the **civil rights movement** to fight this injustice. People like Martin Luther King, Jr., led the movement to end segregation and win rights for African Americans. This success inspired

▼ Which of the wars shown on this time line did not involve open warfare?

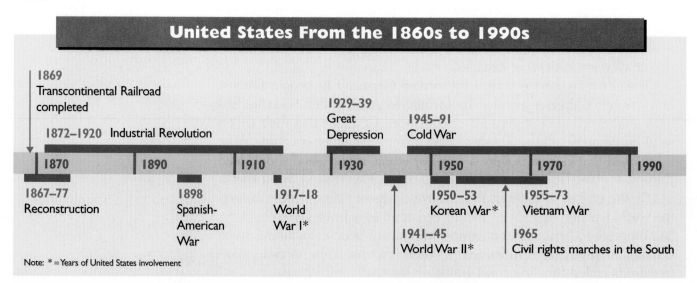

United States From the 1860s to 1990s

1869 Transcontinental Railroad completed

1872–1920 Industrial Revolution

1929–39 Great Depression

1945–91 Cold War

| 1870 | 1890 | 1910 | 1930 | 1950 | 1970 | 1990 |

1867–77 Reconstruction

1898 Spanish-American War

1917–18 World War I*

1950–53 Korean War*

1955–73 Vietnam War

1941–45 World War II*

1965 Civil rights marches in the South

Note: * = Years of United States involvement

A Birthday Celebration

On July 4, 1976, the United States celebrated its bicentennial, or two hundredth birthday. One of the most spectacular events of the celebration was a review of a huge fleet of tall sailing ships sent from the United States and foreign countries. Here, one of the ships sails into New York Harbor. **Critical Thinking** What events do you think would be appropriate for a country's two hundredth birthday? Why?

others who felt they were treated unequally. Mexican American farmworkers, women, and disabled people also made gains in civil rights.

Many challenges remain, however. There are problems of homelessness and hunger, of low wages and pollution. But Americans have faced such problems before. Once, children worked in factories and mines for 12 hours a day, 6 days a week. During the Great Depression, hundreds of thousands of people were out of work. Droughts destroyed farms all through the Plains states. Again, Americans found ways to solve these problems. They did it by harnessing their energy, creativity, and willingness to work hard in the face of any challenge.

SECTION 3 REVIEW

1. **Define** (a) labor force, (b) settlement house, (c) Homestead Act, (d) communism, (e) Cold War, (f) civil rights movement.
2. **Identify** (a) Jacob Riis, (b) Jane Addams, (c) Woodrow Wilson, (d) Franklin D. Roosevelt, (e) Harry S. Truman, (f) Martin Luther King, Jr.
3. List three events that helped make the United States a world power.
4. What gain in equality did African Americans make after World War II?

Critical Thinking
5. **Recognizing Cause and Effect** How did the Homestead Act help settle the Plains of the Midwest?

Activity
6. **Writing to Learn** People who stay home during a war also find ways to help the country. Do research in the library about such things as rationing, volunteer work, and the employment of women during World War II. You can also interview friends or family members about that period. Then write a report about what life was like at home during the war.

SECTION

4

Growth, Settlement, and Independence in Canada

BEFORE YOU READ

Reach Into Your Background

Have you ever seen a commercial for a product—or talked to a friend about some item—then rushed out immediately to buy it? Fads like this can make a company rich. The same thing happened back in the 1600s and 1700s. French businessmen got rich by selling American beaver skins. Many Europeans wanted hats made from the beaver's thick, glossy fur.

Questions to Explore

1. Why were France and Britain rivals in Canada?
2. How did Canada become an independent nation?
3. How did Canada become a world power?

Key Terms

dominion
bilingual

Key People and Places

Louis Papineau
William Mackenzie
Earl of Durham
Ontario
Quebec
Yukon

The Haida people of British Columbia tell this tale. As in many Native American tales, nature plays an important role.

▼ The trade in beaver furs was so profitable during the 1600s and 1700s because beaver hats like this were the height of fashion in Europe.

"**W**hile he was crying and singing his dirge [sad song], a figure emerged from the lake. It was a strange animal, in its mouth a stick that it was gnawing. On each side of the animal were two smaller ones also gnawing sticks. Then the largest figure . . . spoke, 'Don't be so sad! It is I, your wife, and your two children. We have returned to our home in the water. . . . Call me the Beaver woman.**"**

To the Haida and other native peoples in Canada, beavers were especially important. Imagine how they felt when European trappers killed almost all of the beavers to make fur hats.

The Battle of Quebec was a turning point in the Seven Years' War. This painting illustrates how British troops found a path through the cliffs that protected Quebec. **Critical Thinking** Do you think that Quebec would have fallen to the British if troops had not found a path in? Why or why not?

The French and the British in Canada

The profitable fur trade in Canada brought two European powers—France and Great Britain—into conflict there. Actually, the two rivals fought wars all over the world. In 1713, they signed a peace treaty. The treaty gave Great Britain the Hudson Bay region, Newfoundland, and the southeastern corner of Canada, called Acadia.

The peace was uneasy. Against their will, French Catholics in Acadia came under the rule of British Protestants. The French controlled the lowlands south of Hudson Bay and around the St. Lawrence River. Both countries wanted to control the Ohio River Valley, farther to the south. The French wanted its beavers for furs. The British wanted its land for settlement.

The contest for this region was so intense that in 1754, it erupted into the Seven Years' War. In the United States, this conflict is called the French and Indian War. The British won the decisive Battle of Quebec in 1759. The Treaty of Paris, signed four years later, gave Great Britain complete control over Canada. Some French settlers returned to France. Those who stayed resisted English culture. The first two British governors of Canada were sympathetic. They gained passage of the Quebec Act. It gave the French people in Quebec the right to speak their own language, practice their own religion, and follow their own customs.

LINKS ACROSS THE WORLD

Acadia Until 1763, France and Britain claimed land that today is Nova Scotia, New Brunswick, and part of Maine. The French called this region Acadia. When the British took over, Acadians who refused to pledge loyalty to Great Britain were driven from their homes. Some formed a colony in Louisiana. The name *Acadian* came to sound like "cajun." Now the Cajun culture is an important part of life in Louisiana.

Fort York, Toronto

During the War of 1812, United States forces crossed Lake Ontario and occupied York, then Canada's capital, for four days. American soldiers burned government buildings and looted private houses. Today York is called Toronto. Here, in the shadow of Toronto's modern skyline, militia dressed in British uniforms of the period parade at historic Fort York.

During the American Revolution, some Americans did not want independence. They were called British Loyalists. After the war, many Loyalists moved to Canada. But most did not want to live in a French culture. To avoid problems, Great Britain divided the land into two colonies, Upper and Lower Canada. Most Loyalists moved into Upper Canada. It is now called Ontario. French Canadians remained in Lower Canada. It is now Quebec.

During the War of 1812, the French and British groups worked together. This was crucial when the United States tried to invade Canada. The United States had troops on the border between the two countries. The French, British, and native peoples forced the Americans back.

Canada Seeks Self-Rule

Once the war ended, however, Canadians again could not cooperate. Both French Canadians and British Canadians hated British rule. Many felt Britain was too far away to understand their needs. But the two groups did not join in rebellion. In 1837, a French Canadian named Louis Papineau (pah pee NOH) organized a revolt in Lower Canada. His goal was to establish the region as a separate country. The British easily defeated the rebels. The same thing happened in Upper Canada. William Mackenzie led the people against British rule. Again, the British easily defeated the rebels.

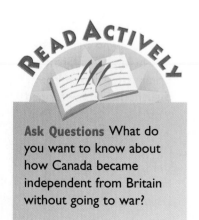

Ask Questions What do you want to know about how Canada became independent from Britain without going to war?

Still, British leaders were afraid more trouble was coming. They sent the Earl of Durham to learn what was wrong. When Durham returned, he had many suggestions. First, he suggested that the Canadians be given more control of their government. He also thought all the Canadian provinces should be united. But the British government united only Upper and Lower Canada to form the Province of Canada. Nova Scotia, Newfoundland, Prince Edward Island, and New Brunswick were not included in this union. If Canada were completely united, the British feared, the Canadians might make a successful rebellion.

But Canadians felt that all provinces should be represented in their government. Otherwise it could not be effective. In 1864, leaders from every province met. Together they worked out a plan to form a union. On July 1, 1867, the British Parliament accepted the plan. It passed the British North American Act. This made Canada "one Dominion under the name of Canada." A **dominion** is a self-governing area. Canada was still subject to Great Britain. But now a central government would run the country. Canadians would solve their own problems. Without a war, Canadians had won the right to control their own government.

After its "peaceful revolution," Canada saw years of growth and change. Skilled European farmers settled Canada's western plains. The region filled with productive farms. Gold and other valuable minerals were discovered in the Yukon in the 1890s. That brought miners to the far northwest. Canada was becoming rich and important.

HEROES

A Voice of Protest In 1869, the Canadian government wanted to finish the cross-country railroad across the flat plains region. Louis Riel, leader of the *métis* (may TEE)—mixed European and Native American people—objected to the plan. The *métis* said the railroad would bring new settlers, who would take away their land. The government refused to stop, so Riel led an armed revolt. It failed, and Riel was executed for treason, but the government did set aside land for the *métis*. Today, French Canadians consider Riel a hero.

▼ On November 7, 1885, Canada's far-flung provinces were tied together as the last spike was driven in, completing the Canadian Pacific Railway.

Canada Takes Its Place in the World When Britain entered World War I, Canadians were still British subjects. Canada, therefore, entered the war, too. Canada willingly sent soldiers and resources overseas. Canada contributed so much to the Allied victory that the young country became a world power. Great Britain recognized Canada's new strength and granted it more independence. During the Great Depression, Canada focused on solving problems at home. But when World War II began in 1939, Canada took part. Once again, Canadian efforts helped win the war.

Canada: Postwar to the Present

During the war, Canadians built factories. They made war supplies and goods like clothes and shoes. Because of the war, people could not get such products from Europe. After the war, Canadian goods found a ready market in Europe.

Also during the postwar years, immigrants poured into Canada. They came from Asia, Europe, Africa, and the Caribbean. The newcomers filled jobs in new factories and other businesses. Soon, Canada became the world's fourth-largest industrial nation.

Rebecca Bond
age 10
Ajax, Ontario, Canada

The CN Tower is a communications and observation tower in downtown Toronto. "I painted the CN Tower," the artist said, "because it's my favorite place in Toronto. You can see the whole city from the top." **Critical Thinking** If you were asked to paint a picture of one of your area's landmarks, which one would you choose? Why?

Toronto and the CN Tower

Industrialization brought back old arguments. British Canadians built new factories in Quebec. That alarmed French Canadians. In 1969, the government passed new laws that made Canada a **bilingual** country. That is, Canada had two official languages— English and French. However, by 1976 some French Canadians were tired of being part of Canada. Quebec, they argued, should be independent. Many people in Quebec still feel that way today.

In 1982, the Canadians wrote a new constitution. It gave Canadians the power to change their constitution without Great Britain's permission. Canada was completely independent.

Canada's government is modeled on the British parliamentary system. It is called a constitutional monarchy. It is also called a parliamentary democracy because the group of representatives that makes its laws is modeled on the English parliament. Another thing ties Canada to Great Britain. Canada belongs to the Commonwealth of Nations. All member countries were once British colonies. Great Britain gives members financial aid, advice, and military support.

Dates Provinces and Territories Joined Canada

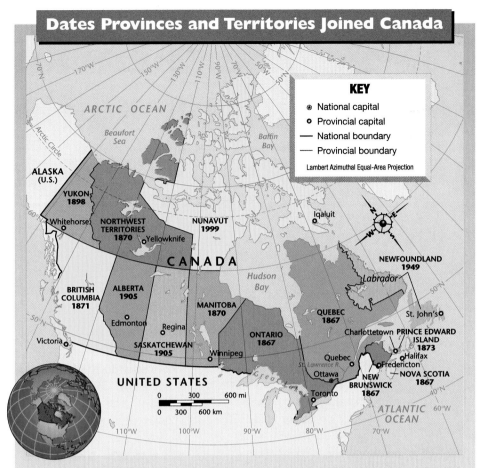

Map Study Canada continued to grow throughout the nineteenth and twentieth centuries as new provinces and territories developed. **Place** Which provinces and territories were developed in the 1900s?

SECTION 4 REVIEW

1. **Define** (a) dominion, (b) bilingual.
2. **Identify** (a) Louis Papineau, (b) William Mackenzie, (c) Earl of Durham, (d) Ontario, (e) Quebec, (f) Yukon.

3. (a) Why was the Ohio River Valley important to the French? (b) Why was it important to the English?
4. How did Canada become an industrial power after World War II?

Critical Thinking
5. **Making Comparisons** Compare the ways in which Canada and the United States became independent nations.

Activity
6. **Writing to Learn** Write a few reasons that a French Canadian might give for separating from British Canada.

SECTION 5 Partners and Friends

THE UNITED STATES AND CANADA TODAY

BEFORE YOU READ

Reach Into Your Background

Think about the land on which your community is built. What do you think it looked like 300 years ago? What natural resources did it have? How have people changed it? Which changes are improvements and which are not? If you had the job of protecting the environment of your community, what would you do?

Questions to Explore

1. What environmental concerns do the United States and Canada share today?
2. What economic ties do the United States and Canada have to each other and to the world?

Key Terms

fossil fuel
acid rain
clear-cut
interdependent
tariff
free trade
NAFTA

Key Places

Cuyahoga River
Lake Erie
Niagara Falls
St. Lawrence Seaway

▼ By 1996, the lake trout population had greatly increased, thanks in large part to the commission's efforts.

The birch-bark canoes paddled into the village of Sault Ste. Marie, on the border of what would later become the United States and Canada. The canoes carried fishing nets made from strands of willow bark, and baskets full of lake trout. The Native American fishermen unloaded their baskets at the shore. Any fish they did not eat that day would be dried on racks and saved for later, or ground up and used as fertilizer for crops.

For centuries, the lake trout of the Great Lakes provided food for both Native Americans and European settlers. By the mid-1950s, lake trout were the most valuable fish in the Upper Great Lakes. Soon lake trout were overharvested. In some of the Great Lakes, the lake trout almost disappeared.

In 1955, Canada and the United States joined to create the Great Lakes Fishery Commission. Members of the commission work together to find ways to protect lake trout and many other species of fish in the Great Lakes. This is just one of the ways the United States and Canada have become cooperative neighbors.

56 THE UNITED STATES AND CANADA

Environmental Issues

Protecting lake trout is one of many environmental issues that concern both the United States and Canada. Both countries share many geographic features—the coasts of the Atlantic and Pacific oceans, the Great Lakes, and the Rocky Mountains, for example. Both countries use natural resources in similar ways. And both have used technology to meet their needs. But technology has left its mark on their water, air, forests, and futures.

Solving Water Problems   Can you picture a river on fire? Impossible, you say? In 1969, a fire started on the Cuyahoga (KY uh hoh guh) River. That river flows past Cleveland, Ohio, and then empties into Lake Erie. Along the way, Cleveland's factories had poured waste, garbage, and oil into the river. The layer of pollutants was so thick that it burned without being put out by the water beneath it.

The Cuyahoga was typical of the rivers that empty into Lake Erie. So much pollution had been dumped into the lake that most of the fish had died. Swimming in the river was unthinkable. But the fire on the Cuyahoga was a wake-up call. The United States and Canada signed a treaty promising to cooperate in cleaning up the lake. Such treaties as this have greatly reduced freshwater pollution in the United States. Today, people again enjoy fishing and boating on the Cuyahoga.

The Cuyahoga River, Yesterday and Today

On August 22, 1969, a fireboat hosed down a burning pier that had been set on fire by flames from the Cuyahoga River (above right). Today, after a huge cleanup campaign, the view is different. Waterfront attractions such as restaurants and cruise boats (above left) offer visitors and residents a chance to enjoy the river views.

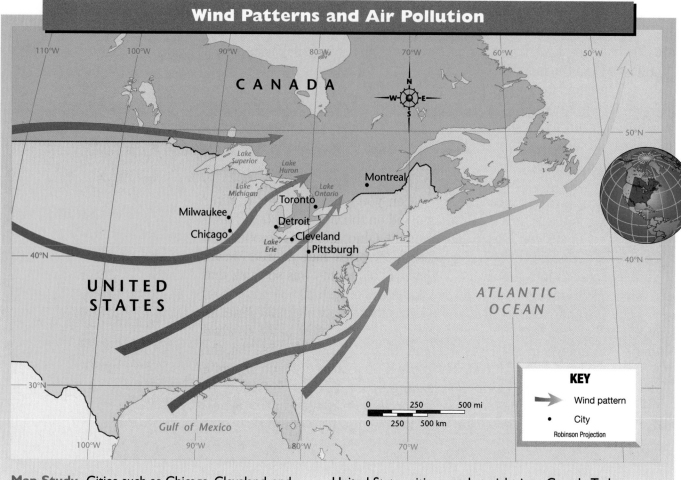

Map Study Cities such as Chicago, Cleveland, and Pittsburgh have been centers of industry since the late 1800s. Factories in these and other Great Lakes cities were powered by burning coal. The wind carried much of the pollution from these factories away from United States cities—and straight into Canada. Today, Canada and the United States cooperate to keep air pollution under control. **Location** What Canadian cities marked on the map lie in the path of winds from industrial cities in the United States?

Predict What happens to the air pollution created in the Northeast or in Great Lakes areas of the United States?

Improving Air Quality On many days, you can look around most big cities and see that the air is filled with a brown haze. This pollution is caused by cars and factories burning **fossil fuels,** such as gasoline and coal. Not only is this air unhealthy for people to breathe, but it can also create other serious problems hundreds of miles away. Wind picks up pollutants in the air, where they combine with moisture to form an acid. When the moisture turns into rain, it is **acid rain.** Acid rain kills plants, trees, and fish. Coal-burning power plants in the Northeast and in Great Lakes areas have caused acid rain.

But polluted winds do not stop at international borders. Acid rain caused by United States power plants has affected forests and lakes in Canada. When the Canadian government protested the situation in the 1980s, the two countries signed agreements to control air quality. A 2000 government report showed that Canada and the United States had reduced rain acidity by up to 25 percent.

Renewing Forests "I'm like a tree—you'll have to cut me down," cried Kim McElroy in 1993. The other demonstrators with her agreed. They were blocking the path of logging trucks trying to enter the forest of Clayoquot Sound on Vancouver Island, British Columbia. The protesters believed that cutting down the trees would damage the environment. In similar forests throughout the United States and Canada, logging companies practiced **clear-cutting,** or cutting down all the trees in an area. Without trees, soil washes away, other plants die, and animals lose their homes.

On the other hand, people need lumber for houses. Paper companies need wood pulp to make their products. People who work for logging companies need their jobs.

The Canadian and American governments want to maintain both the forests and the timber industry. They are working to develop ideas that will do that. For example, British Columbia passed a law that sets aside parts of the Clayoquot Sound's forests for logging. The law also imposes new rules on loggers to prevent damage in the areas where cutting is allowed.

"Economics Has Made Us Partners"

Not all next-door neighbors get along as well as the United States and Canada. President John F. Kennedy once described the relationship this way: "Geography has made us neighbors. History made us friends. Economics has made us partners." With 5,527 miles (8,895 km) of border between the two countries, economic cooperation has benefited both. Part of this cooperation has been in transportation between the countries, particularly around the Great Lakes.

▼ Clear-cutting in Oregon's Mount Hood National Forest scars the land with large bare patches.

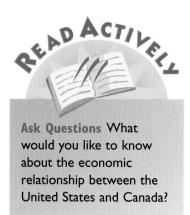

Ask Questions What would you like to know about the economic relationship between the United States and Canada?

The St. Lawrence Seaway   Have you ever heard of someone going over Niagara Falls in a barrel? The barrel would drop about 190 feet (58 m)—a pretty crazy stunt! But suppose you had a cargo of manufactured goods in Cleveland to send to Montreal. You decide to ship by water, because it is the cheapest and most direct means of transportation. Now what do you do? Niagara Falls lies between lakes Erie and Ontario. After that, your cargo would have to travel down a total drop of another 250 feet (76 m) in the St. Lawrence River before it reached Montreal. And once your cargo was unloaded, how would you get the ship back to Cleveland?

To solve this problem, the United States and Canada built the St. Lawrence Seaway. Completed in 1959, it is a system of locks, canals, and dams that allows ships to move from one water level to another. Now, ships can travel from Duluth, Minnesota, on Lake Superior, all the way to the Atlantic Ocean. The St. Lawrence Seaway makes it much easier for the United States and Canada to trade with each other and with Europe.

Trade   What country is the biggest trading partner of the United States? It is Canada. And the United States is Canada's largest trading partner, too. About three fourths of all of Canada's foreign trade—both exports and imports—is with the United States. Our economies are **interdependent**. That means that in order to be successful, each country needs to do business with the other.

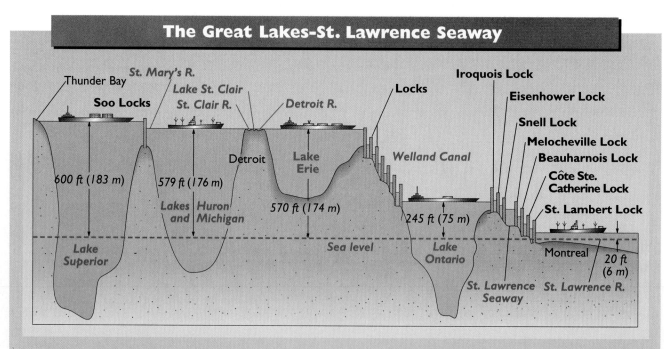

Chart Study Ships traveling from Lake Superior to the Atlantic Ocean must go through a series of locks. A lock is an enclosed part of a canal with a watertight gate at each end. Letting water into the lock raises ships. Letting water out lowers them. This diagram shows the location of locks along the St. Lawrence Seaway. **Critical Thinking** How do you think building the St. Lawrence Seaway affected the economies of the United States and Canada?

This train is taking on a load of wheat from the nearby grain elevator. A grain elevator is a tall building where grain is stored. The train takes the wheat west to the Pacific Coast or east to the Great Lakes. The wheat then is loaded on ships for export. Wheat is one of Canada's most important exports. In fact, Canada is the world's second leading grain exporter. The United States leads the world in grain exports.

Before 1989, both countries charged fees called tariffs on many things they imported from each other. Tariffs raise the cost of goods, so they can limit the amount of trade. In 1989, Canada and the United States agreed to eliminate tariffs and have free trade. And in 1994, Mexico joined the United States and Canada to sign the North American Free Trade Agreement, or NAFTA. The goal of this agreement is to encourage trade and economic growth in all three countries. Trade among all three countries has increased since these agreements were made.

SECTION 5 REVIEW

1. **Define** (a) fossil fuel, (b) acid rain, (c) clear-cut, (d) interdependent, (e) tariff, (f) free trade, (g) NAFTA.

2. **Identify** (a) Cuyahoga River, (b) Lake Erie, (c) Niagara Falls, (d) St. Lawrence Seaway.

3. Why is there disagreement about logging in some forests?

4. Why is acid rain from the United States a problem in Canada?

5. How has geography contributed to the trade partnership between Canada and the United States?

Critical Thinking

6. **Expressing Problems Clearly** Explain briefly why the United States and Canada cooperated to build the St. Lawrence Seaway.

Activity

7. **Writing to Learn** Write a paragraph that explains the main reasons why Canada and the United States are important to each other.

SKILLS ACTIVITY

Interpreting Diagrams

Suppose that your pen pal in Canada wants to know what your school looks like. Which would you rather do, write her a letter describing your school, or send her a photograph?

Many people would probably choose to send the photograph. A photograph would show her in an instant what your school looks like. But writing a letter also has its benefits. You can describe details a photograph might not show.

Which should you do—send a letter or send a photograph? The best solution would be to send both. The photograph would show your pen pal what your school looks like, and the letter would tell her about it. In a way, you would be playing a long-distance game of show-and-tell with your pen pal!

Get Ready

You can also have show-and-tell with a diagram. As you know, a diagram is a picture that shows how something works or is made. It usually includes labels that tell about certain parts of the picture. It is like a combination of the letter and the photograph you would send to your pen pal. A diagram can both show things through a picture and tell about them through labels.

A diagram is like a game of "show-and-tell"—the picture *shows,* and the labels *tell.*

Try It Out

To understand how diagrams are made— and how to learn more from them—make one yourself. Complete these steps:

A. Find a photograph of a bicycle. You can cut one out of an old catalog or a magazine. Look for a photograph that is about the same size as the diagram on the next page.

B. Write a description of the bicycle. Describe in words the bicycle for someone who has never seen one before. Be sure to describe what it looks like, what its different parts are, and how the parts work.

C. Draw a diagram of the bicycle. Using the picture and your paragraph as a reference, draw a diagram of the bicycle. Be sure to label each part and explain how it works.

D. Compare the picture, the paragraph, and the diagram. Which of the three does the best job of showing and explaining what a bicycle is, what its parts are, and how it works?

As you can see, both pictures and words are useful. But nothing works as well as the combination of pictures and words you find in a diagram.

Apply the Skill

Now that you see how a simple diagram can "show and tell," you are ready to see how a more complicated diagram does the same thing. Use the diagram to complete the steps that follow.

1 **Read and look at the diagram below.** Look it over to get a sense of what it is about. What does this diagram illustrate? What do the labels tell?

2 **Study the picture.** What does the picture tell you about how a locomotive works?

3 **Study the words.** What path does the steam take through the engine?

4 **Think about diagrams.** Write a few sentences that explain how this diagram helps you understand locomotives.

How a Locomotive Works

Steam is superheated and goes to the steam chest.

Burning coal turns water in the boiler to steam.

superheater pipes

boiler

steam pipe

steam chest

firebox

drive rods

The pistons move the drive rods, which turn the wheels.

pistons   cylinder

Steam moves into the cylinders, where it pushes the pistons back and forth.

Steam locomotives drove trains for about a century beginning in 1830.

CHAPTER 2 Review and Activities

Reviewing Main Ideas

1. Some scholars say that the first people in North America were not indigenous. According to this theory, how did the first people get here?

2. How did Europeans change Native American ways of life?

3. Name two reasons why early colonists wanted to break away from Great Britain.

4. How did westward expansion affect voting laws?

5. How did the United States become a world power?

6. Besides African Americans, which groups campaigned for civil rights after the 1950s?

7. Why did Canada become more independent from Britain after World War I?

8. After World War II, Canada's influence on the rest of the world increased. Why?

9. How is acid rain produced?

10. What is the value of the St. Lawrence Seaway?

Reviewing Key Terms

Use each key term in a sentence that shows the meaning of the term.

1. indigenous
2. Manifest Destiny
3. immigrant
4. Industrial Revolution
5. abolitionist
6. Reconstruction
7. Cold War
8. civil rights movement
9. dominion
10. bilingual
11. fossil fuel
12. acid rain
13. interdependent
14. tariff
15. free trade

Critical Thinking

1. **Identifying Central Issues** Explain why Southern colonists believed that they needed slaves.

2. **Making Comparisons** Compare the ways in which the United States and Canada gained their independence from Great Britain.

Graphic Organizer

On a sheet of paper, copy this chart and fill in the empty ovals with forces that made the United States a world power.

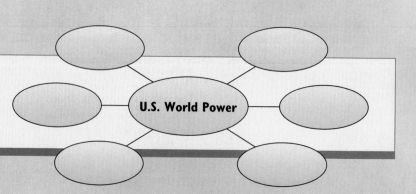

U.S. World Power

Map Activity

Canada
For each place listed below, write the letter from the map that shows its location.

1. Ontario

2. Quebec

3. Yukon

4. Lake Erie

5. St. Lawrence Seaway

Writing Activity

Writing Activity
Think about ways in which the United States and Canada are similar. How are they different? Write a summary comparing the two countries.

Take It to the NET

Activity Read the letters of Civil War soldier Galutia York. What was daily life like for Civil War soldiers? For help in completing this activity, visit www.phschool.com.

Chapter 2 Self-Test To review what you have learned, take the Chapter 2 Self-Test and get instant feedback on your answers. Go to www.phschool.com to take the test.

Skills Review

Turn to the Skills Activity.
Review the four steps for reading a diagram. Then write a few sentences explaining why a diagram is more effective than a paragraph or a picture in providing information.

How Am I Doing?

Answer these questions to help you check your progress.

1. Do I understand how differences between the North and South led to the Civil War?

2. Can I describe how the United States became a world power?

3. Can I recognize the differences between the ways in which the United States and Canada gained their independence?

4. What information from this chapter can I include in my journal?

Transportation

By foot and in flight, in horse-drawn wagons and in locomotives, the people of Canada and the United States have always been on the move.

Transportation has played an important role in the histories of both countries. Early Native Americans spread across the continent on foot, on horseback, and in canoes. European colonists arrived in sailing ships, and settlers traveled west in covered wagons. History has always been affected by the ways in which people have traveled.

Purpose

In this activity, you will conduct an investigation of the ways in which people have crossed the rugged land and vast distances of the United States and Canada.

Find the Routes

Some of the roads in Canada and the United States have existed since Native Americans followed animal trails through the wilderness. Others have only existed since town or city planners decided to build them. Many roads change over time. Footpaths became cement sidewalks or paved highways. Look for different roads and paths in your community. Make a note of even the largest highway or the smallest path across the corner of someone's lawn. How old do you think the different routes are? Make a map of all the routes you take on your way to school.

◀▼ From trails to highways, transportation routes come in many forms.

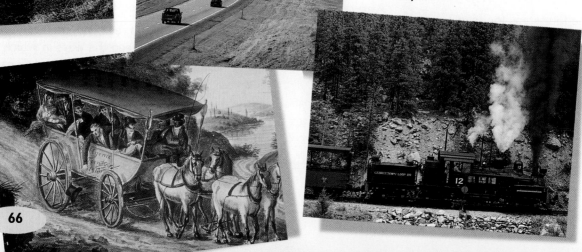

Do a Sailboat Study

Ships with great sails brought the first Europeans to this continent. Read about sailboats and sailing ships to see how they work. Then make a model sailboat. Draw a plan for your sailboat and choose your materials very carefully. Test your sailboat by floating it in water and blowing on it to create wind. Make any changes you need to improve the boat.

Calculate Travel Times

As the United States and Canada have grown older, travel times have become shorter and shorter. The chart below shows how long it has taken to travel from New York to St. Louis, the "Gateway to the West," in various years between 1800 and today. The distance between New York and St. Louis is 870 miles (1400 km).

New York to St. Louis

Year	Method	Approximate Travel Time
1800	stagecoach and horseback	5 weeks
1860	passenger train	3 days
1930	passenger train	1 day
1950	automobile	24 hours
Today	passenger jet	3 hours

Use the chart to see how much travel speeds have improved. First, calculate the average speed in miles per hour of each method of transportation shown in the chart (distance in miles ÷ time in hours = speed in miles per hour). Then, draw a line graph of your results.

Links to Other Subjects

Finding routes	**Geography**
Doing a sailboat study	**Science**
Calculating travel times	**Math**
Singing transportation songs	**Music**
Telling a travel tale	**Language Arts**

Sing Some Transportation Songs

"I've been workin' on the railroad, all the livelong day. . . ." Sound familiar? People have written many folk songs about trains, cars, boats, and other ways of getting around. What other transportation songs can you think of? Find the words and music to a few, and perform them with your classmates.

Tell a Travel Tale

You may not be a world traveler yet, but you have traveled. You've walked, ridden in cars and buses, and perhaps you've even ridden a train, boat, or plane. Write the story of your most exciting journey. Explain how you traveled, and what made the voyage exciting.

ANALYSIS AND CONCLUSION

Write a summary of your investigation. Describe the steps you followed and consider the following questions in your summary.

1. Why is transportation so important?

2. How has transportation affected the histories of the United States and Canada?

3. People are continually trying to make transportation faster and more efficient. Why do you think this is so?

CHAPTER

3

Cultures of the United States and Canada

SECTION 1
The United States
A NATION OF
IMMIGRANTS

SECTION 2
Canada
A MOSAIC

PICTURE ACTIVITIES

In addition to official U.S. holidays, like the Fourth of July, Americans celebrate many ethnic holidays. These people in New York City are enjoying the Puerto Rican Day Parade, which is held every June. To help you think about the mixture of people in the United States, do the following activities.

Take a poll
Ask students in your class where their great-grandparents are from. Many will be from the United States, of course. What other countries are represented?

Study restaurant listings
Use a telephone book to list the kinds of food served in restaurants in your community. How many countries are represented?

The United States

A NATION OF IMMIGRANTS

BEFORE YOU READ

Reach Into Your Background

"So what'll it be tonight? Italian, Mexican, Chinese?" Does someone ask this question when your family is trying to decide on a restaurant or where to get take-out food? A wide variety, or diversity, of food is just one advantage of living in a society made up of different cultures. What else do you like about cultural diversity?

Questions to Explore

1. What influences have made the United States a culturally diverse nation?

2. How does this diversity affect life in the United States?

Key Terms

cultural diversity
cultural exchange
ethnic group

This view of **cultural diversity,** or a wide variety of cultures, comes from Tito, a teenager from Mexico. What do you think of it?

"**M**y parents say, 'You have to learn the American culture.' I listen to them, but then I think about an ideal society where there's a little bit of every culture and it goes together just right. Say there's a part of the United States that's very hot. The problem to solve: What can we do to keep these people from overheating? The people who came here from the tropics have certain secrets of surviving in hot climates. Well, they come along and would say, 'When I lived in the tropics . . . we made our buildings with thick walls and a lot of windows. The buildings were white to reflect away the sun.' And the others would say, 'Hey, what a great idea. It works!' Different ideas would come together and make everything a whole lot better."

▼ A family enjoys dinner at a Mexican restaurant in San Antonio, Texas.

Diverse Cultures in the United States

The United States has always been culturally diverse. The country is geographically diverse, too—that is, it has a variety of landforms, climates, and vegetation. The cultures of the first Americans reflected their environments. Native Americans near the ocean ate a great deal of fish and told stories about the sea. Native Americans in forests learned how to trap and hunt forest animals. Native American groups also traded with each other. When groups trade, they get more than just goods. They also get involved in **cultural exchange.** In this process, different cultures share ideas and ways of doing things.

Cultural Exchange When Europeans came to North America, they changed Native American life. Some changes came from things that Europeans brought with them. For example, there were no horses in the New World when the Spanish explorers came. Once horses arrived, they changed the way that many Native Americans lived and became an important part of Native American culture.

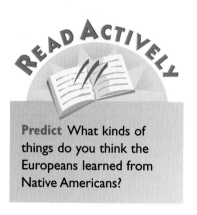

Predict What kinds of things do you think the Europeans learned from Native Americans?

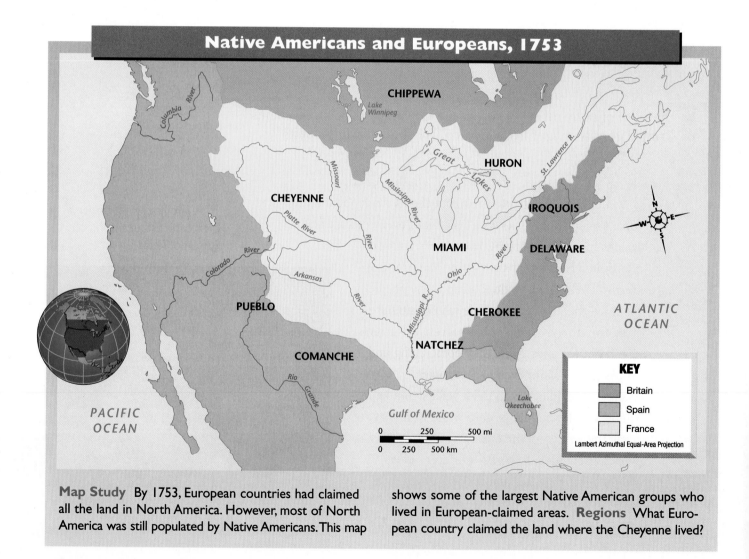

Native Americans and Europeans, 1753

CHIPPEWA

Lake Winnipeg

Columbia River

Great Lakes

HURON

St. Lawrence R.

CHEYENNE

Missouri River

Mississippi River

IROQUOIS

Platte River

MIAMI

DELAWARE

Colorado River

Arkansas River

Ohio River

Mississippi R.

PUEBLO

CHEROKEE

ATLANTIC OCEAN

NATCHEZ

COMANCHE

Rio Grande

Lake Okeechobee

PACIFIC OCEAN

Gulf of Mexico

0   250   500 mi
0   250   500 km

KEY
Britain
Spain
France
Lambert Azimuthal Equal-Area Projection

Map Study By 1753, European countries had claimed all the land in North America. However, most of North America was still populated by Native Americans. This map shows some of the largest Native American groups who lived in European-claimed areas. **Regions** What European country claimed the land where the Cheyenne lived?

Immigration to the United States, 1951–1998

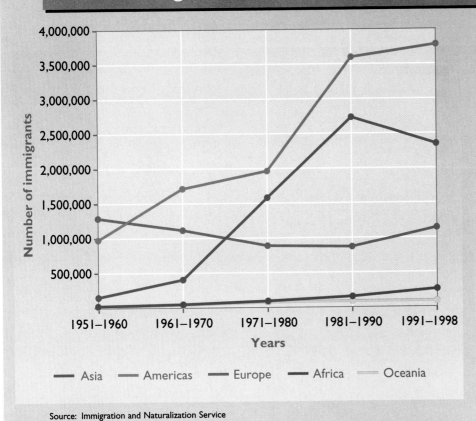

Number of immigrants

4,000,000
3,500,000
3,000,000
2,500,000
2,000,000
1,500,000
1,000,000
500,000

1951–1960   1961–1970   1971–1980   1981–1990   1991–1998

Years

— Asia — Americas — Europe — Africa — Oceania

Source: Immigration and Naturalization Service

Chart Study This chart shows how many immigrants came to the United States from other parts of the world between 1951 and 1998. **Critical Thinking** Between 1951 and 1960, most immigrants to the United States were from Europe. How had things changed by the 1990s?

Cultural exchange occurred in two ways. Native Americans contributed many things to European culture. The French learned how to trap and to survive in the forest. English families learned to grow local foods such as corn and pumpkins. Cultural exchange also took place between enslaved Africans and their owners. The Africans learned English and used European tools. African music and foods entered the daily lives of slave owners.

This give-and-take happens every time immigrants come to a country. When Russian settlers came to the Midwest, they brought a kind of hardy wheat from their home country. Farmers soon learned that this tough wheat grew well in the Midwestern climate. These immigrants helped the Midwest become the leading wheat-growing area in the country today. In fact, so much wheat is grown here that it is called "America's breadbasket." Members of other ethnic groups have made important contributions to American culture, too. An **ethnic group** is a group of people who share a language, history, and culture.

What to Keep and What to Change? When immigrants move from one country to another, they must make difficult decisions. For instance, what things in their original culture should they keep, and what should they change? They must learn the language, laws, and manners of the people in their new home. For some, this is difficult. Others, however, want to forget the life they lived before.

LINKS TO MATH

Using Your Fingers and Toes Native Americans created the first number systems north of the Mexican border. The San Gabrielino in California used "all my hand finished" to mean 10. "All my hand finished and one my foot" was 15. The Chukchee used their fingers to count. Their word for "five" is *hand,* for "ten" *both hands,* and for "twenty" *man—* meaning both hands and both feet.

►Chinese American boy scouts in San Francisco proudly show off a dragon, which symbolizes Chinese New Year. Do you have to be Chinese to observe this holiday? Of course not—Americans of all ethnic backgrounds join in the joyous celebration.

For instance, Florence Benjamin, a third-generation American, asked her grandfather to teach her Russian. He replied, "From the time I came to this country, America has been my home and English my language. It is the only country that has been good to me and to the Jews. It is the one that is best for you. You don't need Russian." This man was grateful because American laws protected him. To him, being an American meant having the freedom *not* to use his native language.

On the other hand, some newcomers have difficulty adjusting to new ways. The United States is so different from their home country. Adults are sometimes afraid that the differences will come between them and their children. Anna, a teenager from Greece, describes the tensions that can grow among family members:

"Once I understood English, once I started to see a whole American world out there that I never knew existed, a world that you don't see in Greece, I felt a little distant from [my parents]. The distance grew. They would be proud of me, but they also began to feel threatened. My new knowledge had no meaning for them. This has been hard and sad for all of us."

Almost all immigrants cling to things that remind them of their former homes. Think about your family or your friends' families. Does someone play an instrument special to your heritage? Do they use special phrases from the language they learned from their parents or grandparents? These customs give people a sense of identity. They also enrich American life.

United States Culture

Have you ever listened to music at a Caribbean carnival or watched a dragon parade amid bursting firecrackers at Chinese New Year? Although these traditions came from other countries, they are now a part of the diverse culture of the United States.

Regions of the United States also have cultural differences. Some things make all places seem alike, such as television and radio. But regional differences remain, in foods, accents, and pastimes. Consider musical styles. There is Cajun zydeco from Louisiana and bluegrass music from the Southeast. These styles "belong" to particular regions. However, people everywhere in the country enjoy them. Exchanging such things helps us appreciate the diversity of American life.

American culture also includes ordinary, everyday items. They often appear in the work of American artists. Composer Aaron Copland used cowboy songs in his ballet *Billy the Kid.* Andrew Wyeth painted haunting pictures of ordinary people in humble country surroundings. In

READ ACTIVELY

Connect What traditions do you think reflect your ethnic heritage?

▼ In small towns—like Elm Grove, Wisconsin—and large cities, people celebrate the Fourth of July with big parades.

Joseph Andereasen
age 11
United States

Sports are very much a part of a nation's culture. Baseball has been called the national pastime of the United States. Perhaps as many as 50 million people attend major league baseball games each season. **Critical Thinking** Who do you think the artist feels is the most important player? Why?

John Steinbeck's novel, *The Grapes of Wrath,* a poor farm family escapes dust storms of the 1930s. The African American poet Langston Hughes described life in Harlem, New York City in the early 1900s.

Cultures around the world also influence America's art. Musicians borrow sounds and ideas from Asia, South America, Africa, and Eastern Europe. Painters use techniques and images from Europe, Africa, and Asia. Writers use themes from the world's folk tales. Like Tito, the boy from Mexico, American artists all believe in different ideas coming together to "make everything a whole lot better."

SECTION 1 REVIEW

1. **Define** (a) cultural diversity, (b) cultural exchange, (c) ethnic group.

2. How has the arrival of immigrants affected the culture of the United States?

3. Why are the cultures in different environments so different from each other?

4. Describe the cultural exchange that occurred between Native Americans and Europeans.

Critical Thinking

5. **Recognizing Cause and Effect** Why do you think Anna's parents felt threatened when she began to feel like a part of American society?

Activity

6. **Writing to Learn** Write a brief poem about a custom that is important to your family or the family of a friend.

Canada

A MOSAIC

BEFORE YOU READ

Reach Into Your Background

Have you ever made a mosaic, or a picture from tiles, beads, or other small bits of material? If you have, you know how satisfying it is to create a single pattern from many different shapes and colors. Canadians are proud of their "mosaic" society. It is the product of different cultures that keep their own identities while contributing to the culture of the whole nation.

Questions to Explore

1. Why do Canadians consider their society a mosaic?
2. How have the indigenous peoples of Canada worked to preserve their cultures?

Key Term
reserve

Key People and Places
Inuits
Nunavut

C hannel-surf Canadian radio or television, and you may be surprised at the different languages you hear. Journalist Andrew H. Malcolm describes the variety of languages in Canada this way:

"One Toronto radio station broadcasts in thirty languages, including announcements of arrival delays for flights from 'back home.' In many Vancouver neighborhoods the street signs are in . . . English and Chinese. One Toronto television station survived simply by broadcasting programs in many languages aimed at many different ethnic communities, including [Pakistani] movies in Urdu with English subtitles. Toronto's city government routinely prepares its annual property tax notices in six languages: English, French, Chinese, Italian, Greek, and Portuguese."

▼ For people across the world, the Royal Canadian Mounted Police, or Mounties, symbolize Canada.

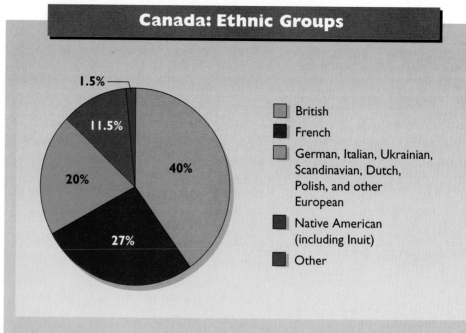

Canada: Ethnic Groups

1.5%

11.5%

40%

20%

27%

- British
- French
- German, Italian, Ukrainian, Scandinavian, Dutch, Polish, and other European
- Native American (including Inuit)
- Other

Chart Study Like the United States, Canada is very ethnically diverse. **Critical Thinking** Hundreds of years ago, Native Americans were the largest ethnic group in Canada. What group is largest today? What percentage of Canada's people are of European descent?

LINKS TO LANGUAGE ARTS

Forming an Identity
Until the 1830s, no French-Canadian poets or novelists had any of their work published in Canada. The Quebec Movement of 1860 was the first attempt to preserve French culture. In the 1960s, Quebec poets worked to create a French-Canadian identity. One example is Paul Chamberland. In his book called *Terre Québec*, which means "the land of Quebec," he uses language to encourage pride in the province's French roots.

The People of Canada

The people who speak these languages came to Canada in search of better lives. Since Canada is the second-largest country in the world, it was attractive to newcomers in search of land and new opportunities. From the beginning, Canada's leaders made immigration easy. At first, they preferred European settlers. Laws set limits on immigrants who were Jews, Asians, or Africans. But that has changed. Today, people of all ethnic groups may move to Canada as long as they can support themselves.

Sometimes the ties among Canadians are not as strong as those among Americans. People in the United States may disagree with one another. But they rarely talk about forming independent states or countries. Some Canadian groups do.

For instance, the French Canadians of Quebec are very concerned about preserving their heritage. They are glad that Canada is a bilingual country. It has two official languages—English and French. In Quebec, special laws promote French culture and language. For instance, all street and advertising signs are written in French. An English translation of the sign appears below the French. But many French Canadians want more. They want Quebec to become a separate country. To show their determination, they have license plates that read *Je me souviens,* or "I remember." This refers to remembering their French heritage.

Canada's indigenous peoples also want to preserve their culture. Most, however, do not want to be independent. Instead, they are trying to fix problems from the past. In Canada, as in the United States, early European settlers took over the indigenous peoples' lands. Many indigenous peoples were sent to **reserves.** These were areas that the government set aside for them. Others were denied equal rights and facilities. In Canada, new laws allow the indigenous peoples to use their own languages in their schools. Now, people want their own languages on the street signs in their communities.

The Chippewa have a special problem. During World War II, the Canadian army took over Chippewa land for a military base. The Chippewa were sent to a reserve. The government said it would return the land after the war. Although the war ended in 1945, the land was not returned. The Chippewa sued the government for breaking its promise. They will use the money awarded to them for many projects. One big project is cleaning up dangerous waste that the military left behind. Chippewa chief Thomas M. Bressette feels his people deserved better treatment from the government:

READ ACTIVELY

Connect How is the history of Canada's indigenous peoples similar to that of Native Americans in the United States?

Remembering Canada's History

The community of Chemainus, British Columbia, is famous for its collection of 33 historical murals. The murals are huge, and the people depicted in them are larger than life. This mural honors the role that the country's indigenous peoples have played in Canada's history.

▼ An Inuit artist uses a drill to put the finishing touches on a soapstone carving. Creating such traditional artwork is one way the Inuits retain their identity.

READ ACTIVELY

Ask Questions What do you want to know about the ways in which Canadians have encouraged artists to express Canadian ideals?

"While our people were giving their lives [in the war] in Europe, the Government here in Canada was taking their land away from them and putting us on postage-stamp [size] reserves. We're asking for a share in the resources. We don't want to appear as beggars dependent on the government handouts, but we are now being denied the resources that we so willingly gave up to support this nation."

Canada's Inuits are also trying to improve their lives. For centuries, these nomadic hunters lived in the Arctic. They had great survival skills and were fine craftworkers and artists. They made everything they needed. Modern technology, however, allows them to buy the clothes, tools, and weapons they once used to make. Many Inuits have lost their traditional skills. As a result, some feel they are losing their identity as Inuits. In the early 1990s, the Inuits convinced the Canadian government to grant them a huge section of land, which was part of the Northwest Territory. On April 1, 1999, the area became an official Canadian territory. The Inuits named it *Nunavut* (NOO nah voot), or "Our Land."

Canadian Culture—The Mosaic

Canada has made a special effort "to recognize all Canadians as full and equal participants in Canadian society." This means that people can be Canadian and express their ethnic heritage at the same time. There is one cultural issue that unites most Canadians. They feel that the United States has too much influence on their culture. This worry is not new. As early as 1939, Canada established the National Film Board. Its job is to support movies with Canadian national themes and concerns.

Canadians still search for ways to express their unique culture. Painters have played a role. In the 1920s and 1930s, several painters formed the "Group of Seven." These artists developed bold new techniques for their paintings of Canada's landscape. The group inspired other Canadian artists to experiment. Many are still doing this today. Some ethnic artists follow other paths. For instance, Inuit printmakers and sculptors give new life to the images and ideas of their ancestors.

Many Canadian writers and musicians are famous for their work. American writer Mark Twain highly praised Lucy Maud Montgomery's *Anne of Green Gables.* The heroine, Anne, was "the dearest and most moving and delightful child since Alice in Wonderland," Twain said. Today, writers such as Margaret Atwood and Alice Munro are praised for their work. "The Wreck of the Edmund Fitzgerald" is a well-known

A Canadian Export

Hockey began in Canada, probably in the mid-1800s. Since that time, the Canadians have exported their national game to the United States. Twenty-four of the 30 teams in the National Hockey League are located in U.S. cities. Also, some 60 percent of players in the NHL are Canadians. Above, Canadian Paul Kariya of the Anaheim Mighty Ducks prepares to move forward with the puck.

folk song about a ship that sank in a storm on Lake Superior. Most people think the song is old. Actually, it was written in the 1970s by Canadian folksinger Gordon Lightfoot.

In sports, Canada has turned the tables. It has influenced the United States. Ice hockey and lacrosse are two of Canada's athletic exports. Every year, hockey teams from the United States and Canada compete for the Stanley Cup, a Canadian prize.

Overcoming Obstacles
Terry Fox never earned millions a year or had an athletic shoe named after him. But he was one of the greatest Canadian athletes. In 1980, for 143 days in a row, he ran a daily marathon, which is 26 miles (42 km) long! Through snow, hail, and intense heat, he ran 3,339 miles (5,374 km). But why? When Terry was 19, his right leg was amputated because of bone cancer. He ran to raise money to help others with the disease. When his "Marathon of Hope" was over, he had raised $25 million for cancer research.

SECTION 2 REVIEW

1. **Define** reserve.

2. **Identify** (a) Inuits, (b) Nunavut.

3. Why can Canadian society be described as a mosaic?

4. How have Canada and Quebec tried to protect French culture?

5. What have the Inuits done to protect their culture?

Critical Thinking

6. **Making Predictions** Think about the Inuits gaining an official Canadian territory. What do you think might happen to their culture? Why?

Activity

7. **Writing to Learn** Write a brief paragraph explaining why you think ice hockey developed in Canada.

Organizing Information

What tools do you use to help you study? You certainly use your books, and you probably use a pencil and paper. Perhaps you use a dictionary or note cards. What about maps? You can make a map of the material you want to learn, and not just for your geography class.

When you think of a map, you might picture a map of a country or a continent from your textbook. Perhaps you think of a globe or of a street map. There are dozens—maybe even hundreds—of different kinds of maps. But there is an entirely different kind of map that you may not know of. It does not show the land or the water or even the sky.

This kind of map is called a concept map. As you read about a new topic, you can draw a concept map of the information. When you take notes, a concept map can help you organize information in a way that can be easier to understand and remember.

Get Ready

A concept map shows how concepts, or ideas, are related to one another. You can make a concept map about almost anything. Look at the concept map below.

The *subject* of this concept map, "lamps," is in the middle. Two important *features* of this subject are identified in the circles. Lines connect the features to the subject to show that they are related.

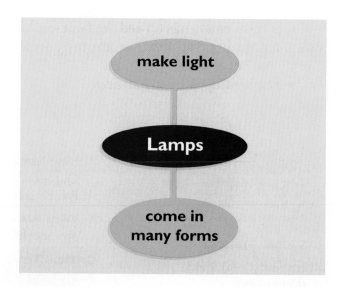

Now look below at how this concept map can grow. Can you see where *details* have been added to each of the features of lamps? Lines connect the details to each feature to show that they are related.

The subject of the concept map is in the middle. The features of the subject are identified at the next level. The final level identifies details of the features. As you get farther away from the middle of a concept map, it becomes more specific.

This type of concept map is sometimes called a "web." Can you see how its shape is similar to that of a spider web?

How do the concept maps show a great deal of information in a simple way? Notice that they show how all the ideas are related to each other. That is what makes concept maps so useful.

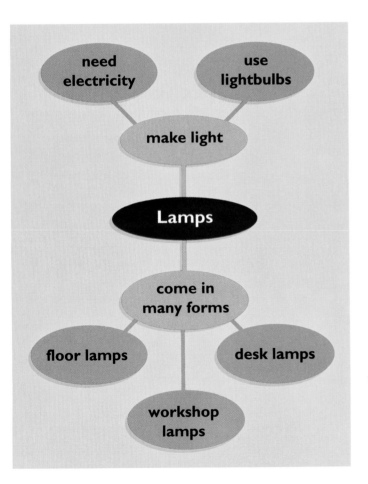

Try It Out

Try drawing your own concept maps. Draw a web for each of the subjects below.
- cars
- school
- music

Start with the subject in the center of the web. Then add features in circles connected to the subject with lines. Next add details of each feature. Some information you could include in a web about cars is shown in the chart.

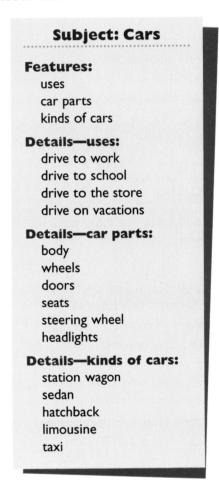

Subject: Cars

Features:
uses
car parts
kinds of cars

Details—uses:
drive to work
drive to school
drive to the store
drive on vacations

Details—car parts:
body
wheels
doors
seats
steering wheel
headlights

Details—kinds of cars:
station wagon
sedan
hatchback
limousine
taxi

Apply the Skill

Concept maps can be especially useful when you use them in your schoolwork. Reread Chapter 3 and create a web for each of the subjects below.
- Nunavut
- immigration
- traditions

Review and Activities

Reviewing Main Ideas

1. What contributions have Native Americans made to American culture?

2. If you went to an ethnic street festival, what kinds of things might you find?

3. What challenges face immigrants who move to the United States?

4. Why did the Chippewa sue the Canadian government?

5. How is Canadian culture similar to a mosaic?

Reviewing Key Terms

Match the definitions in Column I with the key terms in Column II.

Column I

1. the exchange of customs, ideas, or things between two cultures

2. a wide variety of cultures

3. an area set aside for native peoples

4. a group of people who share a language, history, and culture

Column II

a. **cultural diversity**

b. **cultural exchange**

c. **ethnic group**

d. **reserve**

Critical Thinking

1. **Drawing Conclusions** What do you think will be the effect on Canada if Quebec eventually becomes a separate country?

2. **Expressing Problems Clearly** Why do some French Canadians want Quebec to be a separate country?

Graphic Organizer

Immigrants have contributed much to the cultures of the United States and Canada. Copy the chart onto a sheet of paper. Then fill in the empty boxes with examples of regions from which immigrants to the United States and Canada came.

	United States	Canada
Regions from which immigrants came		

Map Activity

Native American Groups
For each Native American group listed below, write the letter from the map that shows its location.

1. Miami

2. Chippewa

3. Cherokee

4. Iroquois

5. Pueblo

6. Cheyenne

7. Comanche

8. Huron

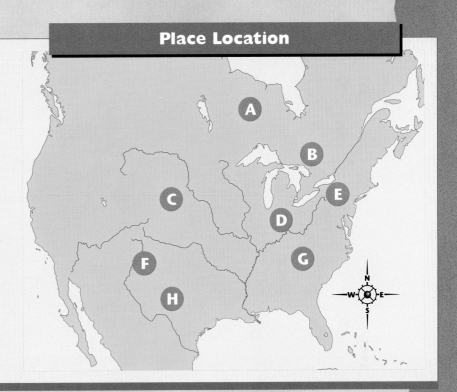

Writing Activity

Writing a Letter
Suppose that Anna and Tito are pen pals. Write a letter from Tito to Anna, suggesting ways she might get her parents more involved in American culture. Remember, Tito believes problems can be solved when different ideas come together. Perhaps he might suggest that her parents contribute ideas to a community project. What kind of project could they participate in? How could participation make Anna's parents feel like they are part of their new society?

Take It to the NET

Activity Explore Canada to learn more about its culture and history. Use the information you gather to create a travel brochure for the country. For help in completing this activity, visit www.phschool.com.

Chapter 3 Self-Test To review what you have learned, take the Chapter 3 Self-Test and get instant feedback on your answers. Go to www.phschool.com to take the test.

Skills Review

Turn to the Skills Activity.
Review how concept maps are used to organize information. Then answer the following questions: (a) What three levels of information are shown on a concept map? (b) What is another name for a concept map?

How Am I Doing?

Answer the following questions to check your progress.

1. Can I identify the important contributions immigrants have made to the United States?

2. Do I understand why Canadian culture is described as a mosaic?

3. Can I describe some challenges faced by immigrants to a country such as the United States or Canada?

4. What information from this chapter can I include in my journal?

Western Wagons

BY STEPHEN VINCENT BENÉT

prairie-schooner a covered wagon used by American pioneers to travel across the country

They went with axe and rifle, when the trail was still to blaze,
They went with wife and children, in the prairie-schooner days,
With banjo and with frying pan—Susanna, don't you cry!
For I'm off to California to get rich out there or die!

We've broken land and cleared it, but we're tired of where we are.
They say that wild Nebraska is a better place by far.
There's gold in far Wyoming, there's black earth in Ioway,
So pack up the kids and blankets, for we're moving out today!

The cowards never started and the weak died on the road,
And all across the continent the endless campfires glowed.
We'd taken land and settled—but a traveler passed by—
And we're going West tomorrow—Lordy, never ask us why!

◀ This photograph was taken in 1866. The colors were hand painted on the photograph. It shows a wagon train on its way through the Strawberry Valley in the Sierra Nevada, a mountain range in California.

We're going West tomorrow, where the promises can't fail.
O'er the hills in legions, boys, and crowd the dusty trail!
We shall starve and freeze and suffer. We shall die, and tame the lands.
But we're going West tomorrow, with our fortune in our hands.

EXPLORING YOUR READING

Look Back

1. In "Western Wagons," what hopes do the people have for their future?

Think It Over

2. What is the mood of the travelers in "Western Wagons"?

Go Beyond

3. This poem mentions men and boys but barely refers to women or girls. Why do you think that is so? How could the poem be changed to include the women and girls who were part of these beginnings?

Ideas for Writing: Poem

4. Think of some important or unusual element of your family, community, or some other group to which you belong. It could be a special custom or a more general way of living. Write a poem that explains how this began, using historical facts or inventing a story.

CHAPTER 4

Exploring the United States

SECTION 1
The Northeast
LAND OF BIG CITIES

SECTION 2
The South
A CHANGING LANDSCAPE

SECTION 3
The Midwest
MOVING FROM THE FARM

SECTION 4
The West
USING RESOURCES WISELY

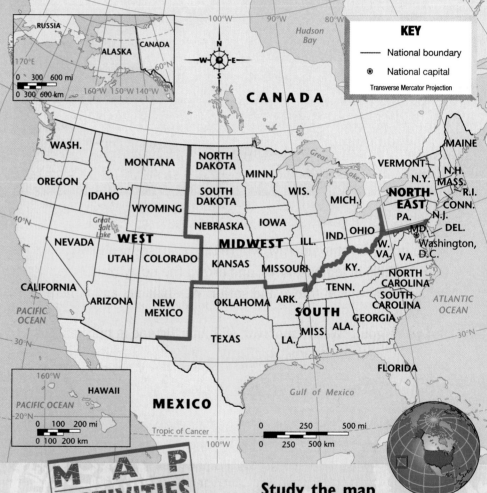

MAP ACTIVITIES

The United States can be divided into distinct regions. These are the Northeast, the South, the Midwest, and the West. To learn more about these regions, do the following activities.

Study the map
Which regions have seacoasts? Which region has the largest states, and which has the smallest?

Look for clues
Think about what it would be like to live in each region. What has attracted people to different parts of the United States? What kinds of work do you think people in different regions do?

The Northeast

LAND OF BIG CITIES

Reach Into Your Background

Draw a quick sketch of your neighborhood. Do the houses have big yards, or are they close together? Do you live in an apartment with other families next door, or is your nearest neighbor some distance away? How do you think closeness to other people affects the ways people live?

Questions to Explore

1. How do the large cities of the Northeast contribute to the economy of the United States?
2. Why is the Northeast a region of many cultures?

Key Terms

commute
megalopolis
population density

Key Places

New York City
Philadelphia
Boston

For at least a century, life in New York City has been described in one way: crowded. One hundred years ago, horse-drawn carriages caused traffic jams. Now, almost 5 million riders squeeze into New York's subway cars every day. Others travel the 1,871 miles (3,011 km) of bus lines or catch one of the city's 12,000 taxis. And many people drive their own cars through the city's busy streets. The ferryboat is another way to travel in New York.

New York is not unique. Washington, D.C., Philadelphia, and Boston are also crowded. In these big cities, millions of people commute, or travel to work, each day. Many drive to work from suburbs that are far from the city's center. Even people who live in the city must travel from one area to another to work.

A Region of Cities

A nearly unbroken chain of cities runs from Boston to New York to Washington, D.C. This coastal region of the Northeast is a megalopolis (meg uh LAHP uh lis). In this type of region, cities and suburbs have

▼ During rush hour, New York City's streets fill with cars. If you are in a hurry, try walking or grabbing a subway train instead of driving.

The Northeast: Population

Urban and Rural Population

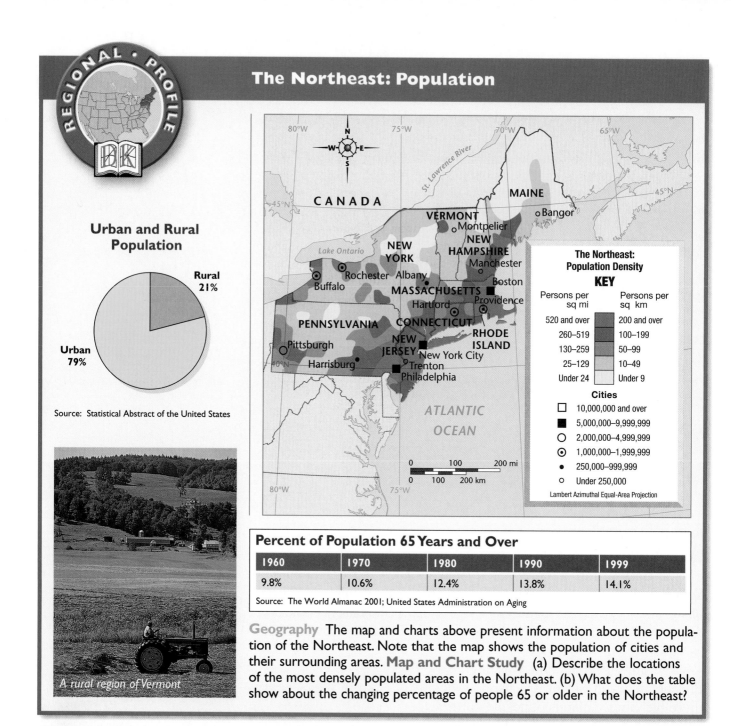

Rural 21%

Urban 79%

Source: Statistical Abstract of the United States

A rural region of Vermont

The Northeast: Population Density

KEY

Persons per sq mi	Persons per sq km
520 and over	200 and over
260–519	100–199
130–259	50–99
25–129	10–49
Under 24	Under 9

Cities

☐	10,000,000 and over
■	5,000,000–9,999,999
○	2,000,000–4,999,999
◉	1,000,000–1,999,999
•	250,000–999,999
○	Under 250,000

Lambert Azimuthal Equal-Area Projection

Percent of Population 65 Years and Over

1960	1970	1980	1990	1999
9.8%	10.6%	12.4%	13.8%	14.1%

Source: The World Almanac 2001; United States Administration on Aging

Geography The map and charts above present information about the population of the Northeast. Note that the map shows the population of cities and their surrounding areas. **Map and Chart Study** (a) Describe the locations of the most densely populated areas in the Northeast. (b) What does the table show about the changing percentage of people 65 or older in the Northeast?

Take It to the NET
Data Update For the most recent data on the Northeast, visit www.phschool.com.

grown so close together that they form one big urban area. Look at the map on the next page to see how large this area is.

The Northeast is the most densely populated region of the United States. A region's **population density** is the average number of people per square mile (or square kilometer). The population is denser in parts of New Jersey than in crowded countries like India or Japan!

The Northeast's economy is based on cities. Many were founded in colonial times, along rivers or near the Atlantic Ocean. These cities began as transportation and trade centers. Today, manufacturing, finance, communications, and government employ millions of urban Northeasterners.

Philadelphia and Boston Philadelphia and Boston were important in our nation's early history. In Philadelphia, America's founders adopted the Declaration of Independence and the Constitution. Some early struggles against the British took place in Boston. In Philadelphia and Boston, you can visit buildings that date from before the American Revolution. Yet you will find that they are very modern cities, too.

Today, Philadelphia is an industrial powerhouse. It is located near the mouth of the Delaware River. Important land and water transportation routes pass through here. Ships, trucks, and trains bring in raw materials from other parts of Pennsylvania and from all over the world. Thousands of factories process food, refine petroleum, and manufacture chemicals. Hundreds of products are then shipped out for sale.

The Boston area is famous for its more than 20 colleges and universities. Cambridge (KAYM brij) is the home of Harvard, which is America's oldest university. The city is also famous for its science and technology centers. Boston's universities and scientific companies often work together to design new products and to carry out medical research.

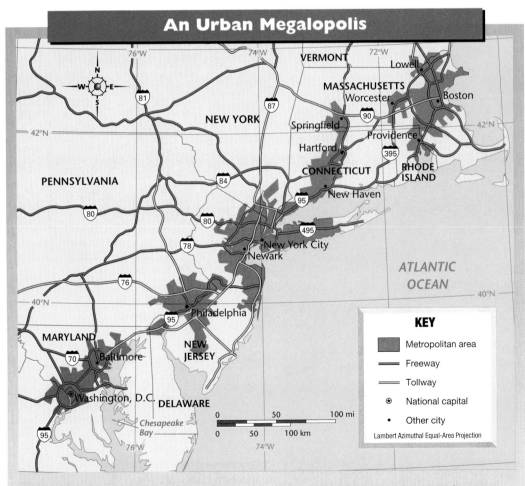

An Urban Megalopolis

KEY
- Metropolitan area
- Freeway
- Tollway
- ⊛ National capital
- • Other city

Lambert Azimuthal Equal-Area Projection

Map Study You can drive from Washington, D.C., to Boston, Massachusetts, almost entirely within urban areas. **Place** Compare this map with the one in the Regional Profile. What similarities are there between the two maps?

EXPLORING TECHNOLOGY

The Brooklyn Bridge

The Brooklyn Bridge is a suspension bridge in New York City. A suspension bridge hangs from cables that are anchored at either end and supported by several towers along the bridge's length. Completed in 1883, the bridge crosses the East River, connecting two boroughs, or sections, of the city—Manhattan and Brooklyn. At the time of its completion, the Brooklyn Bridge was the longest suspension bridge in the world. There are six lanes for traffic. A wide walkway for pedestrians runs along the center of the bridge.

The suspender cables connect the cables and the roadbed.

Each tower is 275 feet (84 m) tall. The two towers are seated firmly in underwater piers buried deep in the riverbed.

The anchorages at either end of the bridge are huge blocks of concrete, set deep in the ground.

The roadbed, or deck, has special braces, called *trusses*, that prevent the bridge from swinging during high winds.

The main cable runs from one anchorage, across two towers, to a second anchorage. This cable is nearly 16 inches (41 cm) thick and is made of steel.

New York City One word describes New York City—huge. In terms of population, it is the largest city in the United States and one of the 10 largest in the world. More than 8 million people live in New York City. Most states do not have populations that large. The city covers an area of about 320 square miles (830 sq km) on islands and the mainland around the mouth of the Hudson River. The various parts of the city are connected by tunnels and bridges. One of the oldest and most interesting bridges is the Brooklyn Bridge. The diagram on the opposite page shows how the Brooklyn Bridge was built.

New York City is our nation's "money capital." The word *millionaire* was invented here. About 500,000 New Yorkers work for banks and other financial institutions. The headquarters of many of the country's wealthiest corporations are in New York. The famous New York Stock Exchange is on Wall Street.

New York is also a center of fashion, publishing, advertising, television, radio, and the arts. New York's Broadway is famous for its plays. About eight million people see plays in New York every year.

◄ New York City's financial district is a maze of skyscrapers. One of the streets hidden among these towers is Wall Street, the heart of New York's banking and financial industries.

A Gateway for Immigrants

On January 1, 1892, 15-year-old Annie Moore made her way down the gangplank of a steamship onto American soil. Annie and her two younger brothers had sailed from Ireland. Annie stepped into the registry room of the Ellis Island Immigrant Station. Here she received a $10 gold piece for being the first immigrant to arrive at the new station.

From 1892 to 1943, the first stop for millions of immigrants to the United States was Ellis Island. From here, immigrants could see the Statue of Liberty, half a mile away in New York Harbor. Today, Ellis Island and the Statue of Liberty are national monuments.

New York and other port cities of the Northeast have been important gateways for immigrants. In the 1800s, many Irish and Germans immigrated to New York. Later, immigrants poured in from Southern and Eastern Europe. During the 1900s, people also have come from the Caribbean, Asia, and Africa. In one recent year, New York City welcomed immigrants from more than 100 different countries.

After entering through the port cities, many immigrants stayed in those cities and built a new life. Today, New York is rich in ethnic diversity. You can visit Little Italy, Little India, and Chinatown. To get a real sense of the ethnic diversity of the United States, just look at a list of restaurants in a big city like New York.

▶ The Statue of Liberty symbolizes the United States' tradition of providing a home to immigrants. The statue stands on Liberty Island in New York Harbor.

SECTION 1 REVIEW

1. **Define** (a) commute, (b) megalopolis, (c) population density.

2. **Identify** (a) New York City, (b) Philadelphia, (c) Boston.

3. (a) How does the population density in the Northeast compare with densities in other regions of the country?

(b) How does population density affect the ways people live and work?

4. If you were looking for work in the Northeast, what kinds of jobs might you find?

5. How have immigrants affected the culture of the Northeast?

Critical Thinking

6. **Making Comparisons** Think about the histories of, and major industries in, Philadelphia and Boston. How are the two cities similar? How have they developed differently?

Activity

7. **Writing to Learn** Which city described in this section are you most interested in learning more about? Make a list of things you would like to learn about this city. Then write a brief paragraph explaining why you want to learn these things.

The South

A CHANGING LANDSCAPE

BEFORE YOU READ

Reach Into Your Background

Think about a time in your life when you experienced a big change. Perhaps you moved to another community or started at a new school. How did you adapt to the change? Did you find yourself thinking and behaving in new ways?

Questions to Explore

1. How are the South's land and water important to its economy?

2. How has the growth of industry changed the South?

Key Terms

petrochemical
industrialization
Sun Belt

Key Places

Atlanta
Washington, D.C.

From July 19 to August 4, 1996, the city of Atlanta, Georgia, was the center of the world. More than two million people from 172 countries visited the city during that time. They came to see a very special event. It was the 1996 Summer Olympic Games.

The people who watched the 1996 Olympics saw more than great athletes. They also saw a world-class city. Atlanta today is a center of trade, transportation, and communication. Atlanta is also in one of the fastest-growing regions of the United States: the South. With strong urban areas like Atlanta, plus rich agriculture, the South is helping to lead the United States into the future.

The Varied Land of the South

People in the South today can make a living in many different ways. The South's geography makes many of these jobs possible. The South is warmer than regions of the United States that are farther north. Most parts of the region also receive plenty of rain. The wide coastal plains along the Atlantic

▼ Famous boxer Muhammad Ali lights the Olympic torch at the 1996 Summer Olympic Games in Atlanta, Georgia.

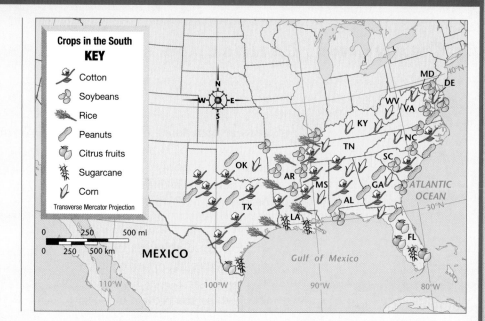

Crops in the South
KEY

- Cotton
- Soybeans
- Rice
- Peanuts
- Citrus fruits
- Sugarcane
- Corn

Transverse Mercator Projection

Growing Seasons

Crop	Growing season
Corn	60–330 days
Cotton	135–180 days
Peanuts	120–140 days
Soybeans	100–150 days
Sugarcane	about 240 days

Source: Encyclopedia Britannica;
MSN Encarta Encyclopedia

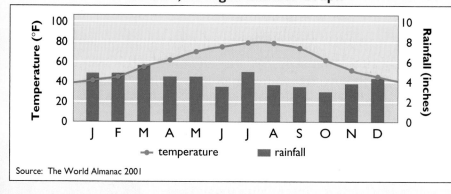

Atlanta, Georgia: Climate Graph

Source: The World Almanac 2001

Cotton harvesting in the South

Geography The map and charts above present information about climate and land use in the South. **Map and Chart Study** (a) What crops are grown in Texas? (b) In what month is the average temperature highest in Atlanta? (c) Why are the crops listed in the growing season chart well-suited to be grown the South?

Take It to the **NET**
Data Update For the most recent data on the South, visit
www.phschool.com.

Ocean and the Gulf of Mexico have rich soil. Together, these features make much of the South a great place for growing crops. Some places in the region are also good for raising animals. People in the South can take advantage of many different natural resources.

Farming in the South Farming has always been one of the most important parts of the South's economy. For years, the South's most important crop was cotton. Southern farmers once depended on cotton as their only source of income. Today, cotton still brings a lot of money to the South, especially to Alabama, Mississippi, and Texas. But

"King Cotton" no longer rules this region. In the 1890s, the boll weevil (bowl WEE vuhl)—a kind of beetle—began to attack cotton plants in the South. Over the next 30 years, it destroyed fields across the area. Without money from cotton, many farmers went bankrupt. Most southern farmers now try to raise more than one crop. Together they produce a wide variety of crops and farm animals.

Some of these crops need very special growing conditions. Citrus fruits require year-round warmth and sunshine. Florida has plenty of both. More oranges, tangerines, grapefruits, and limes are grown here than in any other state. Rice needs warm, moist growing conditions. Farmers in Arkansas, Louisiana, and Mississippi can supply this. They grow rice along the coast of the Gulf of Mexico and in the Mississippi River valley.

Some areas of the South have become famous for their agricultural products. Georgia has taken one of its products as its nickname. It is the Peach State. Georgia is also known for its peanuts and pecans. Texas raises more cattle than any other state. Arkansas raises the most chickens and turkeys. All of these items are just a sample of what southern agriculture produces. You can read about more of the South's farm products in the Regional Profile.

Drilling and Mining in the South In some parts of the South, what is under the soil is as important as what grows in it. In Louisiana, Oklahoma, and Texas, companies drill for oil and natural gas. These can be used as fuel. They are also made into **petrochemicals.** These are substances, like plastics, paint, and asphalt, that come from petroleum. In Alabama, Kentucky, West Virginia, and Tennessee, miners dig for coal. Southern states are also leading producers of salt, sulfur, lead, zinc, and bauxite—a mineral used to make aluminum.

READ ACTIVELY

Predict Think about what happened when oil and natural gas were discovered in Louisiana, Oklahoma, and Texas. How do you think those discoveries affected the economies of those states?

◀ Cotton is no longer the South's major crop, but it still plays an important part in the region's economy.

Southern Fish and Forests People in the South can also make a living in fishing and forestry. The Chesapeake Bay area near Maryland and Virginia is famous for its shellfish. However, the South's fishing industry is strongest in Louisiana and Texas. The timber industry works in every southern state except for Delaware. Softwood trees like southern pine are used for building or for paper. People use hardwood trees to make furniture. North Carolina has the nation's largest hardwood furniture industry.

Southern Cities and Industries

Until recently, people often thought of the South as a slow-moving, mostly rural region. But over the past 50 years, this region has gone through lots of changes. Though the South's rural areas are still important, most people in the South today live in cities. Some work in factories or in high-technology firms. Others work in tourism or in one of the other industries in this region's growing economy. This change from an agriculture-based economy to an industry-based economy is called **industrialization.**

Textiles and Technology One of the most important industries in the South is the textile industry. Textile mills make cloth. They were first built in this region to use the South's cotton. Today, many mills still make cotton cloth. Many others now make cloth from synthetic, or human-made, materials. The textile industry is strongest in Georgia, the Carolinas, and Virginia.

Visualize Visualize how a rural area might change to an urban area. What do you think might be built? What features might disappear?

▼ One of the largest cities in the United States, Dallas, Texas, is a center of banking, industry, and trade.

The tourists on this steamboat are getting a taste of what it was like to travel on the Mississippi River more than 100 years ago. They are taking a trip on the *Natchez*, which sails out of New Orleans, Louisiana. In the 1800s and early 1900s, steamboats were an important form of transportation on rivers in the United States. **Critical Thinking** What part of a steamboat is used to push the ship through the water?

The textile industry was an early arrival in the South. The first mills in the region were built in the 1800s. Now, more than 100 years later, new industries are growing all across the South. One is the high-technology industry. Workers in this industry try to improve computers and figure out better ways to use them. Some centers of high technology are Raleigh, North Carolina, and Austin, Texas. Another forward-looking industry is the aerospace business. In Cape Canaveral, Florida; Houston, Texas; and Huntsville, Alabama, people work for the National Aeronautics and Space Administration (NASA). Some train as astronauts and run the space shuttle program. Atlanta, Georgia, is now a center for the cable television industry. If you watch the news on cable television, you are probably watching a program from Atlanta.

Transportation and Tourism A big part of the South's economy depends on moving goods and people into and out of the region. Most of the South's largest cities play big roles in this transportation industry. Miami, Florida, and New Orleans, Louisiana, are major ports. Miami is a center for goods and people going to and from Central and South America. New Orleans is a gateway between the Gulf of Mexico and the Mississippi River system. It is also an important port for oil tankers.

Some of the people the transportation industry brings to the South come to stay. Thousands come to work in the South's new industries. Thousands more choose to move to the South because of its climate. The South is part of the **Sun Belt.** This broad area of the United States

TO MUSIC

Jazz Jazz music is arguably the South's greatest contribution to the arts in America. Most people consider New Orleans to be the birthplace of jazz. Mainly African in origin, jazz grew out of many different kinds of music. African American work songs, hymns, and spirituals are all part of its roots. Today, musicians in New Orleans play many forms of jazz. One of the most popular is called Dixieland or New Orleans jazz.

stretches from the southern Atlantic Coast to the coast of California. It is known for its warm weather. The population of the Sun Belt has been rising for the past few decades. Some arrivals are older adults who want to retire to places without cold winters. Others come to take advantage of both the weather and the work that the Sun Belt offers.

Warm weather also brings people to the South who only plan to visit. These people fuel the region's tourist industry. In winter, tourists come to enjoy the sunny beaches of Florida and the Gulf Coast. In the summer, they can hike in the mountains of the Appalachians and Ozarks. They can visit historic cities like Charleston, South Carolina, or New Orleans, Louisiana, at any time of the year. In states throughout the South, there are always fun and exciting things to see and to do.

Our Nation's Capital The city of Washington is not in any state. Instead, it is in the District of Columbia, which lies between the states of Maryland and Virginia. This area of land was chosen as the site for the nation's capital in 1790. Located on the shore of the Potomac River, Washington, D.C., was the first planned city in the nation. It has wide avenues, public buildings, and dramatic monuments. Many people consider Washington to be one of the most beautiful cities in the world. As the nation's capital, it is home to the nation's leaders and to hundreds of foreign diplomats.

U.S. Space Camp

Every year, people from ages 10 to 92 come to Huntsville, Alabama, to go to U.S. Space Camp. Here, a student experiences "weightlessness."

SECTION 2 REVIEW

1. **Define** (a) petrochemical, (b) industrialization, (c) Sun Belt.
2. **Identify** (a) Atlanta, (b) Washington, D.C.
3. How have the geography and climate of the South shaped its economy?
4. How has the South changed in the 1900s?

Critical Thinking

5. **Recognizing Cause and Effect** In this section, you have learned that the population of the South is growing. How have the South's geography and economy affected this growth?

Activity

6. **Writing to Learn** You work in an advertising firm in Atlanta, Georgia; Houston, Texas; or Miami, Florida. Create an advertisement to persuade people to move to your city or state. The advertisement can be designed for a newspaper or a magazine. It can also be for radio, television, or the Internet.

The Midwest

MOVING FROM THE FARM

BEFORE YOU READ

Reach Into Your Background

Have you ever introduced a new food or activity to your family? Can you think of a time when you pursued a new interest on your own? In the Midwest, many people are building ways of life very different from the ways their parents lived.

Questions to Explore

1. How is technology changing agriculture in the Midwest?
2. How is the change in agriculture affecting the growth of cities?

Key Terms
mixed-crop farm
recession
corporate farm

Key Places
Chicago
Detroit
St. Louis
Minneapolis-St. Paul

Camille LeFevre grew up in Black River Falls, Wisconsin. Her family included many generations of farmers. Camille spent her childhood on her parents' sheep farm.

> "As a skinny, pigtailed youngster, I spent a lot of time naming lambs, . . . falling off horses named Ginger and Lucky, building hay forts, riding tractors, stuffing freshly sheared wool into gunny sacks and perching on fence gates staring dreamily into space."

Camille remembers her childhood with deep affection. Yet, like thousands of farm children who grew up in the 1980s and 1990s, she did not follow in her parents' footsteps. Farming in the Midwest changed, and Camille chose a different path.

Technology Brings Changes to the Midwest

The Midwest is often called "the heartland" because it is the agricultural center of our nation. The soil is rich, and the climate is suitable for producing corn, soybeans, and livestock. Technology helped make farms productive. Inventions like the

▼ On most farms, sheep-shearing takes place once a year. The wool from this breed of sheep—the Suffolk—is used to make industrial and upholstery fabrics.

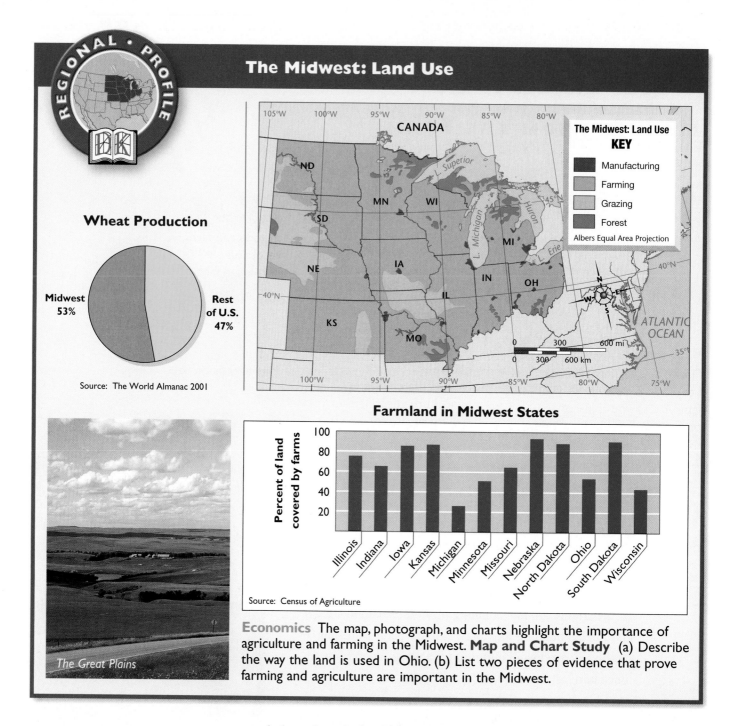

The Midwest: Land Use

Wheat Production

Midwest 53%

Rest of U.S. 47%

Source: The World Almanac 2001

The Great Plains

The Midwest: Land Use
KEY
- Manufacturing
- Farming
- Grazing
- Forest

Albers Equal Area Projection

Farmland in Midwest States

Percent of land covered by farms

Illinois, Indiana, Iowa, Kansas, Michigan, Minnesota, Missouri, Nebraska, North Dakota, Ohio, South Dakota, Wisconsin

Source: Census of Agriculture

Economics The map, photograph, and charts highlight the importance of agriculture and farming in the Midwest. **Map and Chart Study** (a) Describe the way the land is used in Ohio. (b) List two pieces of evidence that prove farming and agriculture are important in the Midwest.

steel plow, the windmill, and barbed wire helped settlers carve out farms on the plains. Today, technology continues to change the way people farm the land.

Take It to the NET
Data Update For the most recent data on the Midwest, visit **www.phschool.com**.

Family Farms Dwindle Until the 1980s, small family farms operated in this region. Many of these farms were **mixed-crop farms.** That is, they grew several different kinds of crops. This was a sensible way for farmers to work. If one crop failed, the farm had others. Camille's family, for example, sometimes raised cattle as well as sheep.

In the 1960s and 1970s, family farms prospered. The world population was rising, and demand for American farm products was high. Farmers felt that they could increase their business if they enlarged their farms. To build bigger farms, farmers bought more land and equipment. But all of this cost money. Many farmers borrowed from local banks.

In the early 1980s, there was a country-wide **recession** (rih SESH un), or a downturn in business activity. The demand for farm products dropped. At the same time, interest rates on loans increased. As a result, many farmers were not able to make enough money to pay their loans. Some families sold or left their farms. Over one million American farmers have left their land since 1980.

Corporate Farms Expand   What happened to the farms that were sold? Many of them were bought by agricultural companies. Small farms were combined to form large ones called **corporate farms.** These large farms could be run more efficiently. Large agricultural companies could afford to buy the expensive land and equipment that modern farming requires. And they could still make a profit.

Corporate farmers rely on machines and computers to do much of the work. This means that corporate farms employ fewer workers. Kansas offers a good example of corporate farming—having fewer

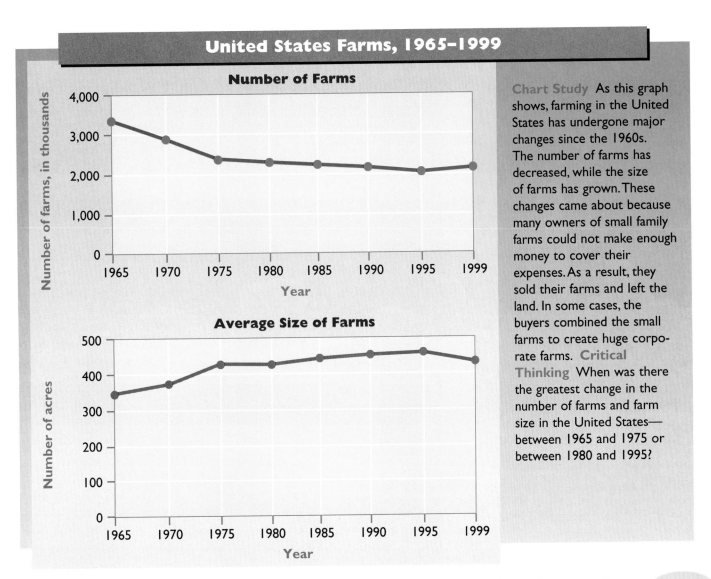

United States Farms, 1965–1999

Number of Farms

Number of farms, in thousands

4,000
3,000
2,000
1,000
0

1965 1970 1975 1980 1985 1990 1995 1999

Year

Average Size of Farms

Number of acres

500
400
300
200
100
0

1965 1970 1975 1980 1985 1990 1995 1999

Year

Chart Study As this graph shows, farming in the United States has undergone major changes since the 1960s. The number of farms has decreased, while the size of farms has grown. These changes came about because many owners of small family farms could not make enough money to cover their expenses. As a result, they sold their farms and left the land. In some cases, the buyers combined the small farms to create huge corporate farms. **Critical Thinking** When was there the greatest change in the number of farms and farm size in the United States— between 1965 and 1975 or between 1980 and 1995?

workers and larger farms. In Kansas, 90 percent of the land is farmland, but less than 10 percent of the people are farmers.

Not every farm in the Midwest is a corporate farm. But most small farms do not earn enough money to support a family. Family farmers usually have another job as well. Camille LeFevre's father, for example, advises other farmers on the best foods for their livestock.

Camille's parents did not lose their farm, but they did sell all their livestock to send Camille to college. When she graduated, she did not go back to the land. Farming these days is a very difficult way to make a living, she explains. She felt that she would have more opportunities in the city.

The Midwest Grows Cities

Camille is not alone. Most people in the Midwest today live in towns and cities. Yet many of these cities got their start as places to process and ship farm products.

Chicago: At the Center of Things   Chicago, Illinois, is a good example. Located on Lake Michigan, it was surrounded by prairies and farms in the mid-1800s. Farmers sent their corn, wheat, cattle, and hogs to Chicago. Mills and meat-packing plants turned these products into foods and shipped them east on the Great Lakes. When railroads were built, Chicago really boomed. By the late 1800s, it had become a steel-making and manufacturing center. What was one of the most important manufactured products made in Chicago? You probably guessed it: farm equipment.

READ ACTIVELY

Ask Questions What questions would you like to ask a person who grew up on a farm and later moved to a city?

▼ This view from the shores of Lake Michigan shows the many skyscrapers in Chicago's downtown area. The Sears Tower, to the left, is the tallest building in the United States.

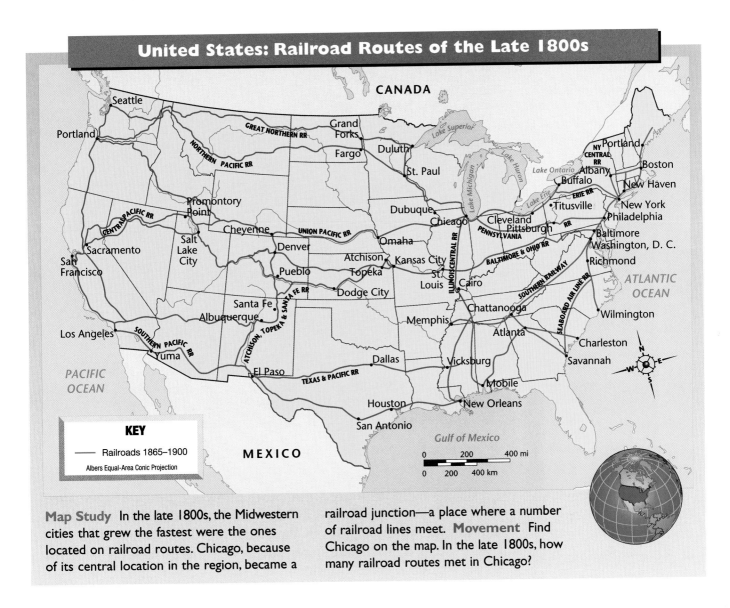

United States: Railroad Routes of the Late 1800s

KEY

— Railroads 1865–1900

Albers Equal-Area Conic Projection

Map Study In the late 1800s, the Midwestern cities that grew the fastest were the ones located on railroad routes. Chicago, because of its central location in the region, became a railroad junction—a place where a number of railroad lines meet. **Movement** Find Chicago on the map. In the late 1800s, how many railroad routes met in Chicago?

Today, Chicago is the biggest city in the heartland. It is known for its ethnic diversity and lively culture. It is the hub of major transportation routes—highways, railroads, airlines, and shipping routes. Chicago is also the home of the first skyscraper—and many other architectural wonders. For a bird's-eye view of Chicago, go to the top of the Sears Tower, one of the tallest buildings in the world.

Other Cities The Midwest has other large cities. Two of them—Detroit and St. Louis—have played an important role in the country's history. Why do you think Detroit, Michigan, is called "the Motor City"? Here, you will find the headquarters of the American automobile industry. General Motors, Ford, and Chrysler have plants here.

Covered wagons, not cars, used to roll through St. Louis, Missouri. Located on the Mississippi River, this city was the starting point for pioneers heading west. Today, a huge stainless steel arch beside the river marks St. Louis as the "Gateway to the West." St. Louis is also a banking and commercial center.

LINKS

ACROSS THE WORLD

Higher and Higher Until 1996, Chicago's Sears Tower, at 1,454 feet (443 m), was the world's tallest building. Now, the Petronas Twin Towers in Malaysia holds that title. It is 1,483 feet (452 m) high. But the world record may change again soon. When completed, the World Financial Center in Shanghai, China, will top out at 1,509 feet (460 m).

THE UNITED STATES AND CANADA   **103**

Suburban Minneapolis–St. Paul

The metropolitan area of Minneapolis–St. Paul covers about 5,051 square miles (8,129 sq km) around the point where the Mississippi and Minnesota rivers join. The area's population stands at more than 2.8 million people and is growing steadily. The greatest population growth has taken place in Minneapolis–St. Paul's suburban areas, like the one pictured here. **Critical Thinking** Compare this photograph with the photograph of Chicago earlier in this section. How are the two scenes different? What similarities, if any, do you see?

Camille LeFevre moved to another Midwestern city, Minneapolis–St. Paul, Minnesota. These "Twin Cities" face each other on opposite sides of the Mississippi River. Publishing, medical, computer, and art businesses are flourishing here. The city's suburbs have replaced the fertile land once used for farming. But the city has offered Camille the opportunity to build a career as a journalist. Camille's father still has his farm, and she visits him on the weekends. Perhaps Camille enjoys the best of both worlds.

SECTION 3 REVIEW

1. **Define** (a) mixed-crop farm, (b) recession, (c) corporate farm.

2. **Identify** (a) Chicago, (b) Detroit, (c) St. Louis, (d) Minneapolis–St. Paul.

3. Why did family farmers face hard times in the 1980s?

4. How are mixed-crop farming and corporate farming different?

Critical Thinking

5. **Identifying Central Issues** Think of how farming has changed with the development of corporate farms. List the advantages and disadvantages of corporate farming.

Activity

6. **Writing to Learn** Suppose you are a farmer and you have decided to sell your farm and move to a city. Write a letter to a friend explaining your decision.

The West

USING RESOURCES WISELY

Reach Into Your Background
Do you and your family take part in a recycling program, try to conserve water, or control the amount of electricity you use? In the western United States, people are trying to improve how they use resources.

Questions to Explore
1. What are the resources of the West?
2. How are people working to balance conservation with the need to use natural resources?

Key Terms
forty-niner
mass transit

Key Places
Sierra Nevada
Pacific Northwest
Portland
San Jose

An American President stood before Congress and made the following statement:

> "The conservation of our natural resources and their proper use constitute the fundamental problem which underlies almost every other problem of our national life. . . . But there must be . . . a realization . . . that to waste, to destroy our natural resources, to skin and exhaust the land instead of using it so as to increase its usefulness, will result in undermining . . . the very prosperity which we ought by right to hand down to [our children]."

Do you think this sounds like a modern plea for the environment? Actually, President Theodore Roosevelt made this statement about one hundred years ago. He understood that the vast resources of the West would not last without proper care.

▼ Congress declared Yosemite a national park in 1890. Yosemite Falls, which drops some 2,425 feet (740 m), is higher than any big-city skyscraper.

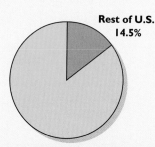

Gold Production

Rest of U.S.
14.5%

West 85.5%

Source: USGS Mineral Production Data

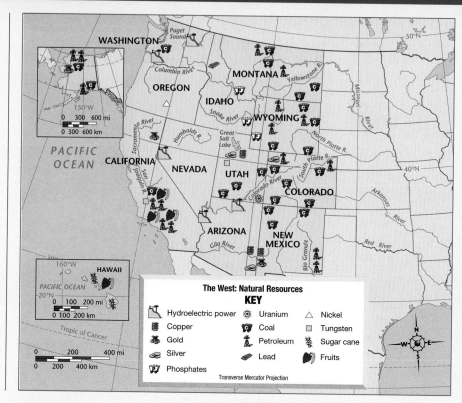

The West: Natural Resources
KEY

⚒ Hydroelectric power	⊛ Uranium	△ Nickel
🔳 Copper	🏭 Coal	⬜ Tungsten
⚜ Gold	⛏ Petroleum	🌿 Sugar cane
🍥 Silver	▭ Lead	🍒 Fruits
🔲 Phosphates		

Transverse Mercator Projection

Top Hydroelectric Power-Producing States in the United States

States	Millions of Megawatt Hours
Washington	💧💧💧💧💧💧💧💧
California	💧💧💧💧💧
Oregon	💧💧💧💧
New York	💧💧💧
Idaho	💧
Arizona	💧
Montana	💧

💧 10 million

Note: States in red are in the West.

Source: Energy Information Administration, US Department of Energy

Economics The map and charts above present information about natural resources and energy in the western United States. **Map and Chart Study** (a) Use the information in the map and chart to write a paragraph about the location and importance of gold mining in the West. (b) Describe the location of the top three hydroelectric power-producing states.

Illustration of the Hoover Dam on the Colorado River

Take It to the NET
Data Update For the most recent data on the West, visit www.phschool.com.

A Land of Precious Resources

An incredible wealth of natural resources has drawn people to the West for well over 400 years. The Spanish were well established on the West Coast even before the Pilgrims settled in New England in the 1620s. Then, after Lewis and Clark's exploration of the Louisiana Territory in the early 1800s, more people began to move westward.

Resources and Population   With the California Gold Rush in 1849, the population of the region exploded. The sleepy port of San Francisco boomed into a prosperous city. Hopeful miners arrived there, bought supplies, and headed off to the Sierra Nevada expecting to strike it rich.

A gold strike in Colorado led to the founding of the city of Denver. Further discoveries of valuable minerals drew more and more people to the region. New settlers here needed homes, and the place to find timber to build them was in the Pacific Northwest. After the Civil War, logging camps, sawmills, and paper mills sprang up in Washington, Oregon, and northern California.

At first, the resources of the West seemed unlimited. The use of these resources did create wealth and many jobs. However, it also created new challenges.

Managing Resources in the Sierras   Do you know the story of the goose that laid the golden egg? Its owner cut the goose open to see what was inside. For many years, people treated the Sierra Nevada in a similar way. The **forty-niners,** the first miners of the Gold Rush, washed small bits of gold from the streams. To get at larger deposits, big mining companies brought in water cannons that could blast away entire hillsides. They got their gold but left behind huge, ugly piles of rock.

After the Gold Rush, California's population soared. To meet the demand for new houses, loggers leveled many forests. Engineers built dams to send water through pipes to coastal cities. Next to the dams, they built hydroelectric (hy droh ee LEK trik) plants. Cities like San Francisco got water and power this way, but the dams flooded whole valleys of the Sierras.

READ ACTIVELY

Visualize What would it be like to be a part of the Gold Rush? What would you see?

▼ The magnificent views at Grand Canyon National Park in Arizona attract crowds of tourists from all over the world.

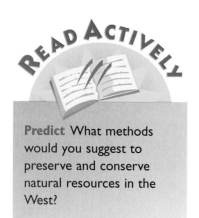

Predict What methods would you suggest to preserve and conserve natural resources in the West?

To save parts of the West as natural wilderness, Congress created several national parks and forests. Yet these, too, have developed problems. Yosemite (yoh SEM ut ee) National Park now gets so many visitors that it has traffic jams and air pollution in the summer.

Westerners are wrestling with new ways to manage the West's resources. For example, Yosemite now limits the number of campers in the park. Dam-building has stopped. Laws protect the habitats of certain animals. In addition, logging companies are limited in the amount of timber they can cut down.

The Urban West

Most Westerners today are not miners, farmers, or loggers. Rather, they work and live in cities. Their challenge is to figure out how to use natural resources wisely.

Portland, Oregon   "Your town or mine?" two land developers asked each other in 1845. The two developers were at the same site and predicted the development of a major port city. With such a great location near the junction of the Willamette and Columbia rivers, how could they lose? Francis W. Pettigrove of Portland, Maine, won the coin toss. He named the site after his hometown in the East.

Portland became a trade center for lumber, furs, grain, salmon, and wool. In the 1930s, new dams produced cheap electricity. Portland attracted many manufacturing industries. Over time, the factories polluted the Willamette River. Federal, state, and local governments—and industries—have worked to clean up this valuable resource.

A Black Bear in Its Natural Habitat

Many Westerners are working to preserve the land areas where black bears and other wild animals live. Parts of the West have been made into national parks, forests, and wilderness areas. In addition, logging companies are working to preserve the environment by planting new trees to replace the ones that have been cut down.

Phoenix, Arizona

Half of Arizona's people live in Phoenix, which is Arizona's capital and an important industrial center. As the city has grown, it has sprawled out across the surrounding desert.

San Jose, California   Urban sprawl is a problem in San Jose. The area around San Jose was known as "Valley of the Heart's Delight" for its beautiful orchards and farms. Now it is called "Silicon Valley," because it is the heart of the computer industry.

Instead of good soil and climate, San Jose's most valuable resource is its people. They come from all parts of the world. The greater population density has created crowded freeways and air pollution. To counter these problems, San Jose has built a light-rail **mass transit** system. Mass transit replaces individual cars with energy-saving buses or trains.

CITIZEN HEROES

To Be a Leader Cesar Chavez and his family made a living as migrant farmworkers. Pay was low, and working conditions were hard. Chavez wanted to build a better future for migrant farmworkers. He helped to set up a farmworkers' union. Chavez's union organized national boycotts of farm products. As a result, farm owners agreed to improve pay and working conditions. Chavez had achieved his goal—fair treatment of migrant farmworkers.

SECTION 4 REVIEW

1. Define   (a) forty-niner, (b) mass transit.

2. Identify   (a) Sierra Nevada, (b) Pacific Northwest, (c) Portland, (d) San Jose.

3. (a) How have people used the resources of the West?
(b) How are these resources being protected today?

4. What natural resources made Portland a good location for a city?

Critical Thinking

5. Recognizing Cause and Effect   How has rapid urban growth affected the natural resources of the West?

Activity

6. Writing to Learn   Do you think that there are better ways to use natural resources in your community? Write a letter to your representative in Congress expressing your ideas. To help you in this task, think about the efforts in the West to preserve and conserve resources.

SKILLS ACTIVITY

Understanding Circle Graphs

Chris walked across the playground with his new friend Kyung, who had just moved to Texas from Korea. Kyung looked up at the burning sun.

"Boy, it's really hot here. Does the whole United States get weather like this?"

"It depends," said Chris. "Let me think ... in the Northwest it rains a lot, and I don't think it gets quite as hot as here. But Arizona and New Mexico do, for sure. In the Midwest, they have some really hot summers, but freezing cold winters. They have tornadoes, too. And then there's Alaska—their summers don't get too hot, even though the sun shines all night long. You know, it's hard to say. This country gets a lot of different weather."

▼ A typical sunny day in Myakka River State Park, Florida

Get Ready

Trying to describe the weather of the United States is no easy task. The United States has a great variety of weather. It can be hard to keep it all straight, but graphs can make it easier.

One common type of graph is a circle graph. Circle graphs show proportion, or the parts of a whole. The entire circle represents all, or 100 percent, of something. Half the circle represents 50 percent. Smaller slices represent smaller amounts, and larger slices represent larger amounts.

Try It Out

The best way to understand how circle graphs work is to try making one yourself. Working with a few other students, make a circle graph showing last week's weather. Follow the steps on the next page.

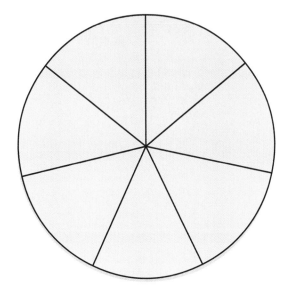

A. Record last week's weather. Write the days of the week in a column down the left-hand side of a sheet of paper. Working with your group, recall last week's weather. Which days had precipitation? Which days did not? Next to each day, note that day's weather activity as either *precipitation* or *no precipitation*. Now count the number of days with precipitation and with no precipitation and make a note of each on your paper.

B. Draw your circle graph. On another sheet of paper, copy the circle above. For your graph, the circle represents one week. Notice how the circle is divided into seven sections, one for each day of the week.

C. Fill in your circle graph. Using one color for each weather category, fill in your circle graph. You should color in one section of the graph for every day. For example, suppose there were three rainy days last week and you chose blue to represent precipitation. Color three sections blue. Be sure to keep the sections with the same color together.

D. Label your circle graph. Finally, label each color on your circle graph or create a key to show what each color stands for. Give your graph a title that tells what the graph is about.

E. Study your circle graph. Your graph lets you quickly see what proportion of last week had precipitation and what proportion did not. How would you describe last week's weather—as mostly wet or mostly dry?

Apply the Skill

A circle graph can show more than two categories of data. It can also be compared with other graphs showing the same kind of data, like the graphs on this page. Use the graphs to answer the questions below.

1 **Become familiar with the illustration.** Read the title. What is the subject of these two graphs? Read the graph key. What data do the graphs provide?

2 **Study the graphs.** Look at the graph for Los Angeles. How would you describe the weather in Los Angeles? Now study the graph for Boston. What percent of the year had no precipitation in this city?

3 **Use the graphs to make comparisons.** Which city has the most rain? What other comparisons can you make?

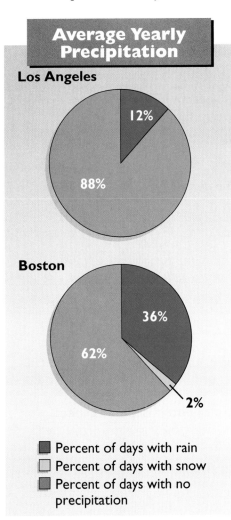

CHAPTER 4 Review and Activities

Reviewing Main Ideas

1. What are some of the large cities of the Northeast?
2. How does the Northeast serve as a gateway to the country?
3. How do people in the South make a living?
4. How does warm weather affect the economy of the South?
5. What major changes have occurred in the Midwest since the 1980s?
6. Describe the differences between family farms and corporate farms.
7. What are the main natural resources of the West?
8. How has life in the West changed since the days of the California Gold Rush?
9. How has the way people manage natural resources in the West changed since the 1800s?

Reviewing Key Terms

Use each key term below in a sentence that shows the meaning of the term.

1. commute
2. megalopolis
3. population density
4. petrochemical
5. industrialization
6. Sun Belt
7. mixed-crop farm
8. recession
9. corporate farm
10. forty-niner
11. mass transit

Critical Thinking

1. **Making Comparisons** Identify at least one major trend that two or more regions of the United States have in common.
2. **Drawing Conclusions** If the unwise use of resources continues in the West, what are some likely results?

Graphic Organizer

Copy the chart onto a separate sheet of paper. Then, using information from the chapter, fill in the empty boxes.

	Resources	Cities	Current Industries
Northeast			
South			
Midwest			
West			

Map Activity

United States

For each place listed below, write the letter from the map that shows its location.

1. Boston
2. New York City
3. Washington, D.C.
4. Atlanta
5. Chicago
6. Detroit
7. Portland
8. San Jose

Place Location

Writing Activity

Writing a Travel Guide
If you had friends who were visiting the United States for the first time, what information would you want to share with them? Which cities would you tell them to visit? Write a brief travel guide for your friends that takes them to all four regions of the United States. Do research to plan the trip. Suggest activities for each region. Provide background information to help your friends understand the history and culture of each region.

Take It to the NET

Activity Make state maps that show urban areas, ethnic groups, and other information about culture and geography. For help in completing this activity, visit www.phschool.com.

Chapter 4 Self-Test To review what you have learned, take the Chapter 4 Self-Test and get instant feedback on your answers. Go to www.phschool.com to take the test.

Skills Review

Turn to the Skills Activity.
Review how special graphs can give information. Then complete the following: (a) Explain what a circle graph shows. (b) Give two examples of kinds of information that could be shown in a circle graph.

How Am I Doing?

Answer these questions to help you check your progress.

1. Do I understand the history and economic development of the four regions of the United States?
2. Can I describe the major cities in the Northeast?
3. Can I identify the major resources and economic challenges in the South, the Midwest, and the West?
4. What information from this chapter can I include in my journal?

Childtimes

BY ELOISE GREENFIELD AND LESSIE JONES LITTLE, WITH MATERIAL BY PATTIE RIDLEY JONES

BEFORE YOU READ

Reach Into Your Background

How much do people know about the lives of their grandparents? What about the lives of their parents as children? Suppose someone wanted to write a history of his or her family—how could they find information?

You can learn a lot from seeing how a single family lives through several generations. Every family history reflects the history of the country or region where that family lives. The following excerpts come from a book written by a mother and daughter, with help from the grandmother. They have written a *memoir,* or a true story of personal experience. This memoir tells the story of their family, and it also takes a peek into the history of the growth of their hometown, Parmele, North Carolina.

Questions to Explore

1. How does the town of Parmele change over three generations?
2. What do the memoirs of the three generations have in common?

Pattie Frances Ridley Jones
Born in Bertie County, North Carolina, December 15, 1884

Parmele, North Carolina

Towns build up around work, you know. People go and live where they can find jobs. And that's how Parmele got started.

At first, it was just a junction, a place where two railroads crossed. Two Atlantic Coast Line railroads, one running between Rocky Mount and Plymouth, and one running between Kinston and Weldon. Didn't too many people live around there then, and those that did were pretty much spread out.

Well, around 1888, a Yankee named Mr. Parmele came down from New York and looked the place over, and he saw all those big trees and decided to start a lumber company. Everybody knew what that meant. There were going to be jobs! People came from everywhere to get work. I was right little at that time, too little to know what was going on, but everybody says it was something to see how fast that town grew. All those people moving in and houses going up. They named the town after the man who made the jobs, and they called it *Pomma-lee.*

The lumber company hired a whole lot of people. They hired workers to lay track for those little railroads they call tram roads that they were going to run back and forth between the town and the woods. They hired lumberjacks to chop the trees down and cut them up into logs and load them on the tram cars. They hired men to build the mill and put the machinery in, and millworkers to run the machines that would cut the logs into different sizes and dry them and make them nice and smooth.

Lessie Blanche Jones Little
Born in Parmele, North Carolina,
October 1, 1906

Parmele

I used to hear Papa and Mama and their friends talking about the lumber mill that had been the center of life in Parmele before I was born, but there wasn't any mill when I was growing up. The only thing left of it

was the sawdust from all the wood they had sawed there. The sawdust was about a foot thick on the land where the mill had been. I used to love to walk on it. It was spongy, and it made me feel like I was made of rubber. I'd take my shoes off and kind of bounce along on top of it. But that was all that was left of the mill.

My Parmele was a train town. The life of my town moved around the trains that came in and out all day long. About three hundred people lived in Parmele, most of them black. There were three black churches, a Baptist, a Methodist, and a Holiness, and one white church. Two black schools, one white. There wasn't even one doctor, and not many people would have had the money to pay one, if there had been. If somebody got down real bad sick, a member of the family would go by horse and buggy to a nearby town and bring the doctor back, or sometimes the doctor would ride on his own horse.

Most of the men and women in Parmele earned their living by farming. Some did other things like working at the tobacco factory in Robersonville, but most worked on the farms that were all around in the area, white

▼ These people were picking peppers in 1921 on a farm in Louisiana.

115

▲ Going to church in the South in the 1930s

READ ACTIVELY

Ask Questions What more would you like to know about farm life?

Pamlico Sound (PAM lih koh sound) a long body of water off the coast of North Carolina that separates the Hatteras Islands from the mainland

people's farms usually. When I was a little girl, they earned fifty cents a day, a farm day, sunup to sundown, plus meals. After they got home, they had all their own work to do, cooking and cleaning, laundry, chopping wood for the woodstove, and shopping.

***

Parmele had trains coming in and going out all day long. Passenger trains and freight trains. There was always so much going on at the station that I wouldn't know what to watch. People were changing trains and going in and out of the cafe and the restaurant. They came from big cities like New York and Chicago and Boston, and they were all wearing the latest styles. Things were being unloaded, like furniture and trunks and plows and cases of fruit and crates of clucking chickens, or a puppy, or the body of somebody who had died and was being brought back home. And every year around the last two weeks in May, a special

train would come through. It had two white flags flying on the locomotive, and it was carrying one hundred carloads of white potatoes that had been grown down near Pamlico Sound, where everybody said the soil was so rich they didn't even have to fertilize it.

The train station was a gathering place, too. A lot of people went there to relax after they had finished their work for the day. They'd come downtown to pick up their mail, or buy a newspaper, and then they'd just stand around laughing and talking to their friends. And on Sundays fellas and their girls would come all the way from other towns, just to spend the afternoon at the Parmele train station.

***

It was hard for Papa to find work. Not long after Sis Clara died, we moved to Mount Herman, a black section of Portsmouth, Virginia. Papa worked on the docks there, and even though he didn't make much money, the work was steady. But when we moved back to Parmele, it was hard for him to find any work at all.

***

Eloise Glynn Little Greenfield
Born in Parmele, North Carolina, May 17, 1929

Daddy Makes a Way

When I was three months old, Daddy left home to make a way for us. He went North, as thousands of black people had done, during slavery and since.

They went North looking for safety, for justice, for freedom, for work, looking for a good life. Often one member of a family would go ahead of the others to make a way—to find a job and a place to live. And that's what my father did.

In the spring of 1926, Daddy had graduated from high school, Parmele Training School. He had been offered a scholarship by Knoxville College in Tennessee, but he hadn't taken it. He and Mama had gotten married that fall, and now they had Wilbur and me to take care of. Mama had been teaching school since her graduation from Higgs, but she had decided to stop.

Nineteen twenty-nine was a bad time for Daddy to go away, but a worse time for him not to go. The Great Depression was about to begin, had already begun for many people. All over the United States, thousands of people were already jobless and homeless.

In Parmele, there were few permanent jobs. Some seasons of the year, Daddy could get farm work, harvesting potatoes and working in the tobacco fields. Every year, from August to around Thanksgiving, he worked ten hours a day for twenty-five cents an hour at a tobacco warehouse in a nearby town, packing tobacco in huge barrels and loading them on the train for shipping. And he and his father were house movers. Whenever somebody wanted a house moved from one place to another, Daddy and Pa would jack it up and attach it to a windlass, the machine that the horse would turn to move the house. But it was only once in a while that they were called on to do that.

So, one morning in August 1929, Mama went with Daddy to the train station and tried to hold back her tears as the Atlantic Coast Line train pulled out, taking him toward Washington, D.C. Then she went home, sat in the porch swing, and cried.

In Washington, friends helped Daddy find a room for himself and his family to live in, and took him job hunting. He found a job as a dishwasher in a restaurant, and in a few weeks, he had saved enough money for our train fare.

READ ACTIVELY

Visualize Picture the trains arriving at the station and the people and goods as they come off board.

Great Depression a period of time in the 1930s when businesses did not do well, causing many people to lose their jobs

EXPLORING YOUR READING

Look Back

1. How did the town of Parmele first begin to grow? What did adding a lumber company do that made more people come to the town?

Think It Over

2. Why were trains such an important part of Parmele?

Go Beyond

3. What do these memoirs tell you about the time period they cover?

Ideas for Writing: Memoir

4. Write a memoir of your own childhood from the point of view of yourself as an older person. What forces have most shaped your life?

CHAPTER 5

Exploring Canada

SECTION 1
Ontario and Quebec
CONNECTING TWO CULTURES

SECTION 2
The Canadian Plains
CANADA'S BREADBASKET

SECTION 3
British Columbia
TIES TO THE PACIFIC RIM

SECTION 4
The Atlantic Provinces
UNITED BY THE SEAS

SECTION 5
The Northern Territories
NEW FRONTIERS

MAP ACTIVITIES

Canada is a nation of many cultures. People from all over the world have immigrated to Canada. This has given each region a distinct cultural identity. To get acquainted with some of these regions, do the following activities.

Study the map
Find the provinces of Quebec, Saskatchewan, and British Columbia on the map. Using information on the map, describe the relative location of each province.

Make historical connections
Which of the three provinces do you think was first settled by Europeans? Explain your answer.

Ontario and Quebec

CONNECTING TWO CULTURES

BEFORE YOU READ

Do friends and neighbors' families celebrate different ones than those of your family?

Reach Into Your Background

Every ethnic group has traditions and customs that are unique to its culture. What traditions and holidays does your family celebrate?

Questions to Explore

1. How has Canada's form of government been shaped by its history?
2. What is the structure of the Canadian federation?
3. What have French Canadians in Quebec done to preserve their culture?

Key Terms

Canadian Shield
federation
autonomous
Francophone
Quiet Revolution
separatist
referendum

Key People and Places

Ottawa
Toronto
Jacques Cartier
Stadacona
Montreal

Much of the border between Ontario and Quebec is formed by the Ottawa River. The Macdonald-Cartier Bridge stretches across the river, connecting the two provinces. The bridge is named for two Canadian political leaders, one an English speaker and one a French speaker. While the bridge links the two provinces, its very name characterizes the differences between the provinces—English is primarily spoken in Ontario, while people in Quebec mostly speak French.

In spite of this significant distinction, Ontario and Quebec have much in common. They are home to Canada's two largest cities—Toronto, Ontario and Montreal, Quebec. They are the two most populous provinces in Canada. Canada's capital, Ottawa, is located in Ontario. But the city of Hull, Quebec, located on the other end of the Macdonald-Cartier bridge, is considered Ottawa's "sister city" because a number of federal government buildings dot its landscape.

▼ The Macdonald-Cartier bridge is the busiest bridge between Quebec and Ontario.

Ontario

The province of Ontario is perhaps Canada's most diverse province geographically. Located on the United States border, it reaches from the Hudson Bay in the north to the Great Lakes in the south. Ontario's northern region is part of the **Canadian Shield**, which has rocky terrain, rugged winters, and is sparsely populated. The province's southern lowlands have milder winters and warm summers. About one third of Canada's entire population lives in this southern area.

The Seat of Government Canada is a federation, or union, of 13 provinces and territories. In the Canadian federation, each province has its own government. Each of these governments must answer to Canada's central government, located in Ottawa. Although Canada's head of state is the monarch of Britain, Canada has complete power over its own government. Unlike in the United States, where the president is head of government as well as head of state, in Canada, there is a separate head of government, called the prime minister. The prime minister is part of Canada's central legislature—the Canadian Parliament.

Visualize Picture the land of Ontario as if you were in a plane flying above it.

READ ACTIVELY

The Parliament Buildings in Ottawa

The Parliament Buildings are an example of the Gothic style of architecture, which is a style that is characterized by medieval buildings. This type of architecture developed in Western Europe between the 12th and 16th centuries.
Critical Thinking How do the Parliament Buildings reflect Canada's heritage?

Ontario: Population

Ethnic Origin

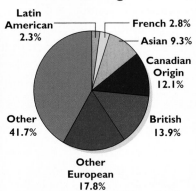

- Latin American 2.3%
- French 2.8%
- Asian 9.3%
- Canadian Origin 12.1%
- British 13.9%
- Other European 17.8%
- Other 41.7%

Source: Statistics Canada

Eastern Ontario

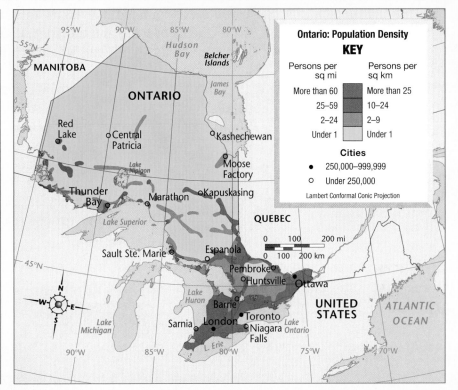

Ontario: Population Density
KEY

Persons per sq mi	Persons per sq km
More than 60	More than 25
25–59	10–24
2–24	2–9
Under 1	Under 1

Cities
- 250,000–999,999
- Under 250,000

Lambert Conformal Conic Projection

Population by Age Group and Sex

Female		Age	Male	
3.2%		75+	1.9%	
4.0%		65–74	3.4%	
10.9%		45–64	10.6%	
16.6%		25–44	15.9%	
6.4%		15–24	6.6%	
10.0%		Under 15	10.6%	

Source: Statistics Canada

Geography The map and charts above present information about the people of Ontario and where they live. **Map and Chart Study** (a) According to the map, which region is the most densely populated? Which region is the least populated? (b) Study the two charts. Write three sentences describing the population of Ontario.

Ottawa has been a capital city since the middle of the nineteenth century, when Upper and Lower Canada—present-day Ontario and Quebec—formed the Province of Canada. Ottawa was selected as the capital because it was located on the border of the two territories. In 1867, Nova Scotia and New Brunswick joined Ontario and Quebec to become the Dominion of Canada, a totally **autonomous**, or self-governing, member of the British Empire. Ottawa continued to be Canada's capital.

Take It to the NET
Data Update For the most recent data on Ontario, visit **www.phschool.com**.

Ask Questions What questions would you like to ask an immigrant to Toronto?

Provincial Capital, Cultural Mosaic Each of Canada's provinces has a capital. Toronto is the capital of Ontario. It is also Canada's largest city and its commercial, cultural, and financial center. Toronto was founded in 1793 as York, and its location on Lake Ontario made it a major trade and transportation center. Toronto has come to be identified by its CN Tower, which is one of the world's tallest freestanding structures.

Toronto has matured into a cultural mosaic with a very diverse population—42 percent of its residents are foreign-born. After World War II, a large number of Europeans immigrated to Canada, with many settling in Toronto. The most recent wave of immigrants included a large number of people from Asia, and Chinese now make up more than 10 percent of Toronto's residents. British, Italian, Native Canadian, Portuguese, East Indian, Greek, German, Ukrainian, Polish, and French are among the other ethnic groups that make up Toronto's population.

Toronto Skyline

The bustling city of Toronto is located on Lake Ontario. The city's skyline is dominated by the CN Tower which stands 1,815 feet (553 m) tall (pictured left). The white dome next to the tower is the SkyDome, where the Toronto Blue Jays baseball team plays. The SkyDome was the first dome stadium built with a roof that opens and closes.

French Influence in Quebec

French culture has dominated Quebec since the 1500s, when Jacques Cartier (zhahk kahr TYAY), a French explorer, sailed along the St. Lawrence River and landed in a village called Stadacona (stad uh KOH nuh). The Iroquois, the native people of the area, inhabited the village. Today the site of that village is the city of Quebec, capital of the province of Quebec.

Cartier claimed the region we now know as Quebec for France and named it New France. Great Britain, however, was also interested in the region. French and British forces fought for the land in four separate wars over a period of nearly 80 years. The last of the battles were part of the French and Indian War, which ended in 1763 with the British capturing the city of Quebec. Within four years, France surrendered all of its North American land to the British.

Despite Great Britain's victory, tens of thousands of French colonists remained in the region, and their descendants make up the majority of Quebec's population today. They are called **Francophones** (FRANG koh fohnz), or people who speak French as their first language. In Quebec's largest city, Montreal, and surrounding areas, about 67 percent of the population are Francophones.

Quebec—Distinct Society within Canada In the 1960s, many Francophones began to express concern that their language and culture might die, because English was spoken in the schools and at work. They also believed that opportunities for Francophones in

Predict What problems developed when Britain took over French colonies in Canada?

◀ The influence of French culture in Quebec can be seen on this street in the capital city where most of the storefront signs are printed in French.

Quebec: Population

Ethnic Origin

- British 2.4%
- Latin American 1.8%
- Asian 2.4%
- Other European 6.4%
- Canadian Origin 37.7%
- Other 20%
- French 29.3%

Source: Statistics Canada

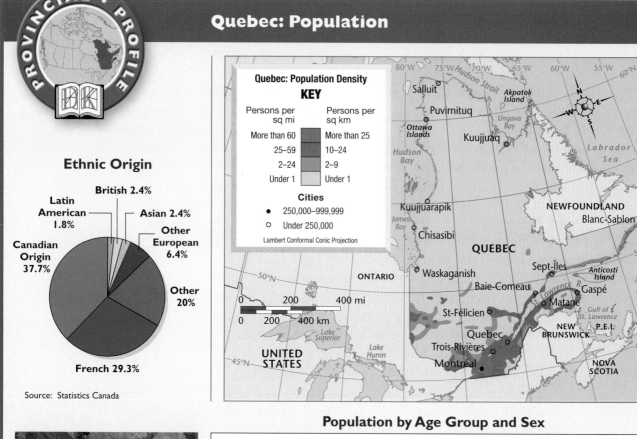

Quebec: Population Density

KEY

Persons per sq mi		Persons per sq km
More than 60		More than 25
25–59		10–24
2–24		2–9
Under 1		Under 1

Cities

- ● 250,000–999,999
- ○ Under 250,000

Lambert Conformal Conic Projection

0   200   400 mi
0   200   400 km

Population by Age Group and Sex

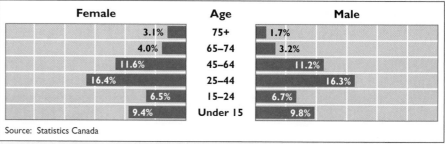

Female	Age	Male
3.1%	75+	1.7%
4.0%	65–74	3.2%
11.6%	45–64	11.2%
16.4%	25–44	16.3%
6.5%	15–24	6.7%
9.4%	Under 15	9.8%

Source: Statistics Canada

Geography The map and charts above present information about the people of Quebec and where they live. **Map and Chart Study** (a) Which area of Quebec has the highest population density? (b) Compare the charts above with those from the Ontario profile on page 121. Write down two similarities and two differences about their populations.

Chinatown in Montreal, Quebec

Take It to the NET
Data Update For the most recent data on Quebec, visit **www.phschool.com**.

Quebec were not equal to those for English speakers. For the most part, Francophones got only low-paying jobs. So they set out to create change in a movement that was similar to the civil rights movement in the United States in the 1960s. In 1960, the Liberal party, which supported Francophones, came to power in Quebec. Prime Minister Jean Lesage led the government in creating better job opportunities for Francophones and in modernizing education and health care in Quebec. This period of change became known as the **Quiet Revolution** because great changes were brought about peacefully.

Just before the 1995 referendum, a Quebec resident (right) displays her opposition to separation. She has a "no" sign on her forehead and the maple leaf—the symbol of Canada—on her cheeks. Other people carrying signs calling for "independence" and "sovereignty," rallied to support the split from Canada (above). By the narrowest of margins, Quebec residents voted to remain part of Canada. **Critical Thinking** Why do you think that so many people in Quebec want their province to be an independent country?

The Separatist Movement During the Quiet Revolution, the separatist movement began to grow. **Separatists** are people who want to see Quebec break away from the rest of Canada and become an independent country. French-Canadian separatists saw important victories in the 1970s as French became the official language of Quebec and immigrants to the province were required to learn French. But still, Quebec remained a province of Canada.

Not everyone in Quebec supported the idea of separation from Canada. In 1980, the provincial government held a referendum. In a **referendum**, voters cast ballots for or against an issue. This referendum asked voters whether Quebec should become a separate nation. A majority voted no.

In 1995, Quebec held another referendum. Again, Quebec's people voted to remain part of Canada. But this time the margin was very slim—50.6 percent voted against separation while 49.4 percent voted for it. Since then, separatists have increasingly lost power and positions in government, but vow that they will continue to fight for Quebec's independence.

READ ACTIVELY

Connect Suppose that California or New York state wanted to leave the United States and become a separate nation. What would be your response?

▶ During Quebec's Winter Carnival, artists compete to make the best sculptures of ice or packed snow.

ACROSS THE WORLD

A Copy of St. Peter's Basilica One sign of Quebec's religious heritage is Montreal's Cathedral-Basilica of Mary, Queen of the World. Built in 1870, this church was designed to look like Saint Peter's Basilica in Vatican City, in Rome, Italy. Montreal's church is one third as large as St. Peter's.

Preserving Quebec's Culture

One of the ways in which Quebec's people celebrate their culture is through festivals. The *Fête des Neiges* (fet day NEZH), or winter festival, lasts 17 days. Fantastic ice sculptures adorn the city, and canoe races take place among the ice floes in the St. Lawrence River.

Another Quebec festival honors Jean Baptiste (zhahn bah TEEST), the patron saint, or special guardian, of French Canadians. This festival is held June 24. All over the province, people celebrate with bonfires, firecrackers, and street dances.

French style and cooking are alive in Quebec—with Quebec variations. Sugar pie, for example, uses maple sugar from the province's forests. Quebec has French architecture—with Quebec variations as well. All in all, Quebec has a lively culture to preserve and protect.

SECTION 1 REVIEW

1. **Define** (a) Canadian Shield, (b) federation, (c) autonomous, (d) Francophone, (e) Quiet Revolution, (f) separatist, (g) referendum.

2. **Identify** (a) Ottawa, (b) Toronto, (c) Jacques Cartier, (d) Stadacona, (e) Montreal.

3. Describe the geography of Ontario.

4. How does Canada's government differ from that of the United States?

5. What steps have many Canadians taken to preserve French culture?

Critical Thinking

6. **Expressing Problems Clearly** Explain why many people in Quebec want to separate from Canada.

Activity

7. **Writing to Learn** List some features of Quebec and Ontario culture you would like to learn more about.

The Canadian Plains

CANADA'S BREADBASKET

BEFORE YOU READ

Reach Into Your Background
Think about something you heard that led you to believe that some experience was going to be wonderful. Were you ever disappointed when the real experience turned out to be less than you had hoped for? What did you do?

Questions to Explore
1. Why did many immigrants from central and Eastern Europe come to the Prairie Provinces in the mid-1800s?

2. How did the arrival of Europeans change life for the indigenous people of Canada's plains?

Key Terms
descent
immunity

Key Places
Regina
Calgary

One day in 1821, after a long, difficult journey, about 195 Swiss immigrants reached their new land. It was chilly on the Hudson Bay in northern Canada. The Swiss watchmakers, mechanics, pastry cooks, and musicians wanted to become Canadian farmers in this region called "Rupert's Land." Later, the region became parts of several provinces including Saskatchewan (suh SKATCH uh wahn), Alberta, and all of Manitoba. The settlers heard the vast plains had good land and an excellent climate. But no shelter, food, or supplies awaited them. The settlers survived only because the native people of the region, the Saulteaux (sawl TOH), helped them.

The Rindisbacher (RIN dis baw kur) family was part of the group of settlers. All of them—father, mother, and seven children—later moved to what is now the province of Manitoba. One of the children, 15-year-old Peter, loved to draw. He sketched and painted detailed pictures of life on the Canadian plains.

Rindisbacher's pictures tell about the hard lives of the settlers. During harsh winters they fought snow and ice. In summer they fought drought, floods, and swarms of grasshoppers. There were few trees on the plains, so many people built homes out of sod—clumps of soil and grass. They cut prairie sod into blocks and piled them up to make walls. "Soddies" were cheap, but if it rained, the roofs leaked! Few settlers had farming experience, and they did not anticipate such hardships.

▼ This photograph, taken in 1928, shows a group of young men on board the ship *Montcalm*. They are on their way to Canada to start a new life in the Prairie Provinces.

Young Provinces, Ancient Lands

Take It to the NET

Data Update For the most recent data on the Prairie Provinces, visit **www.phschool.com**.

Manitoba, Saskatchewan, and Alberta are located on the largest prairie in the world, stretching across the three provinces and down into the central United States. As a result, these provinces are often called the Prairie Provinces. The Prairie Provinces are more recent members of the Dominion of Canada. Manitoba joined the federation in 1870, and Saskatchewan and Alberta each became Canadian provinces in 1905. However, these provinces occupy lands where indigenous peoples have lived for centuries.

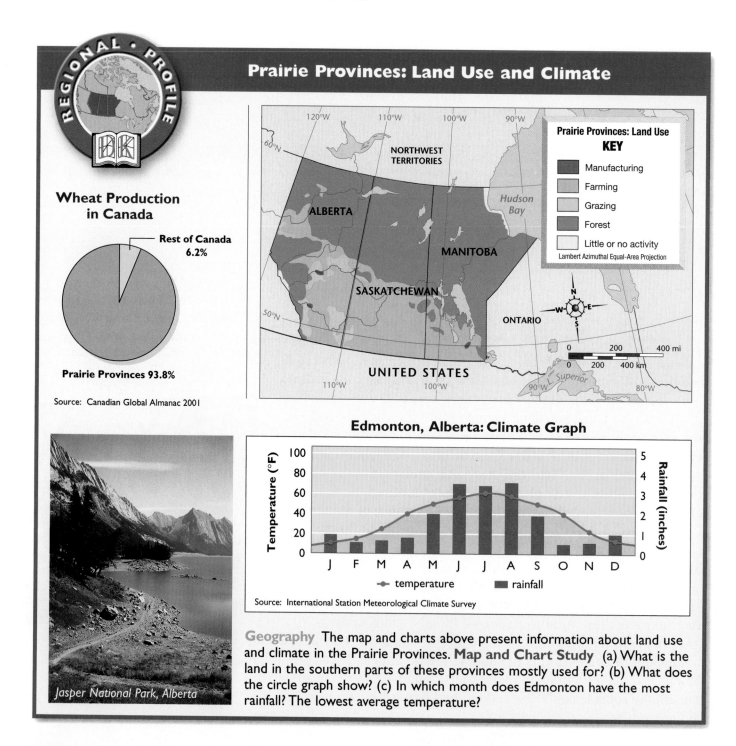

REGIONAL · PROFILE

Prairie Provinces: Land Use and Climate

Wheat Production in Canada

Rest of Canada 6.2%

Prairie Provinces 93.8%

Source: Canadian Global Almanac 2001

Prairie Provinces: Land Use KEY
- Manufacturing
- Farming
- Grazing
- Forest
- Little or no activity

Lambert Azimuthal Equal-Area Projection

NORTHWEST TERRITORIES

ALBERTA

Hudson Bay

MANITOBA

SASKATCHEWAN

ONTARIO

UNITED STATES

L. Superior

Edmonton, Alberta: Climate Graph

Temperature (°F) / Rainfall (inches)

J F M A M J J A S O N D

temperature / rainfall

Source: International Station Meteorological Climate Survey

Jasper National Park, Alberta

Geography The map and charts above present information about land use and climate in the Prairie Provinces. **Map and Chart Study** (a) What is the land in the southern parts of these provinces mostly used for? (b) What does the circle graph show? (c) In which month does Edmonton have the most rainfall? The lowest average temperature?

The Cree and Saulteaux were among the indigenous peoples who lived on the plains in what became Manitoba. The Cree, Blackfoot, and Assiniboine (uh SIN uh boyn) lived on the plains of present-day Alberta. The Chipewyan (chip uh WY uhn) and Sioux are native to Saskatchewan. These native peoples were deeply connected to the plant and animal life of their lands. Buffaloes, in particular, were the foundation of their daily lives. Buffalo meat provided food and their hides were made into clothing. Regina, now the capital of Saskatchewan, was once a place the Cree called *Oscana*, which means "pile of bones." Here people collected and cleaned buffalo bones which could be made into tools.

A Way of Life Lost In the late 1870s, the ways of life of many indigenous peoples in the Plains region of North America came to an end. For centuries, these people had built their lives around the buffalo. People of European **descent**, or ancestry, who were moving into the area, began killing off the buffalo herds. In a few years, nearly all the buffalo were gone. At the same time, the government of Canada began to take over the indigenous peoples' land. Most agreed to give up their land and live on reserves. Indigenous peoples in Canada usually did not go to war to protect their land as they did in the United States.

LINKS
TO SCIENCE

Sanctuary Visitors to Saskatchewan's Grasslands National Park see some of North America's last untouched prairies. Ancient grasses called wheat grass, snowberry, and silver sage blow in the wind. The park is also home to 12 endangered and threatened species. They include certain kinds of hawks, burrowing owls, and short-horned lizards.

Buffalo Hunting in the Plains

By the 1730s, Plains Indians were able to trade for horses. This helped the Plains Indians more effectively hunt the buffalo that provided them with clothing, food, and tools.

Connect If you wanted to move to a new location, what kinds of things would attract you?

Free Land Draws Newcomers The population of the indigenous peoples was shrinking. This happened, in part, because European immigrants brought diseases to which the Plains Indians did not have **immunity**, or natural resistance. At the same time, the European population swelled. Many early settlers like the Rindisbacher family moved away, but more immigrants replaced them. The new people were equally eager to farm the prairie. The Canadian government wanted even more people to settle there. Newcomers would help the economy grow. In the late 1800s and early 1900s, Canada advertised free land in European newspapers. The advertisements worked, and immigration increased.

Until then, most Canadians were indigenous peoples or settlers from France or Britain. That quickly changed. The newcomers were from many ethnic groups. German, French, Belgian, Ukrainian, Swedish, Hungarian, and Scandinavian immigrants all came to the Prairie Provinces. These immigrants farmed, mined, ranched, and participated in the fur trade.

Many of the European immigrants became wheat farmers. Today, more than three-fourths of Canada's farmland is in the three Prairie Provinces. Wheat is the major crop. Canada is one of the world's leading exporters of wheat. It is no wonder then, that the region is known as "Canada's Breadbasket."

Wheat Fields Near Saskatoon

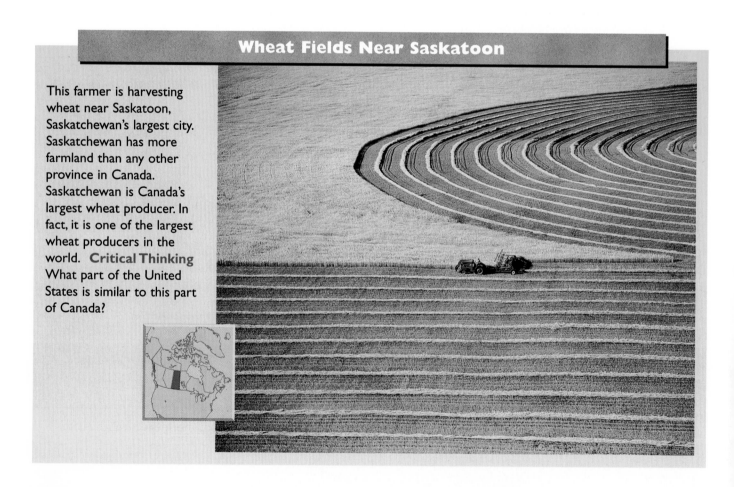

This farmer is harvesting wheat near Saskatoon, Saskatchewan's largest city. Saskatchewan has more farmland than any other province in Canada. Saskatchewan is Canada's largest wheat producer. In fact, it is one of the largest wheat producers in the world. **Critical Thinking** What part of the United States is similar to this part of Canada?

Nurturing Traditions

Each year, cities of the Prairie Provinces celebrate their ethnic or cultural heritage. In Calgary, Alberta, the Calgary Stampede commemorates the area's ranching legacy. This 10-day rodeo event has been held in Calgary since 1912. It offers a large variety of events such as chuckwagon races and bull riding. Festival du Voyageur is held each February in Winnipeg, the capital of Manitoba. It honors the French Canadian fur-trading heritage of the area with tons of traditional food, arts and crafts, and exhibits. And in Weyburn, Saskatchewan, residents pay tribute to wheat as the area's vital crop with the Weyburn Wheat Festival. A great deal of fun at this festival comes from harvesting competitions and plant shows. The smell of fresh-baked bread from outdoor ovens adds to the atmosphere.

▲ Rodeo events at the Calgary Stampede draw large crowds.

SECTION 2 REVIEW

1. **Define** (a) descent, (b) immunity.

2. **Identify** (a) Regina, (b) Calgary.

3. What attracted thousands of European immigrants to the Prairie Provinces?

4. How did the lives of indigenous people in the Canadian plains change after the Europeans arrived?

5. How have European immigrants influenced the culture of the Prairie Provinces?

Critical Thinking

6. **Drawing Conclusions** Many immigrants came to the Canadian plains in the 1800s. What advantages and disadvantages do you think this move had for them?

Activity

7. **Writing to Learn** Suppose that it is the year 1900. You want to encourage people to come to the Prairie Provinces to start farms. The government will give 160 acres of land to those willing to try. Make a poster advertising free land. Describe conditions that would make settlers want to come.

British Columbia

TIES TO THE PACIFIC RIM

BEFORE YOU READ

Reach Into Your Background

Think about the ways in which people use natural resources. How do we benefit from natural resources? What are some of the problems that using natural resources can cause?

Questions to Explore

1. Before the 1880s, what major events influenced British Columbia's culture?
2. Why does British Columbia have such a diverse population?
3. How does geography tie British Columbia to the Pacific Rim?

Key Terms
totem pole
boomtown

Key Places
Vancouver
Fraser River
Victoria
Cariboo Mountains
Pacific Rim

▼ Brightly painted totem poles are sometimes used to tell the history of a family or tribe.

A visitor starts her day at a tiny coffee shop. All around her, people are speaking Dutch, Japanese, Spanish, German, and English. After having breakfast, the visitor gets into her car. On the radio, she hears country music—sung in French. Driving downtown, she passes street signs in Chinese, Indian men wearing turbans, a Korean travel agency, and a Thai restaurant. Where in the world is she? It may seem like the United Nations. But it is Vancouver (van KOO vur), British Columbia—a truly international city.

Fishers, Hunters, Traders, Miners

The first people came to what is now British Columbia about 10,000 to 12,000 years ago. They belonged to several ethnic groups and spoke many different languages. Each group had its own customs and a complex society. The people along the coast caught fish, whales, and clams. They also carved giant **totem poles,** which were symbols for a group, a clan, or a family. Other groups lived and hunted game

132

British Columbia: Natural Resources

Wood and Paper Products Production

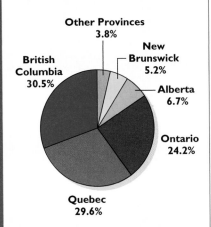

Other Provinces 3.8%

New Brunswick 5.2%

British Columbia 30.5%

Alberta 6.7%

Ontario 24.2%

Quebec 29.6%

Source: Canadian Global Almanac 2001

British Columbia: Natural Resources KEY

- 🌲 Timber
- 🪙 Silver
- 💰 Gold
- C Coal
- Copper
- Iron Ore
- 🔥 Natural Gas
- Petroleum
- Lead
- Zinc
- Hydroelectric power

Lambert Conformal Conic Projection

Income from Mining

Types of Minerals	Income
Copper	🪙🪙🪙🪙🪙🪙🪙🪙🪙
Gold	🪙🪙🪙🪙🪙🪙🪙
Zinc	🪙🪙🪙🪙
Silver	🪙🪙🪙
Lead	🪙

🪙 $50 million

Source: Statistics Canada

Economics The map and charts above show natural resources and their contribution to the economy in British Columbia. **Map and Chart Study** (a) In total, how much income does British Columbia receive from mining copper, gold, zinc, silver, and lead? (b) Use the map and the pie chart to describe the location of timber and its impact on British Columbia's economy.

Pacific Rim National Park

in the dense inland forests. Some groups traded with each other and got along well. Others fought.

New Arrivals In the late 1500s, Spanish, British, and Russian explorers began to arrive in the area to trade. In 1778, James Cook, a British explorer, sailed to Vancouver Island, off the coast of British Columbia. A group of Nootka (NOOT kuh) people met the British and agreed to trade. These coastal people wanted iron tools, while the

Take It to the NET

Data Update For the most recent data on British Columbia, visit www.phschool.com.

READ ACTIVELY

Predict How did the discovery of gold affect life in British Columbia?

British wanted furs. When the British built a fur-trading post on the island, trade began to flourish.

Trade did not change the indigenous peoples' lives a great deal, however. Fur traders came and went. They did not settle. Then in 1858, everything changed. Someone discovered gold along Fraser River.

The Gold Rush A few years earlier, the British had established Victoria, a trading village on Vancouver Island. It was a tidy town of traders and farmers. Its citizens attended church and cultivated lovely gardens. Then, one Sunday morning in April 1858, an American paddle-wheeler entered Victoria's harbor. It dropped off 450 men in red shirts. They carried packs, blankets, spades, pickaxes, knives, and pistols. These rugged-looking characters had come to mine gold. In a single morning, they more than doubled Victoria's population.

Within weeks, tens of thousands more had arrived. Victoria quickly became a "stumptown"—which meant that all of its great trees had been chopped down to build shacks and boats.

Two years later, miners also struck gold in the Cariboo Mountains. Another wave of miners came from China, Europe, and the United States. Because the Cariboo region was hard to reach, the government built a 400-mile (644-km) highway to it. Almost overnight, settlements called **boomtowns** sprang up along it. A boomtown's only purpose was to meet the miners' needs. When the gold rush was over, many boomtowns died out.

Changes for Indigenous Peoples

The indigenous peoples, said the governor of Victoria, were "naturally annoyed" that thousands were coming and taking gold from their land—even taking over the land itself. In 1888, the British government wanted to confine some indigenous peoples to a small reserve. The indigenous peoples protested. They had always lived on the land where the reserve was located. How, they asked, could the government now "give" it to them?

The indigenous peoples had little choice. In a few short years, they had gone from being the great majority to being the smallest minority of the population. They were pushed onto small reserves. Laws banned many of their customs, religions, and languages. Children were taken from their parents to be raised in European-run schools.

▲ This photograph, taken in 1900, shows a group of people looking for gold at Pine Creek, British Columbia. During the gold rush, most people mined gold from creeks and streams, not by digging deep into the ground.

Recently, the indigenous peoples of British Columbia have found new pride in their history and culture. They are demanding land and political rights, and their art is thriving.

The Canadian Pacific Railway In the spring of 1881, Canadians began work on an enormous project—building a railroad all the way from Montreal to Vancouver. The goal of the project was to unite Canada. Look at the physical map of Canada in the Activity Atlas and you may see what a major task this was. There were countless obstacles—soaring mountains, steep valleys, freezing weather, and glaciers. Workers built 600 bridges and blasted 27 tunnels through the mountains.

The railroad project brought more change. Immigrants from all over the world came to work on the railroad. Towns grew up along the railroad, and more newcomers moved in. All this activity attracted criminals, too. They caused so much trouble that the Mounted Police were brought in. In a few short years, British Columbia went from being a sparsely inhabited region to a settled one, complete with cities.

Trapping Shells Many native peoples of the Northwest used a shell called *dentalia* as money. The shells were difficult to gather. They lie on the ocean bottom, in beds 50 to 60 feet (15 to 18 m) deep. Native peoples would lower a broom-like device from a canoe. Stabbing the broom into the sand, they would trap a few shells at a time.

Hauling Freight

A huge freight train heads for Vancouver along the banks of the Thompson River, high in the mountains of British Columbia. **Critical Thinking** What difficulties do you think faced the workers who laid the railroad along the Thompson River?

British Columbia Today

The Canadian Pacific Railroad did unite all of Canada. However, the mountains have always been a big barrier between British Columbia and the rest of the country. Today, about two thirds of British Columbians live along the coast, west of the mountains. Many feel that their future lies with Pacific Rim countries—nations that border the Pacific Ocean—not with the rest of Canada.

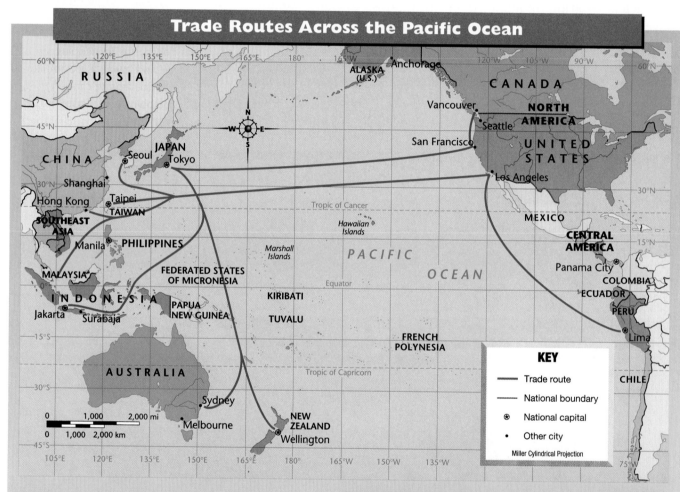

Trade Routes Across the Pacific Ocean

KEY
— Trade route
— National boundary
⊛ National capital
• Other city
Miller Cylindrical Projection

Map Study Traditionally, the United States and Europe have been Canada's most important trade partners. However, Canada is developing a thriving relationship with the countries that border the Pacific Ocean. In the mid-1970s, Japan replaced the United Kingdom as the second largest market for Canadian exports. Most of Canada's Pacific Rim trade passes through British Columbia's major port, Vancouver (right). **Movement** Name three Pacific countries, other than Japan, with which Canada might trade.

◄ The water in Vancouver's harbor never freezes. As a result, Vancouver is one of Canada's most important ports. Many people call Vancouver Canada's "Gateway to the Pacific" because almost all of Canada's trade with Asian countries is handled by this port.

Another link between British Columbia and the Pacific Rim is British Columbia's diverse people. About 11 percent have Asian ancestors. Trade is still another link between British Columbia and the Pacific Rim. Forty percent of the province's trade is with Asian countries. British Columbia wants good relationships with them. As a result, in British Columbian schools, students learn Asian languages. They learn Japanese, Cantonese Chinese, or Mandarin Chinese. Some even learn Punjabi (pun JAH bee), a language of India and Pakistan.

SECTION 3 REVIEW

1. **Define** (a) totem pole, (b) boomtown.

2. **Identify** (a) Vancouver, (b) Fraser River, (c) Victoria, (d) Cariboo Mountains, (e) Pacific Rim.

3. What brought Europeans to British Columbia between the late 1500s and the late 1800s?

4. Explain the effects of the gold rush on British Columbia.

5. What ties are there between the people of British Columbia and the Pacific Rim?

Critical Thinking

6. **Identifying Central Issues** What was the importance of the completion of the Canadian Pacific Railroad?

Activity

7. **Writing to Learn** What do you think it would be like to be a gold prospector in one of the gold rushes in Canada? Write a journal entry describing a gold prospector's typical workday.

The Atlantic Provinces

UNITED BY THE SEAS

BEFORE YOU READ

Reach Into Your Background

Think about a time when you remembered having an item that you really liked, but could not find it anywhere. Finally, you found it stashed in the back of your closet or in a corner of the attic. How did you feel when you found it? Did you do something to ensure you would not lose it again?

Questions to Explore

1. How have the natural resources of the Atlantic Provinces influenced their economies?

2. How have the economies of the Atlantic Provinces changed over time?

Key Terms

exile
maritime
aquaculture

Key Places

L'Anse aux Meadows
Acadia

▲ Some historians believe Leif Ericsson may have landed here at L'Anse aux Meadows about 1,000 years ago.

Modern-day Norwegian explorer Helge Ingstad was aboard a ship in 1961 that stopped at a barren, rocky peninsula in Newfoundland. The land formation was similar to what he had seen on ancient maps, and the scenery reminded him of descriptions he had read in Viking legends. After spotting what appeared to be the outlines of old building foundations, Ingstad believed he might be at the site of the first known Viking settlement in North America. Seven years of archeological digs proved that Ingstad had truly unearthed a Viking settlement—possibly the very one that Leif Ericsson reached and named Vinland around the year 1000. Many artifacts were found at the site including a kiln, or oven, and a pit where iron may have been heated and formed into tools.

The Viking settlement is now called L'Anse aux Meadows (lahns oh meh DOH). Viking buildings and artifacts have been reconstructed, and the historic site has become a popular tourist attraction. In 2000, ceremonies and festivals were held to commemorate the 1,000th anniversary of the Vikings' landing in North America. As part of the celebration, a replica of Ericsson's Viking ship recreated the explorer's journey from Iceland to Newfoundland, anchoring at L'Anse aux Meadows.

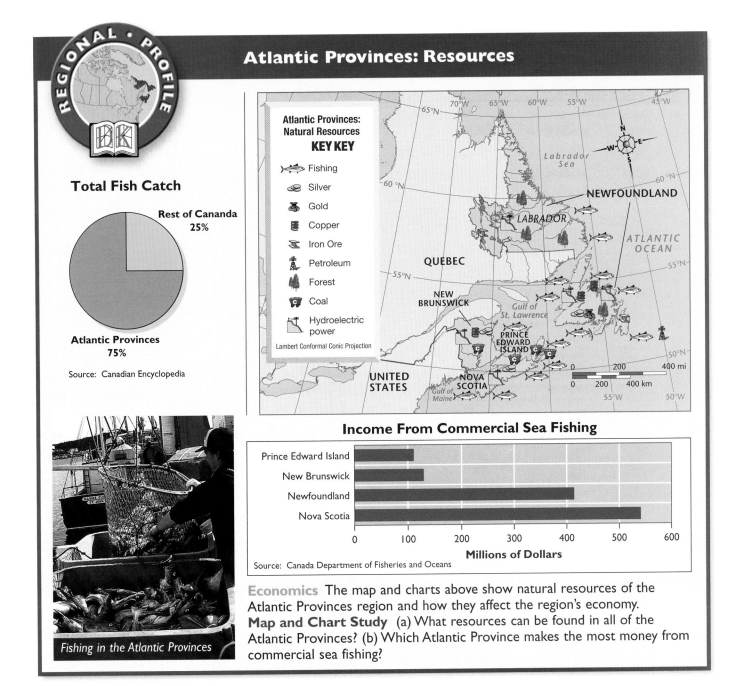

Total Fish Catch

Rest of Cananda
25%

Atlantic Provinces
75%

Source: Canadian Encyclopedia

Atlantic Provinces: Natural Resources KEY KEY

- Fishing
- Silver
- Gold
- Copper
- Iron Ore
- Petroleum
- Forest
- Coal
- Hydroelectric power

Lambert Conformal Conic Projection

Income From Commercial Sea Fishing

Prince Edward Island
New Brunswick
Newfoundland
Nova Scotia

Millions of Dollars

Source: Canada Department of Fisheries and Oceans

Fishing in the Atlantic Provinces

Economics The map and charts above show natural resources of the Atlantic Provinces region and how they affect the region's economy. **Map and Chart Study** (a) What resources can be found in all of the Atlantic Provinces? (b) Which Atlantic Province makes the most money from commercial sea fishing?

Living on the Coast

Today Newfoundland, along with Prince Edward Island, New Brunswick, and Nova Scotia, make up the Atlantic Provinces. These provinces are located in eastern Canada where they all share at least part of their border with the Atlantic Ocean. Most of the people in these provinces live on the coast, with the exception of Prince Edward Island where the population is evenly spread across the island. The people in the Atlantic Provinces are mainly of British, Irish, Scottish, and French descent.

Acadia Eastern Canada was once almost entirely populated by people of French descent. Nova Scotia, New Brunswick, and Prince Edward Island were part of Acadia. It was here that the first permanent

Take It to the NET Data Update For the most recent data on the Atlantic Provinces, visit **www.phschool.com**.

The World's Highest Tides

The Bay of Fundy lies between New Brunswick and Nova Scotia. Its unique funnel shape—narrow with shallow water at the north end of the bay and wide with deep water where the bay opens into the ocean—causes some of the highest tides in the world. Water in the bay can rise as high as 60 feet at high tide. These exceptional tides carry about 100 billion tons of water in and out of the bay each day.

French settlement in North America was established in the early 1600s. French control of the area, however, did not last long. The British wanted this land and the two countries fought over it many times. Parts of the area shifted from under each country's control more than once. During the fighting, Acadians remained neutral.

In 1755, a time when Britain controlled the area, Britain feared that the French inhabitants of Acadia might secretly be loyal to France. As a result, Acadians were **exiled**, or forced to leave the area. Some exiled Acadians settled in Quebec, some moved to France, and still others moved to present-day Louisiana, then a French settlement, where their descendants are known as Cajuns. Britain gained permanent control over Acadia in 1763. Many Acadians returned to the area only to find that the British had taken control of the fertile lands they had once farmed. So they took up fishing and lumbering to support themselves instead.

Maritime Pursuits

Maritime means "related to navigation or commerce on the sea," and there is perhaps no term that better sums up the focus of life in the Atlantic Provinces. Much of the economy of the Atlantic Provinces is dependent on fishing, and has been for a long time. In the 1800s, the demand for fishing vessels brought about the growth of another important industry for the Atlantic Provinces—shipbuilding. The region led Canada in ship construction through most of the 1800s. The growing forestry industry in the area kept shipbuilders well-supplied. Both industries helped the region's economy boom. In the 1880s, ships were

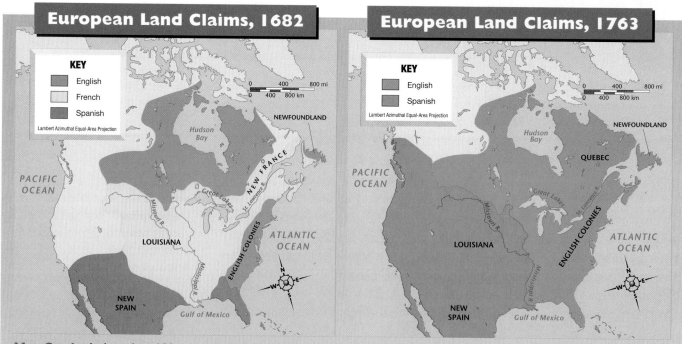

Map Study In less than 100 years, France lost its land claims in the United States and Canada. **Regions** In 1763, who controlled the areas once controlled by France?

Hard Times for Fishermen

In 1992, cod fishing was banned in Newfoundland because cod were nearing extinction. Newfoundland's fishing industry lost millions of dollars as a result of the ban. The federal government set up a program that provided assistance to unemployed cod fishers for several years, ending in 1999.

increasingly being made of steel and the economy slowed considerably. The provinces could, however, still rely on the fishing industry.

The Atlantic Fishing Industry Today The fishing industry continues to be a major industry in the Atlantic Provinces. In fact, as much as 75 percent of Canada's total catch comes from the region. The industry provides employment for thousands of residents.

The fishing industry has changed over the years. In some provinces, like Prince Edward Island, processing fish now brings in more money than catching fish. Fish processing—freezing, salting, smoking, and canning—is an important part of the fishing industry in Nova Scotia and New Brunswick as well. In Newfoundland, cod had been the primary catch until cod fishing was banned in 1992. Today, the province has turned its attention toward other types of fish and parts of the industry to try to make up for loss of revenue from cod. Fish farming, or **aquaculture**, is also a growing industry in some of the Atlantic Provinces. Mussels are grown on Canada's eastern coast, and salmon farms are operating in New Brunswick.

READ ACTIVELY

Predict What role might the fishing industry play in the Atlantic Provinces' economy in the future?

SECTION 4 REVIEW

1. **Define** (a) exile, (b) maritime, (c) aquaculture.

2. **Identify** (a) L'Anse aux Meadows (b) Acadia.

3. How did the lives of the Acadians change after the British gained control over Acadia in 1763?

4. What industries did fishing help to grow in the 1800s?

5. How has the fishing industry in the Atlantic Provinces changed in recent years?

Critical Thinking

6. **Drawing Conclusions** In this section, you learned that many people in the Atlantic Provinces live along the coast. What are the advantages of living in coastal settlements?

Activity

7. **Writing to Learn** You are a French farmer living in Acadia in 1755. The British have told you that you must move to Louisiana. Write a journal entry describing how you feel about the move and why you think you should be allowed to stay in Acadia.

The Northern Territories

NEW FRONTIERS

BEFORE YOU READ

Reach Into Your Background

Suppose you and your classmates wanted to have an area designated as a student lounge. How would you, as a group, go about proposing it? What procedures might you have to follow to convince the principal that the idea was worthwhile?

Questions to Explore

1. Who are the native peoples of Canada's Northern Territories?

2. How does a territory's form of government differ from that of a province?

Key Term
aurora borealis

Key Places
Dawson
Iqaluit

The northern lights, or **aurora borealis** (uh ROR uh bor ee AL uhs), are a spectacular natural light show that can be seen in the Northern Hemisphere. The farther north you travel, the better your chance of seeing these colorful bands of light. Some of Canada's indigenous peoples believed the lights were spirits. One folktale described the lights as spirits playing games. Others said that if you whistled loudly, the spirits would whisk you away.

Scientists today believe that the lights are caused by the reaction that occurs when winds from the sun hit gases in Earth's atmosphere. The beauty of the lights still attracts many sky-gazers. Some of the most dazzling displays can be seen in the Yukon and Northwest Territories.

A Unique Part of Canada

In addition to its provinces, Canada has three territories—the Northwest Territories, Yukon, and Nunavut. Together these territories make up over one third of Canada's total land area and stretch far north into the Arctic Ocean. Despite this,

▼ In the north, the best times to see the northern lights are March, late September, and early October.

Northern Territories: Ethnic Groups and Population

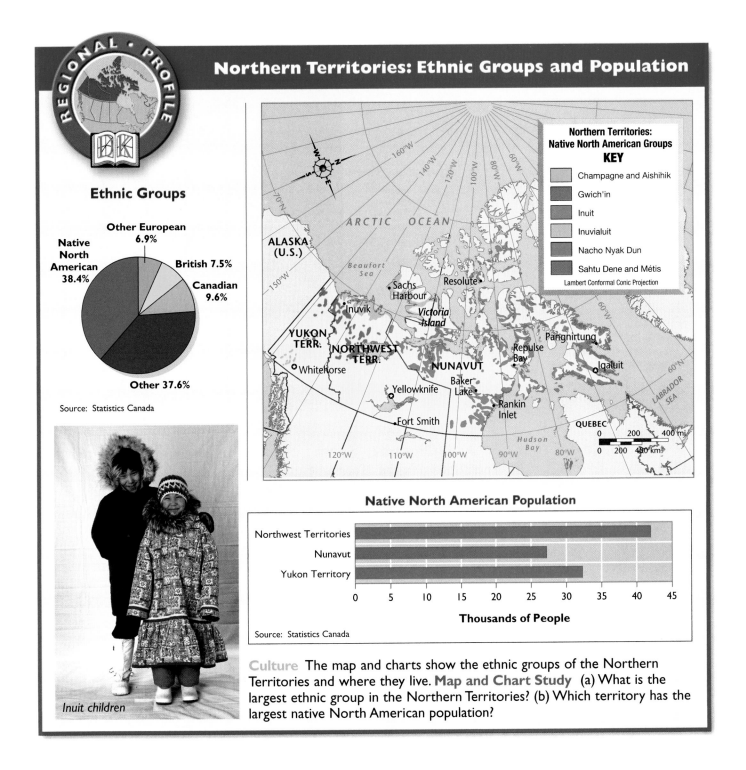

Ethnic Groups

Native North American 38.4%

Other European 6.9%

British 7.5%

Canadian 9.6%

Other 37.6%

Source: Statistics Canada

Northern Territories: Native North American Groups KEY

- Champagne and Aishihik
- Gwich'in
- Inuit
- Inuvialuit
- Nacho Nyak Dun
- Sahtu Dene and Métis

Lambert Conformal Conic Projection

ARCTIC OCEAN

ALASKA (U.S.)

Beaufort Sea

Sachs Harbour

Resolute

Inuvik

Victoria Island

YUKON TERR.

NORTHWEST TERR.

Whitehorse

Repulse Bay

Pangnirtung

NUNAVUT

Iqaluit

Baker Lake

Yellowknife

Rankin Inlet

Fort Smith

QUEBEC

Hudson Bay

LABRADOR SEA

0 200 400 mi
0 200 400 km

Native North American Population

	Thousands of People
Northwest Territories	~42
Nunavut	~27
Yukon Territory	~32

0 5 10 15 20 25 30 35 40 45

Thousands of People

Source: Statistics Canada

Inuit children

Culture The map and charts show the ethnic groups of the Northern Territories and where they live. **Map and Chart Study** (a) What is the largest ethnic group in the Northern Territories? (b) Which territory has the largest native North American population?

the people of these territories comprise less than one percent of the nation's population. The main reason for the low population is the region's rugged terrain and climate. The majority of the area is made up of tundra with little vegetation, icy waters, and subarctic forests.

Another characteristic unique to this region is the large number of indigenous people who live there. For example, in the Northwest Territories, almost 50 percent of the population is made up of indigenous peoples such as the Dene, Metis, and Inuit.

Take It to the NET
Data Update For the most recent data on the Northern Territories, visit **www.phschool.com**.

These miners worked tirelessly to mine gold on "Gold Hill" near Dawson in the Yukon Territory.

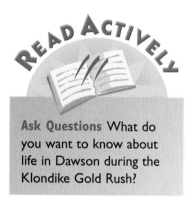

Ask Questions What do you want to know about life in Dawson during the Klondike Gold Rush?

A Different Form of Government The Northwest Territories, Yukon Territory, and Nunavut do not have the same relationship with Canada's federal government that the provinces do. Both territories and provinces are represented in the federal government by members of the House of Commons, a part of the Canadian Parliament. Each territory has its own legislative, or law-making, body similar to those of the provinces. But the federal government has slightly more control over the territories. While territories do have control over many of the same local concerns as provinces, such as education, the federal government controls some other areas, such as certain natural resources. Territories also have less power to tax than the provinces do.

Exploring a Remote Region

The Yukon Territory is well known for its Klondike Gold Rush. After gold was discovered in a branch of the Klondike River in 1896, thousands of prospectors immigrated to the area from all over the world. Within two years, the town's population swelled to about 30,000. In the town of Dawson, saloons, banks, theaters and dance halls sprung up. Dawson began to be called "Paris of the North." It was amazing that so many people were able to get to the area, because one of the main routes was the treacherous Chilkoot Pass, known as "the meanest 32 miles in the world." It became less than three feet wide and very steep toward its end. But the Yukon's era of prosperity was short-lived. By the end of 1898 the rush began to slow, and the population of the settlement declined quickly. Today, fewer than 1,300 people live in Dawson.

A brand new building was constructed in Iqaluit to house Nunavut's legislature.

Forming a New Territory

The Yukon Territory was once a district of the Northwest Territories. In 1898, an act of Parliament made it a separate territory. Then, in 1993, the area now known as Nunavut was carved out of the eastern portion of the Northwest Territories. A constitutional act officially made Nunavut the third Canadian territory in 1999.

The Inuit, who make up a large portion of Nunavut's population, proposed the formation of Nunavut in the 1970s. Nunavut means "our land" in Inuktitut (i NOOK ti toot), the native language of the Inuit. When the matter came to a vote in 1982, residents favored the creation of their own territory by a four-to-one margin.

The construction of Nunavut's new capital, Iqaluit (ee KA loo eet), provided many jobs for people. But Nunavut still faces many challenges. The territory will have to figure out how to keep its economy strong in the face of its remote location and harsh climate. The modernization of the area, which now has an Internet provider and cellular phone service, may be a step in the right direction.

SECTION 5 REVIEW

1. **Define** (a) aurora borealis.
2. **Identify** (a) Dawson, (b) Iqaluit.

3. How do the governments of provinces and territories differ? How are they the same?
4. What is the newest territory in Canada?

Critical Thinking
5. **Cause and Effect** What caused the growth of Dawson?

Activity
6. **Writing to Learn** Suppose you have just moved to the capital of Nunavut. Describe what it is like living in a brand new town that is just beginning to grow.

Writing for a Purpose

Think about the last three or four conversations you have had.

You might have been talking with friends at school, a teacher, family members, a clerk in a store, or a friend. Chances are, the conversations were all very different. However, they probably also had something in common.

No matter what you talked about, or with whom you spoke, one of you probably *informed* the other. To inform someone simply means to give someone information. You might have informed a friend about how you were feeling, informed a store clerk about what you wanted to buy, or informed your mother that you had basketball practice after school.

People often write to inform, too. This entire book, for example, was written to inform you about the United States and Canada.

Get Ready

As a student and as an adult, you will often write to inform your readers. You may write reports to inform your teacher about a subject you have researched. You may write letters to inform friends about your life. You may fill in a job application to inform an employer about your work experience.

Try It Out

Writing to inform means writing to provide information. It involves five basic steps. As you read through the following steps, think about a one-page paper you could write to inform someone about something. Complete the activity at the end of each step.

A. Choose your topic. What will you write about? What do you want to tell your readers? Of course, there are millions of subjects. You can write about anything you want—a hobby, your last weekend, or a football game. Write down a few possibilities, then circle the one you like best.

Writing to Inform

about a process

Organize your writing around the steps in the process.

B. Choose your audience. You need to know to whom you are writing. You would write differently for a group of second-graders than you would for your parents. For this paper, your audience will be your teacher and your classmates.

C. Research your topic. In order to inform your audience, you have to first inform yourself. Read and take notes from books, magazines, newspapers, and other sources of information. Gather your information and know what you want to write before you begin the next step.

D. Plan your paper. This is how you will inform your audience. When you write to inform, you should organize your paper in the way that will make your topic easiest for your audience to understand. The box to the right tells you how to choose the best way.

Will you write about a process, an event, or a thing? How will you organize your paper? Write it down.

E. Write. Now you can start writing a one-page paper to inform. Make an outline before you start. Make sure it is organized in the same way that you will organize your final paper. Try to start your paper with an interesting opening and write clearly.

Apply the Skill

Now write a one-page paper to inform your teacher and classmates about a subject in this chapter of your textbook. Choose one of the following ideas, or choose your own subject.

- The immigration of Chinese Americans and other Americans to Canada from California (a process)
- The election to decide on Quebec's independence (an event)
- A wheat farm in Saskatchewan (a thing)

about a thing

Write about the object's purpose and its parts.

about an event

Organize your writing in chronological order, or order based on time.

CHAPTER 5 Review and Activities

Reviewing Main Ideas

1. What is the largest cultural group in Quebec?
2. Describe the structure of Canada's government.
3. What did many immigrants do for a living in the Prairie Provinces?
4. Identify different groups of people who have shaped British Columbia's culture.
5. How has geography affected the economy of the Atlantic Provinces?
6. Why are the Northern Territories not heavily populated?

Reviewing Key Terms

Use each key term below in a sentence that shows the meaning of the term.

1. Francophone
2. Quiet Revolution
3. descent
4. totem pole
5. boomtown
6. exile
7. maritime

Critical Thinking

1. **Recognizing Viewpoints** The slogans "Masters of our Own House" and "United from Sea to Sea" are from the dispute over Quebec. Determine which side of the issue each slogan supports.
2. **Recognizing Cause and Effect** Identify several different events in western Canada that led to the decline of the native peoples' cultures.

Graphic Organizer

Immigrants have affected all of the regions mentioned in this chapter in many ways. Copy this chart and fill in the blanks with these ways.

Ontario and Quebec	
Prairie Provinces	
British Columbia	
Atlantic Provinces	
Northern Territories	

Map Activity

Canada
For each place listed below, write the letter from the map that shows its location.

1. Quebec

2. Ottawa

3. Saskatchewan

4. Winnipeg

5. Vancouver

6. Prince Edward Island

7. Iqaluit

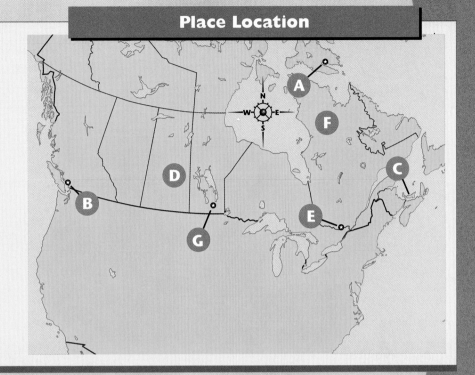

Place Location

Writing Activity

Writing a Paragraph
Make a list of the distinguishing characteristics of Quebec, Saskatchewan, British Columbia, Newfoundland, and Nunavut.

Then chose one and write a letter to a friend, trying to convince your friend to move to that province or territory.

Take It to the NET

Activity Use the Internet to help you describe French culture in Quebec. For help in completing this activity, visit www.phschool.com.

Chapter 5 Self-Test To review what you have learned, take the Chapter 5 Self-Test and get instant feedback on your answers. Go to www.phschool.com to take the test.

Skills Review

Turn to the Skills Activity.
Review the basic steps of writing to inform. Then complete the following: (a) Name some types of writing that inform. (b) Tell how you could organize informative writing about a process, an event, or an object.

How Am I Doing?

Answer these questions to help you check your progress.

1. Can I explain why French Canadians are determined to preserve their culture?

2. Can I visualize what life was like in the Prairie Provinces in the past?

3. Can I explain the difference between territories and provinces?

4. What information from this chapter can I include in my journal?

THE UNITED STATES AND CANADA

PROJECT POSSIBILITIES

As you study the United States and Canada, you will be reading and thinking about these important questions.

☞ **GEOGRAPHY** How has physical geography affected the cultures of the United States and Canada?

☞ **HISTORY** How have historical events affected the cultures of the United States and Canada?

☞ **CULTURE** How has the variety of people in the United States and Canada benefited and challenged the two nations?

☞ **GOVERNMENT** How do the governments of the United States and Cananda differ? How are they alike?

☞ **ECONOMICS** How did the United States and Canada become two of the wealthiest nations in the world?

What do you know about the United States and Canada? It's time to show it.

GEO CLEO

Project Menu

The chapters in this book have some answers to these questions. Now you can find your own answers by doing projects on your own or with a group. Here are some ways to make your own discoveries about the United States and Canada.

Write a Children's Book Choose a topic from this book that interests you. Then write a short book about it for younger students. Take careful notes before you write, to be sure you get all the facts right. Write with simple language that younger children can understand. Include the main points of this topic in your book, along with a few interesting details.

Illustrate your book with drawings and magazine photographs. Draw at least one map of the area you are writing about. Be sure to use the kind of map—physical, political, or other—that shows the right information for your topic. Finally, design a book cover, and bind your book. Share the book with younger students in your school.

From Questions to Careers

PARK RANGER

The national parks of the United States and Canada preserve and protect many of the great treasures of these two countries. Some parks preserve natural wonders, like deep forests and unusual geological formations. Other parks preserve important historic sites. Some simply give people a place to picnic, play, and camp outside.

Many people work for the park services in all kinds of jobs. Tour guides show visitors around historic sites, telling the story of each place. Scientists and park rangers often work together to keep wildernesses healthy and to protect the original land, water, plants, and animals. Writers create brochures for park visitors. On top of all that, the parks always hire people to work in gift shops, visitor offices, and snack bars, to help the thousands of people who visit the parks every year.

▼ This United States park ranger shows the famous cracked Liberty Bell to visitors in Philadelphia, Pennsylvania.

Set Up a Weather Station Set up a weather station to measure and record your local weather as you read this book. Measure the temperature each day at the same time. Also record the amount of precipitation and wind direction. Record all of your findings in a weather log.

Each day, compare your local weather with the weather in other parts of the country. You can get this information from television, radio, the newspaper, or the Internet. When you have finished your measurements and recordings, create graphs to display your local readings. In the end, compare your findings with the climate map in the Activity Atlas.

Make a Time Line of Local History Create a time line of the history of your community. What do you know about it? When was it founded? What famous people have lived there? What important events have shaped its history?

Find the answers to these and other questions about the history of your town, village, city, or county. Read about its history at the local public library. Write down the dates and descriptions of the most important events. Try to find between 10 and 20 events. On a sheet of paper, list the events in the order in which they happened. Then, make a time line large enough to hang on the wall of your classroom. Draw a picture of each event and place it next to its description on the time line. Add several major events of United States history.

Create a Diorama Make a diorama that represents a physical map of the United States and Canada, or of a smaller geographic region within the two countries. Use clay or dough to sculpt the major geographic forms, such as mountain ranges, valleys, rivers, and large bodies of water. Make your diorama with as much detail as possible, showing forests, farms, towns, and other landscapes. You can use materials such as rocks, twigs, and miniature buildings. Make a key that explains what each material represents. Display your finished diorama for the class.

Reference

TABLE OF CONTENTS

Map and Globe Handbook　153

How do you find your way around the world? The Map and Globe Handbook features the skills every geographer needs.

Regional Database　170

Want to find out more about the United States and Canada? The Regional Database includes maps and detailed information about each state, province, and territory.

Atlas　192

Where in the world is it? The Atlas provides physical and political maps of the world and its continents.

The World: Political 192
The World: Physical 194
United States: Political 196
North and South America: Political 198
North and South America: Physical 199
Europe: Political 200
Europe: Physical 201
Africa: Political 202
Africa: Physical 203
Asia: Political 204
Asia: Physical 205
Australia, New Zealand, and the Pacific Islands:
　Physical-Political 206
The Arctic and Antarctica 207

Glossary of Geographic Terms　208
Gazetteer　210
Glossary　212
Index　216
Acknowledgments　226

MAP AND Handbook GLOBE

This Map and Globe Handbook is designed to help you develop some of the skills you need to be a world explorer. These can help you whether you explore from the top of an elephant in India or from a computer at school.

You can use the information in this handbook to improve your map and globe skills. But the best way to sharpen your skills is to practice. The more you practice the better you'll get.

GEO CLEO and GEO LEO

Table of Contents

Five Themes of Geography	154
Understanding Movements of the Earth	156
Maps and Globes Represent the Earth	157
Locating Places on a Map or a Globe	158
Map Projections	160
Parts of a Map	162
Comparing Maps of Different Scale	163
Political Maps	164
Physical Maps	165
Special Purpose Maps	166
Landforms, Climate Regions, and Natural Vegetation Regions	167

Five Themes of Geography

Studying the geography of the entire world can be a huge task. You can make that task easier by using the five themes of geography: location, place, human-environment interaction, movement, and regions. The themes are tools you can use to organize information and to answer the where, why, and how of geography.

1 Location answers the question, "Where is it?" You can think of the location of a continent or a country as its address. You might give an absolute location such as "22 South Lake Street" or "40°N and 80°W." You might also use a relative address, telling where one place is by referring to another place. "Between school and the mall" and "eight miles east of Pleasant City" are examples of relative locations.

2 Place identifies the natural and human features that make one place different from every other place. You can identify a specific place by its landforms, climate, plants, animals, people, or cultures. You might even think of place as a geographic signature. Use the signature to help you understand the natural and human features that make one place different from every other place.

1. Location
Chicago, Illinois, occupies one location on the Earth. No other place has exactly the same absolute location.

2. Place
Ancient cultures in Egypt built distinctive pyramids. Use the theme of place to help you remember features that exist only in Egypt.

3 Human-Environment Interaction focuses on the relationship between people and the environment. As people live in an area, they often begin to make changes to it, usually to make their lives easier. For example, they might build a dam to control flooding during rainy seasons. Also, the environment can affect how people live, work, dress, travel, and communicate.

4 Movement answers the question "How do people, goods, and ideas move from place to place?" Remember that, often, what happens in one place can affect what happens in another. Use the theme of movement to help you trace the spread of goods, people, and ideas from one location to the next.

5 Regions is the last geographic theme. A region is a group of places that share common features. Geographers divide the world into many types of regions. For example, countries, states, and cities are political regions. The people in these places live under the same type of government. Other features can be used to define regions. Places that have the same climate belong to a particular climate region. Places that share the same culture belong to a cultural region. The same place can be found in more than one region. The state of Hawaii is in the political region of the United States. Because it has a tropical climate, Hawaii is also part of a tropical climate region.

PRACTICE YOUR WORLD EXPLORER SKILLS

1. What is the absolute location of your school? What is one way to describe its relative location?

2. What might be a "geographic signature" of the town or city you live in?

3. Give an example of human-environment interaction where you live.

4. Name at least one thing that comes into your town or city and one that goes out. How is each moved? Where does it come from? Where does it go?

5. What are several regions you think your town or city belongs in?

3. Human-Environment Interaction
Peruvians have changed steep mountain slopes into terraces suitable for farming. Think how this environment looked before people made changes.

4. Movement
Arab traders brought not only goods to Kuala Lumpur, Malaysia, but also Arab building styles and the Islamic religion.

5. Regions
Wheat farming is an important activity in Kansas. This means that Kansas is part of a farming region.

Understanding Movements of the Earth

Planet Earth is part of our solar system. The Earth revolves around the sun in a nearly circular path called an orbit. A revolution, or one complete orbit around the sun, takes 365 1/4 days, or a year. As the Earth revolves around the sun, it is also spinning around in space. This movement is called a rotation. The Earth rotates on its axis—an invisible line through the center of the Earth from the North Pole to the South Pole. The Earth makes one full rotation about every 24 hours. As the Earth rotates, it is daytime on the side facing the sun. It is night on the side away from the sun.

The Earth's axis is tilted at an angle. Because of this tilt, sunlight strikes different parts of the Earth at certain points in the year, creating different seasons.

Earth's Revolution and the Seasons

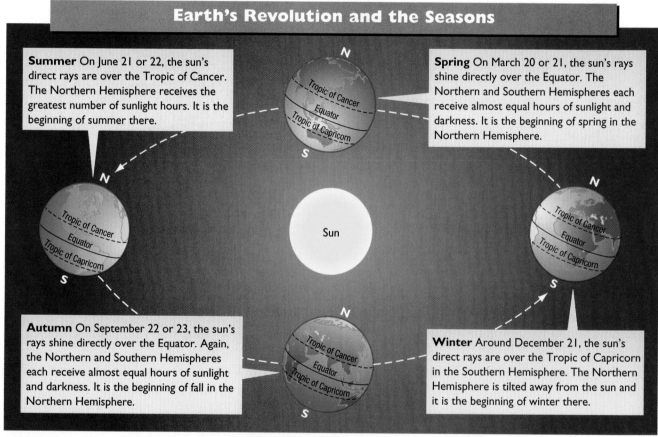

Summer On June 21 or 22, the sun's direct rays are over the Tropic of Cancer. The Northern Hemisphere receives the greatest number of sunlight hours. It is the beginning of summer there.

Spring On March 20 or 21, the sun's rays shine directly over the Equator. The Northern and Southern Hemispheres each receive almost equal hours of sunlight and darkness. It is the beginning of spring in the Northern Hemisphere.

Autumn On September 22 or 23, the sun's rays shine directly over the Equator. Again, the Northern and Southern Hemispheres each receive almost equal hours of sunlight and darkness. It is the beginning of fall in the Northern Hemisphere.

Winter Around December 21, the sun's direct rays are over the Tropic of Capricorn in the Southern Hemisphere. The Northern Hemisphere is tilted away from the sun and it is the beginning of winter there.

▲ **Location** This diagram shows how the Earth's tilt and orbit around the sun combine to create the seasons. Remember, in the Southern Hemisphere the seasons are reversed.

PRACTICE YOUR WORLD EXPLORER SKILLS

❶ What causes the seasons in the Northern Hemisphere to be the opposite of those in the Southern Hemisphere?

❷ During which two months of the year do the Northern and Southern Hemispheres have about equal hours of daylight and darkness?

Maps and Globes Represent the Earth

Globes

A globe is a scale model of the Earth. It shows the actual shapes, sizes, and locations of all the Earth's landmasses and bodies of water. Features on the surface of the Earth are drawn to scale on a globe. This means a smaller unit of measure on the globe stands for a larger unit of measure on the Earth.

Because a globe is made in the true shape of the Earth, it offers these advantages for studying the Earth.

- The shape of all land and water bodies are accurate.
- Compass directions from one point to any other point are correct.
- The distance from one location to another is always accurately represented.

However, a globe presents some disadvantages for studying the Earth. Because a globe shows the entire Earth, it cannot show small areas in great detail. Also, a globe is not easily folded and carried from one place to another. For these reasons, geographers often use maps to learn about the Earth.

Maps

A map is a drawing or representation, on a flat surface, of a region. A map can show details too small to be seen on a globe. Floor plans, mall directories, and road maps are among the maps we use most often.

While maps solve some of the problems posed by globes, they have some disadvantages of their own. Maps flatten the real round world. Mapmakers cut, stretch, push, and pull some parts of the Earth to get it all flat on paper. As a result, some locations may be distorted. That is, their size, shape, and relative location may not be accurate. For example, on most maps of the entire world, the size and shape of the Antarctic and Arctic regions are not accurate.

PRACTICE YOUR WORLD EXPLORER SKILLS

1. What is the main difference between a globe and a map?

2. What is one advantage of using a globe instead of a map?

Global Gores

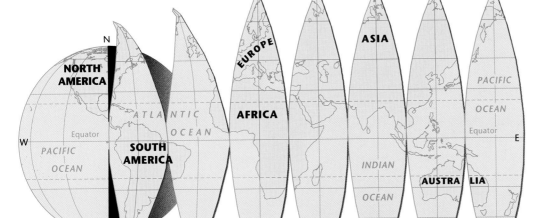

◀ **Location**
When mapmakers flatten the surface of the Earth, curves become straight lines. As a result, size, shape, and distance are distorted.

The Hemispheres

Another name for a round ball like a globe is a sphere. The Equator, an imaginary line halfway between the North and South Poles, divides the globe into two hemispheres. (The prefix *hemi* means "half.") Land and water south of the Equator are in the Southern Hemisphere. Land and water north of the Equator are in the Northern Hemisphere.

Mapmakers sometimes divide the globe along an imaginary line that runs from North Pole to South Pole. This line, called the Prime Meridian, divides the globe into the Eastern and Western Hemispheres.

Northern Hemisphere

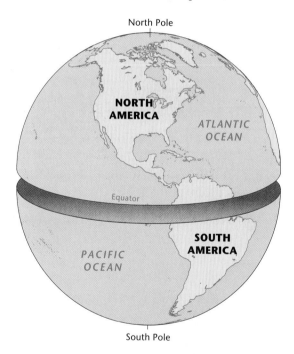

Southern Hemisphere

▲ The Equator divides the Northern Hemisphere from the Southern Hemisphere.

Western Hemisphere **Eastern Hemisphere**

▲ The Prime Meridian divides the Eastern Hemisphere from the Western Hemisphere.

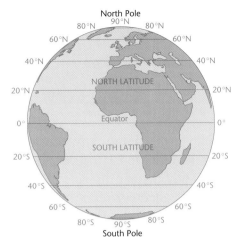

Parallels of Latitude

The Equator, at 0° latitude, is the starting place for measuring latitude or distances north and south. Most globes do not show every parallel of latitude. They may show every 10, 20, or even 30 degrees.

Meridians of Longitude

The Prime Meridian, at 0° longitude, runs from pole to pole through Greenwich, England. It is the starting place for measuring longitude or distances east and west. Each meridian of longitude meets its opposite longitude at the North and South Poles.

The Global Grid

Two sets of lines cover most globes. One set of lines runs parallel to the Equator. These lines, including the Equator, are called *parallels of latitude*. They are measured in degrees (°). One degree of latitude represents a distance of about 70 miles (112 km). The Equator has a location of 0°. The other parallels of latitude tell the direction and distance from the Equator to another location.

The second set of lines runs north and south. These lines are called *meridians of longitude*. Meridians show the degrees of longitude east or west of the Prime Meridian, which is located at 0°. A meridian of longitude tells the direction and distance from the Prime Meridian to another location. Unlike parallels, meridians are not the same distance apart everywhere on the globe.

Together the pattern of parallels of latitude and meridians of longitude is called the global grid. Using the lines of latitude and longitude, you can locate any place on Earth. For example, the location of 30° north latitude and 90° west longitude is usually written as 30°N, 90°W. Only one place on Earth has these coordinates—the city of New Orleans, in the state of Louisiana.

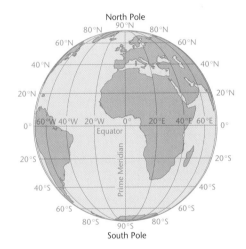

The Global Grid

By using lines of latitude and longitude, you can give the absolute location of any place on the Earth.

1. Which continents lie completely in the Northern Hemisphere? The Western Hemisphere?

2. Is there land or water at 20°S latitude and the Prime Meridian? At the Equator and 60°W longitude?

Map Projections

I *magine trying to flatten out a complete orange peel. The peel would split. The shape would change. You would have to cut the peel to get it to lie flat. In much the same way, maps cannot show the correct size and shape of every landmass or body of water on the Earth's curved surface. Maps shrink some places and stretch others. This shrinking and stretching is called* distortion—*a change made to a shape.*

To make up for this disadvantage, mapmakers use different map projections. Each map projection is a way of showing the round Earth on flat paper. Each type of projection has some distortion. No one projection can accurately show the correct area, shape, distance, and direction for the Earth's surface. Mapmakers use the projection that has the least distortion for the information they are studying.

Same-Shape Maps

Some map projections can accurately show the shapes of landmasses. However, these projections often greatly distort the size of landmasses as well as the distance between them.

One of the most common same-shape maps is a Mercator projection, named for the mapmaker who invented it. The Mercator projection accurately shows shape and direction, but it distorts distance and size. In this projection, the northern and southern areas of the globe appear stretched more than areas near the Equator. Because the projection shows true directions, ships' navigators use it to chart a straight line course between two ports.

Mercator Projection

Equal-Area Maps

Some map projections can show the correct size of landmasses. Maps that use these projections are called equal-area maps. In order to show the correct size of landmasses, these maps usually distort shapes. The distortion is usually greater at the edges of the map and less at the center.

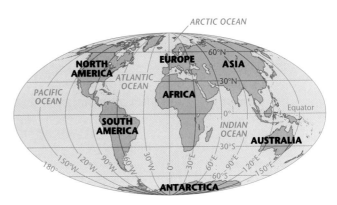

Equal-Area Projection

Robinson Maps

Many of the maps in this book use the Robinson projection. This is a compromise between the Mercator and equal-area projections. It gives a useful overall picture of the world. The Robinson projection keeps the size and shape relationships of most continents and oceans but does distort size of the polar regions.

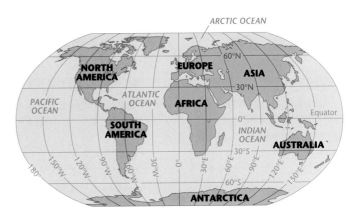

Robinson Projection

Azimuthal Maps

Another kind of projection shows true compass direction. Maps that use this projection are called azimuthal maps. Such maps are easy to recognize—they are usually circular. Azimuthal maps are often used to show the areas of the North and South Poles. However, azimuthal maps distort scale, area, and shape.

1. What feature is distorted on an equal-area map?

2. Would you use a Mercator projection to find the exact distance between two locations? Tell why or why not.

3. Which would be a better choice for studying the Antarctic—an azimuthal projection or a Robinson projection? Explain.

Azimuthal Projection

Parts of a Map

Mapmakers provide several clues to help you understand the information on a map. As an explorer, it is your job to read and interpret these clues.

Compass

Many maps show north at the top of the map. One way to show direction on a map is to use an arrow that points north. There may be an N shown with the arrow. Many maps give more information about direction by displaying a compass showing the directions, north, east, south, and west. The letters N, E, S, and W are placed to indicate these directions.

Title

The title of a map is the most basic clue. It signals what kinds of information you are likely to find on the map. A map titled *West Africa: Population Density* will be most useful for locating information about where people live in West Africa.

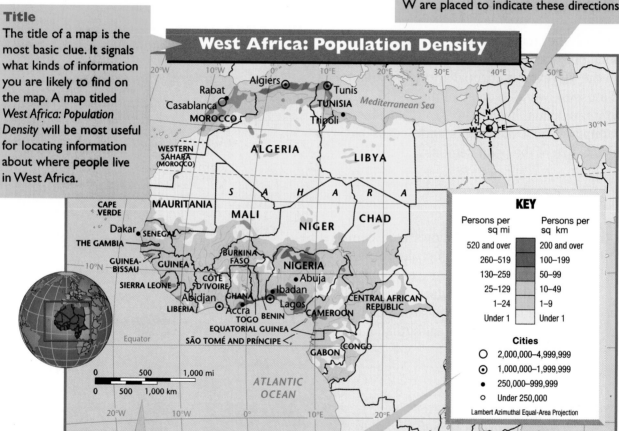

West Africa: Population Density

KEY

Persons per sq mi	Persons per sq km
520 and over	200 and over
260–519	100–199
130–259	50–99
25–129	10–49
1–24	1–9
Under 1	Under 1

Cities

◯	2,000,000–4,999,999
◉	1,000,000–1,999,999
•	250,000–999,999
○	Under 250,000

Lambert Azimuthal Equal-Area Projection

Scale

A map scale helps you find the actual distances between points shown on the map. You can measure the distance between any two points on the map, compare them to the scale, and find out the actual distance between the points. Most map scales show distances in both miles and kilometers.

Key

Often a map has a key, or legend, that shows the symbols used on the map and what each one means. On some maps, color is used as a symbol. On those maps, the key also tells the meaning of each color.

PRACTICE YOUR WORLD EXPLORER SKILLS

1. What part of a map tells you what the map is about?

2. Where on the map should you look to find out the meaning of this symbol? •

3. What part of the map can you use to find the distance between two cities?

Comparing Maps of Different Scale

ere are three maps drawn to three different scales. The first map shows Moscow's location in the northeastern portion of Russia. This map shows the greatest area—a large section of northern Europe. It has the smallest scale (1 inch = about 900 miles) and shows the fewest details. This map can tell you what direction to travel to reach Moscow from Finland.

Find the red box on Map 1. It shows the whole area covered by Map 2. Study Map 2. It gives a closer look at the city of Moscow. It shows the fea-

tures around the city, the city's **boundary,** and the general shape of the city. This **map can** help you find your way from the airport to the center of town.

Now find the red box on **Map 2.** This box shows the area shown on Map 3. **This** map moves you closer into the city. Like the **zoom** on a computer or camera, Map 3 shows the smallest area but has the greatest detail. This map has the largest scale (1 inch = about 0.8 miles). This is the map to use to explore downtown Moscow.

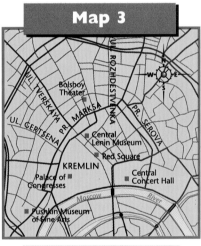

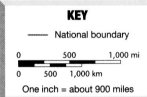

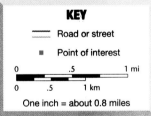

1. Which map would be best for finding the location of Red Square? Why?

2. Which map best shows Moscow's location relative to Poland? Explain.

3. Which map best shows the area immediately surrounding the city?

Political Maps

Mapmakers create maps to show all kinds of information. The kind of information presented affects the way a map looks. One type of map is called a political map. Its main purpose is to show continents, countries, and divisions within countries such as states or provinces. Usually different colors are used to show different countries or divisions within a country. The colors do not have any special meaning. They are used only to make the map easier to read.

Political maps also show where people have built towns and cities. Symbols can help you tell capital cities from other cities and towns. Even though political maps do not give information that shows what the land looks like, they often include some physical features such as oceans, lakes, and rivers.

Political maps usually have many labels. They give country names, and the names of capital and major cities. Bodies of water such as lakes, rivers, oceans, seas, gulfs, and bays are also labeled.

PRACTICE YOUR WORLD EXPLORER SKILLS

1 What symbol shows the continental boundary?

2 What symbol is used to indicate a capital city? A major city?

3 What kinds of landforms are shown on this map?

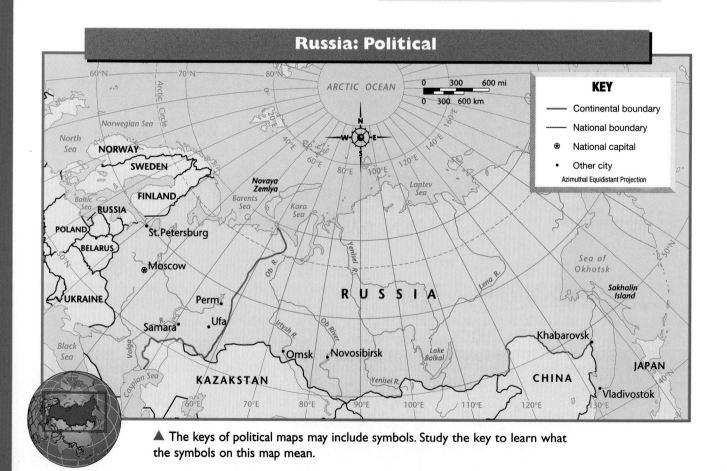

Russia: Political

KEY
- —— Continental boundary
- ——— National boundary
- ⊛ National capital
- • Other city

Azimuthal Equidistant Projection

▲ The keys of political maps may include symbols. Study the key to learn what the symbols on this map mean.

Physical Maps

Like political maps, physical maps show country labels and labels for capital cities. However, physical maps also show what the land of a region looks like by showing the major physical features such as plains, hills, plateaus, or mountains. Labels give the names of features such as mountain peaks, mountains, plateaus, and river basins.

In order to tell one landform from another, physical maps often show elevation and relief.

Elevation is the height of the land above sea level. Physical maps in this book use color to show elevation. Browns and oranges show higher lands while blues and greens show lands that are at or below sea level.

Relief shows how quickly the land rises or falls. Hills, mountains, and plateaus are shown on relief maps using shades of gray. Level or nearly level land is shown without shading. Darkly shaded areas indicate steeper lands.

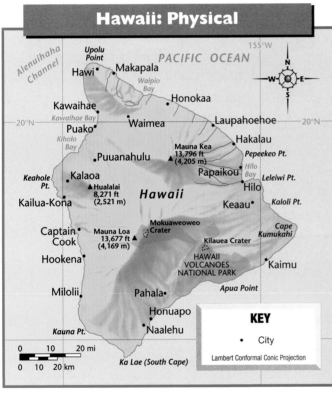

Hawaii: Physical

KEY

• City

Lambert Conformal Conic Projection

▲ On a physical map, shading is sometimes used to show relief. Use the shading to locate the mountains in Hawaii.

PRACTICE YOUR WORLD EXPLORER SKILLS

1 How is relief shown on the map to the left?

2 How can you use relief to decide which areas will be the most difficult to climb?

3 What information is given with the name of a mountain peak?

▼ Mauna Kea, an extinct volcano, is the highest peak in the state of Hawaii. Find Mauna Kea on the map.

Special Purpose Maps

As you explore the world, you will encounter many different kinds of special purpose maps. For example, a road map is a special purpose map. The title of each special purpose map tells the purpose and content of the map. Usually a special purpose map highlights only one kind of information. Examples of special purpose maps include land use, population distribution, recreation, transportation, natural resources, or weather.

The key on a special purpose map is very important. Even though a special purpose map shows only one kind of information, it may present many different pieces of data. This data can be shown in symbols, colors, or arrows. In this way, the key acts like a dictionary for the map.

Reading a special purpose map is a skill in itself. Look at the map below. First, try to get an overall sense of what it shows. Then, study the map to identify its main ideas. For example, one main idea of this map is that much of the petroleum production in the region takes place around the Persian Gulf.

PRACTICE YOUR WORLD EXPLORER SKILLS

1. What part of a special purpose map tells what information is contained on the map?

2. What part of a special purpose map acts like a dictionary for the map?

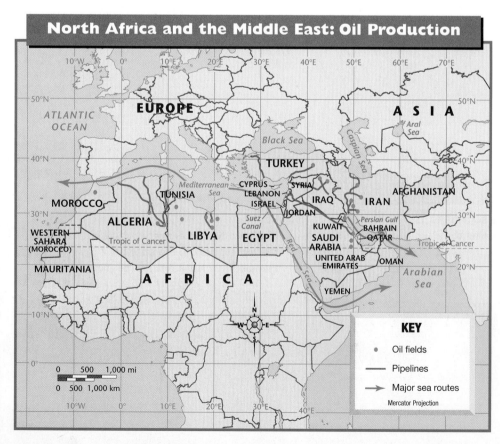

North Africa and the Middle East: Oil Production

KEY
- Oil fields
- Pipelines
- Major sea routes

Mercator Projection

◄ The title on a special purpose map indicates what information can be found on the map. The symbols used on the map are explained in the map's key.

Landforms, Climate Regions, and Natural Vegetation Regions

aps that show landforms, climate, and vegetation regions are special purpose maps. Unlike the boundary lines on a political map, the boundary lines on these maps do not separate the land into exact divisions. A tropical wet climate gradually changes to a tropical wet and dry climate. A tundra gradually changes to an ice cap. Even though the boundaries between regions may not be exact, the information on these maps can help you understand the region and the lives of people in it.

Landforms

Understanding how people use the land requires an understanding of the shape of the land itself. The four most important landforms are mountains, hills, plateaus, and plains. Human activity in every region in the world is influenced by these landforms.

- **Mountains** are high and steep. Most are wide at the bottom and rise to a narrow peak or ridge. Most geographers classify a mountain as land that rises at least 2,000 feet (610 m) above sea level. A series of mountains is called a mountain range.

- **Hills** rise above surrounding land and have rounded tops. Hills are lower and usually less steep than mountains. The elevation of surrounding land determines whether a landform is called a mountain or a hill.
- A **plateau** is a large, mostly flat area of land that rises above the surrounding land. At least one side of a plateau has a steep slope.
- **Plains** are large areas of flat or gently rolling land. Plains have few changes in elevation. Many plains areas are located along coasts. Others are located in the interior regions of some continents.

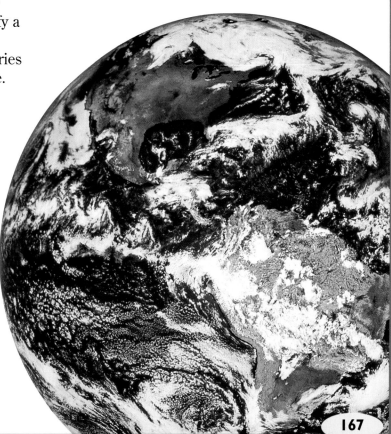

▶ A satellite view of the Earth showing North and South America. What landforms are visible in the photograph?

Climate Regions

Another important influence in the ways people live their lives is the climate of their region. Climate is the weather of a given location over a long period of time. Use the descriptions in the table below to help you visualize the climate regions shown on maps.

Climate	Temperatures	Precipitation
Tropical		
Tropical wet	Hot all year round	Heavy all year round
Tropical wet and dry	Hot all year round	Heavy when sun is overhead, dry other times
Dry		
Semiarid	Hot summers, mild to cold winters	Light
Arid	Hot days, cold nights	Very light
Mild		
Mediterranean	Hot summers, cool winters	Dry summers, wet winters
Humid subtropical	Hot summers, cool winters	Year round, heavier in summer than in winter
Marine west coast	Warm summers, cool winters	Year round, heavier in winter than in summer
Continental		
Humid continental	Hot summers, cold winters	Year round, heavier in summer than in winter
Subarctic	Cool summers, cold winters	Light
Polar		
Tundra	Cool summers, very cold winters	Light
Ice cap	Cold all year round	Light
Highlands	Varies, depending on altitude and direction of prevailing winds	Varies, depending on altitude and direction of prevailing winds

Natural Vegetation Regions

Natural vegetation is the plant life that grows wild without the help of humans. A world vegetation map tells what the vegetation in a place would be if people had not cut down forests or cleared grasslands. The table below provides descriptions of natural vegetation regions shown on maps. Comparing climate and vegetation regions can help you see the close relationship between climate and vegetation.

Vegetation	Description
Tropical rain forest	Tall, close-growing trees forming a canopy over smaller trees, dense growth in general
Deciduous forest	Trees and plants that regularly lose their leaves after each growing season
Mixed forest	Both leaf-losing and cone-bearing trees, no type of tree dominant
Coniferous forest	Cone-bearing trees, evergreen trees and plants
Mediterranean vegetation	Evergreen shrubs and small plants
Tropical savanna	Tall grasses with occasional trees and shrubs
Temperate grassland	Tall grasses with occasional stands of trees
Desert scrub	Low shrubs and bushes, hardy plants
Desert	Little or no vegetation
Tundra	Low shrubs, mosses, lichens; no trees
Ice cap	Little or no vegetation
Highlands	Varies, depending on altitude and direction of prevailing winds

1 How are mountains and hills similar? How are they different?

2 What is the difference between a plateau and a plain?

United States

RUSSIA

ARCTIC OCEAN

ALASKA

CANADA

Anchorage

Bering Sea

Gulf of Alaska

Juneau

250 500 mi

250 500 km

110°W

100°W

90°W

80°W

70°W

CANADA

Presque Isle

MAINE

Augusta

150 300 mi

150 300 km

Olympia

Seattle

WASHINGTON

Spokane

Portland

MONTANA

Minot

NORTH DAKOTA

MINNESOTA

Duluth

Sault Ste. Marie

MICHIGAN

Lake Superior

Portland

Montpelier

NEW HAMPSHIRE

Concord

Salem

OREGON

Helena

Billings

Bismarck

MICHIGAN

Lake Huron

Lake Ontario

VERMONT

NEW YORK

Albany

MASSACHUSETTS

Providence

RHODE ISLAND

Boston

IDAHO

Boise

Sheridan

SOUTH DAKOTA

Pierre

Minneapolis

St. Paul

WISCONSIN

Milwaukee

Madison

Lansing

Detroit

Lake Erie

Buffalo

Cleveland

Hartford

New Haven

CONNECTICUT

NEW YORK CITY

Klamath Falls

Eureka

Winnemucca

Great Salt Lake

Salt Lake City

WYOMING

Jackson

Twin Falls

Snake River

Rapid City

NEBRASKA

Cheyenne

Omaha

Lincoln

IOWA

Des Moines

Cedar Rapids

Chicago

ILLINOIS

Springfield

INDIANA

Indianapolis

OHIO

Columbus

Cincinnati

Pittsburgh

PENNSYLVANIA

Harrisburg

Philadelphia

Trenton

NEW JERSEY

Dover

DELAWARE

Baltimore

Washington, D.C.

Annapolis

MARYLAND

Sacramento

Carson City

NEVADA

UTAH

Denver

Grand Junction

COLORADO

Pueblo

Topeka

Kansas City

KANSAS

Wichita

MISSOURI

Jefferson City

St. Louis

Louisville

Frankfort

KENTUCKY

WEST VIRGINIA

Charleston

Richmond

VIRGINIA

Norfolk

San Francisco

CALIFORNIA

Las Vegas

Cedar City

Colorado River

Arkansas River

Nashville

TENNESSEE

Memphis

Raleigh

NORTH CAROLINA

Charlotte

ATLANTIC OCEAN

Los Angeles

San Diego

ARIZONA

Phoenix

Albuquerque

Santa Fe

NEW MEXICO

Roswell

OKLAHOMA

Oklahoma City

Tulsa

ARKANSAS

Little Rock

Pine Bluff

Birmingham

MISSISSIPPI

Columbus

GEORGIA

Atlanta

Columbia

SOUTH CAROLINA

Charleston

Savannah

PACIFIC OCEAN

Tucson

El Paso

Rio Grande

Red River

Dallas

TEXAS

Austin

San Antonio

Shreveport

Jackson

ALABAMA

Montgomery

Hattiesburg

LOUISIANA

Baton Rouge

Houston

New Orleans

Tallahassee

Jacksonville

FLORIDA

Tampa

Miami

Lake Okeechobee

MEXICO

Gulf of Mexico

30°N

160°W

155°W

Honolulu

PACIFIC OCEAN

HAWAII

Hilo

20°N

50 100 mi

50 100 km

155°W

Data compiled from the *Dorling Kindersley World Desk Reference*, the CIA Factbook, and the *Infoplease Internet Encyclopedia.*

Arches National Park, Utah

GEOFACTS

United States

Capital: Washington, D.C.

Area: 3,539,224 sq mi/9,166,600 sq km

Population: 281,421,906

Most Populated City: New York City (8,008,278)

Largest State: Alaska (570,374 sq mi/ 1,477,267 sq km)

Smallest State: Rhode Island (1,045 sq mi/ 2,706 sq km)

Highest Point: Mount McKinley (20,320 ft/ 6,194 km)

Lowest Point: Death Valley (-282 ft/-86 m)

Longest River: Missouri River (2,565 mi/4,130 km)

Mount Rushmore, South Dakota

Northeast

KEY

— National boundary

— State boundary

⊚ State capital

• Other city

Albers Equal Area Projection

0 100 200 mi
0 100 200 km

CANADA

MAINE

Bangor

Augusta

Lake Champlain · Burlington

Watertown · Montpelier ⊚

VERMONT · Lewiston

Isle au Haut

NEW HAMPSHIRE

Niagara Falls · Lake Ontario · Rochester · Syracuse

Portland · Gulf of Maine

Auburn

Schenectady · Concord · Portsmouth

Lake Erie · Buffalo

NEW YORK

Albany ⊚ · MASSACHUSETTS

Erie

Ithaca

Springfield · Boston

Massachusetts Bay

Hartford · Providence · Cape Cod

PENNSYLVANIA · Scranton

CONNECTICUT

Nantucket Island

State College · Wilkes-Barre

New Haven

Martha's Vineyard

Pittsburgh · Altoona

Newark

New York

RHODE ISLAND

Harrisburg

Trenton · Philadelphia

NEW JERSEY · Atlantic City

ATLANTIC OCEAN

Delaware Bay

Connecticut

Year of Statehood: 1788

Capital: Hartford

Land area: 4,845 sq mi/12,550 sq km

Population: 3,405,565

Largest City: Bridgeport

Ethnic Groups: 77.5% white; 9.4% Hispanic/Latino; 8.7% African American; 2.4% Asian; 0.2% American Indian/Alaska Native; 1.8% other

Agriculture: poultry, fruit, dairy products, tobacco, nursery stock, sweet corn

Industry: computers, office machines, ball and roller bearings, turbines, engines

---

Maine

Year of Statehood: 1820

Capital: Augusta

Land area: 30,865 sq mi/79,939 sq km

Population: 1,274,923

Largest City: Portland

Ethnic Groups: 96.5% white; 0.7% Hispanic/Latino; 0.5% African American; 0.7% Asian; 0.5% American Indian/Alaska Native; 1.0% other

Agriculture: dairy products, poultry and egg production, potatoes, blueberries, hay, apples, aquaculture

Industry: paper and wood products, transportation equipment, leather goods, granite, sand, gravel, zinc, peat, stone

---

Massachusetts

Year of Statehood: 1788

Capital: Boston

Land area: 7,838 sq mi/20,300 sq km

Population: 6,349,097

Largest City: Boston

Ethnic Groups: 81.9% white; 6.8% Hispanic/Latino; 5% African American; 3.7% Asian; 0.2% American Indian/Alaska Native; 2.4% other

Agriculture: cranberries, dairy products, poultry, nursery and greenhouse produce

Industry: computers, medical devices, electric and electronic equipment

---

Background Photo: Brooklyn Bridge, New York

Note: Percentages may not equal 100 due to rounding

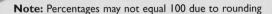

New Hampshire

Year of Statehood: 1788

Capital: Concord

Land area: 8,969 sq mi/3,231 sq km

Population: 1,235,786

Largest City: Manchester

Ethnic Groups: 95.1% white; 1.7% Hispanic/Latino; 0.7% African American; 1.3% Asian; 0.2% American Indian/Alaska Native; 1.1 % other

Agriculture: dairy products, poultry, corn, potatoes, hay

Industry: tourism, machinery, textiles, plastics, pulp, paper products, stone and clay products

Pennsylvania

Year of Statehood: 1787

Capital: Harrisburg

Area: 44,820 sq mi/116,083 sq km

Population: 12,281,054

Largest City: Philadelphia

Ethnic Groups: 84.1% white; 3.2% Hispanic/Latino; 9.8% African American; 1.8% Asian; 0.1% American Indian/Alaska Native; 1% other

Agriculture: dairy products, cattle, hay, corn, wheat, oats, mushrooms, poultry

Industry: metal products, transportation equipment, machinery, chemicals, steel

New Jersey

Year of Statehood: 1787

Capital: Trenton

Land area: 7,419 sq mi/19,215 sq km

Population: 8,414,350

Largest City: Newark

Ethnic Groups: 66% white; 13.3% Hispanic/Latino; 13% African American; 5.7% Asian; 0.1% American Indian/Alaska Native; 1.8% other

Agriculture: cranberry and blueberry culture, potatoes, corn, hay, peaches

Industry: chemicals, pharmaceuticals, machinery, electronic equipment, printed materials, processed foods

Rhode Island

Year of Statehood: 1790

Capital: Providence

Land area: 1,045 sq mi/ 2,706 sq km

Population: 1,048,319

Largest City: Providence

Ethnic Groups: 81.9% white; 8.7% Hispanic/Latino; 4% African American; 2.2% Asian; 0.4% American Indian/Alaska Native; 2.8% other

Agriculture: dairy products, poultry, nursery and greenhouse items, fishing

Industry: finance, jewelry, silverware, textiles, metals, machinery

New York

Year of Statehood: 1788

Capital: Albany

Land area: 47,224 sq mi/122,310 sq km

Population: 18,976,457

Largest City: New York

Ethnic Groups: 62% white; 15.1% Hispanic/Latino; 14.8% African American; 5.5% Asian; 0.3% American Indian/ Alaska Native; 2.4% other

Agriculture: apples, grapes, strawberries, cherries, pears, onions and potatoes

Industry: finance, printed materials, apparel, food products, machinery

Vermont

Year of Statehood: 1791

Capital: Montpelier

Land area: 9,249 sq mi/23,956 sq km

Population: 608,827

Largest City: Burlington

Ethnic Groups: 96.2% white; 0.9% Hispanic/Latino; 0.8% Asian; 0.5% African American; 0.4% American Indian/Alaska Native; 1.2% other

Agriculture: dairy products, apples, cheese, maple syrup, greenhouse and nursery products

Industry: nonelectric machinery, machine tools, precision instruments, textiles

South

Alabama

Year of Statehood: 1819

Capital: Montgomery

Land area: 50,750 sq mi/131,443 sq km

Population: 4,447,100

Largest City: Birmingham

Ethnic Groups: 70.3% white; 25.9% African American; 1.7% Hispanic/Latino; 0.7% Asian; 0.5% American Indian/Alaska Native; 1% other

Agriculture: poultry, cattle, cotton, greenhouse plants, peanuts, vegetables

Industry: pulp and paper products, chemicals, electronics, textiles, processed foods, automobiles, oil, gas

Arkansas

Year of Statehood: 1836

Capital: Little Rock

Area: 52,075 sq mi/134,874 sq km

Population: 2,673,400

Largest City: Little Rock

Ethnic Groups: 78.6% white; 15.6% African American; 3.2% Hispanic/Latino; 0.7% Asian; 0.6% American Indian/Alaska Native; 1.2% other

Agriculture: soybeans, rice, cotton, poultry, dairy goods, catfish

Industry: petroleum, bromine, natural gas, bauxite, food products, chemicals, lumber, paper goods, electrical equipment

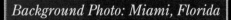

Background Photo: Miami, Florida

Delaware

Year of Statehood: 1787

Capital: Dover

Land area: 1,955 sq mi/5,153 sq km

Population: 783,600

Largest City: Wilmington

Ethnic Groups: 72.5% white; 18.9% African American; 4.8% Hispanic/Latino; 2.1% Asian; 0.3% American Indian/Alaska Native; 1.5% other

Agriculture: poultry, soybeans, corn, dairy products, potatoes, clams, oysters

Industry: chemical products, clothing, processed foods, rubber and plastic products, transportation equipment

Kentucky

Year of Statehood: 1792

Capital: Frankfort

Land area: 39,732 sq mi/102,907 sq km

Population: 4,041,769

Largest City: Louisville

Ethnic Groups: 89.3% white; 7.3% African American; 1.5% Hispanic/Latino; 0.7% Asian; 0.2% American Indian/Alaska Native; 1.1% other

Agriculture: tobacco, horses, cattle, corn, dairy products, hay, soybeans

Industry: electrical equipment, food products, automobiles, nonelectrical machinery, chemicals, apparel, printing

Florida

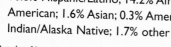
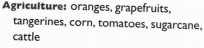

Year of Statehood: 1845

Capital: Tallahassee

Land area: 54,153 sq mi/140,256 sq km

Population: 15,982,378

Largest City: Jacksonville

Ethnic Groups: 65.4% white; 16.8% Hispanic/Latino; 14.2% African American; 1.6% Asian; 0.3% American Indian/Alaska Native; 1.7% other

Agriculture: oranges, grapefruits, tangerines, corn, tomatoes, sugarcane, cattle

Industry: tourism, defense and scientific research, construction, electric and electronic equipment

Louisiana

Year of Statehood: 1812

Capital: Baton Rouge

Area: 43,566 sq mi/112,836 sq km

Population: 4,468,976

Largest City: New Orleans

Ethnic Groups: 62.5% white; 32.3% African American; 2.4% Hispanic/Latino; 1.2% Asian; 0.5% American Indian/Alaska Native; 1% other

Agriculture: sweet potatoes, rice, sugarcane, soybeans, cotton, dairy products

Industry: salt, sulfur, petroleum, natural gas, timber, oil refining, chemicals, lumber, paper

Georgia

Year of Statehood: 1788

Capital: Atlanta

Area: 57,919 sq mi/150,010 sq km

Population: 8,186,453

Largest City: Atlanta

Ethnic Groups: 62.6% white; 28.5% African American; 5.3% Hispanic/Latino; 2.1% Asian; 0.2% American Indian/Alaska Native; 1.2% other

Agriculture: peanuts, tobacco, corn, cotton, poultry, eggs, cattle

Industry: textiles, transportation equipment, food processing, paper products

Maryland

Year of Statehood: 1788

Capital: Annapolis

Land area: 9,775 sq mi/25,316 sq km

Population: 5,296,486

Largest City: Baltimore

Ethnic Groups: 62.1% white; 27.7% African American; 4.3% Hispanic/Latino; 4% Asian; 0.3% American Indian/Alaska Native; 1.6% other

Agriculture: corn, hay, tobacco, soybeans, poultry, dairy goods, horses

Industry: fishing, electrical and electronic machinery, primary metals, food products, missiles

Mississippi

Year of Statehood: 1817

Capital: Jackson

Land area: 46,914 sq mi/121,506 sq km

Population: 2,844,658

Largest City: Jackson

Ethnic Groups: 60.7% white; 36.2% African American; 1.4% Hispanic/Latino; 0.6% Asian; 0.4% American Indian/Alaska Native; 0.7% other

Agriculture: cotton, rice, soybeans, poultry, aquaculture, dairy products

Industry: petroleum, natural gas, chemicals, plastics, foods, wood products, fishing, seafood processing

Oklahoma

Year of Statehood: 1907

Capital: Oklahoma City

Land area: 68,679 sq mi/177,877 sq km

Population: 3,450,654

Largest City: Oklahoma City

Ethnic Groups: 74.1% white; 7.7% American Indian/Alaska Native; 7.5% African American; 5.2% Hispanic/Latino; 1.3% Asian; 4.2% other

Agriculture: wheat, cotton, hay, peanuts, grain, sorghum, soybeans, corn, pecans

Industry: natural gas, petroleum, nonelectrical machinery, transportation

North Carolina

Year of Statehood: 1789

Capital: Raleigh

Land area: 48,718 sq mi/126,180 sq km

Population: 8,049,313

Largest City: Charlotte

Ethnic Groups: 70.2% white; 21.4% African American; 4.7% Hispanic/Latino; 1.4% Asian; 1.2% American Indian/Native Alaska; 1.1% other

Agriculture: tobacco, chickens, hogs, turkeys, greenhouse products, sweet potatoes

Industry: furniture, lumber, textiles, electrical machinery, computers, chemicals

South Carolina

Year of Statehood: 1788

Capital: Columbia

Land area: 30,111 sq mi/77,988 sq km

Population: 4,012,012

Largest City: Columbia

Ethnic Groups: 66.1% white; 29.4% African American; 2.4% Hispanic/Latino; 0.9% Asian; 0.3% American Indian/Alaska Native; 0.9% other

Agriculture: tobacco, soybeans, cotton, broiler chickens, cattle, peanuts, pecans

Industry: tourism, pulp and paper, chemicals, machinery, clothing, automobiles

Tennessee

Year of Statehood: 1796

Capital: Nashville

Land area: 41,220 sq mi/106,759 sq km

Population: 5,689,283

Largest City: Memphis

Ethnic Groups: 79.2% white; 16.3% African American; 2.2 % Hispanic/Latino; 1% Asian; 0.2% American Indian/Alaska Native; 1.1% other

Agriculture: cotton, soybeans, tobacco, cattle, dairy products, hogs

Industry: chemicals and related products, foods, electrical machinery, primary metals, automobiles, textiles, aluminum

Virginia

Year of Statehood: 1788

Capital: Richmond

Land area: 39,598 sq mi/102,558 sq km

Population: 7,078,515

Largest City: Virginia Beach

Ethnic Groups: 70.2% white; 19.4% African American; 4.7% Hispanic/Latino; 3.7% Asian; 0.3% American Indian/Alaska Native; 1.8% other

Agriculture: tobacco, grains, corn, soybeans, peanuts, sweet potatoes, cotton, apples

Industry: coal, stone, cement, sand, gravel, shipbuilding, computers, tourism

Texas

Year of Statehood: 1845

Capital: Austin

Land area: 261,914 sq mi/678,358 sq km

Population: 20,851,820

Largest City: Houston

Ethnic Groups: 52.4% white; 32% Hispanic/Latino; 11.3% African American; 2.7% Asian; 0.3% American Indian/Alaska Native; 1.3% other

Agriculture: cattle, cotton, grains, rice, cattle, dairy products, greenhouse products

Industry: oil, natural gas, helium, salt, sulfur, clays, chemicals, petroleum, transportation equipment, machinery, metals

West Virginia

Year of Statehood: 1863

Capital: Charleston

Land area: 24,087 sq mi/62,384 sq km

Population: 1,808,344

Largest City: Charleston

Ethnic Groups: 94.6% white; 3.1% African American; 0.7% Hispanic/Latino; 0.5% Asian; 0.2% American Indian/Alaska Native; 0.9% other

Agriculture: apples, peaches, hay, corn, tobacco, poultry, cattle, dairy products

Industry: coal, natural gas, stone, cement, salt, oil, glass, chemical and high-technology industries, metals, machinery

Midwest

CANADA

Lake of the Woods

NORTH DAKOTA
Minot
Grand Forks
Bismarck

MINNESOTA
Duluth
Lake Superior

SOUTH DAKOTA
Rapid City
Pierre
Sioux Falls

St. Cloud
Minneapolis St. Paul
Rochester

WISCONSIN
Wausau
Fond du Lac
Madison
Milwaukee

Lake Michigan

MICHIGAN
Saginaw
Port Huron
Lansing Detroit
Lake Huron
Lake St. Clair
Lake Erie
Cleveland

NEBRASKA
Grand Island
Omaha
Lincoln

Sioux City
Fort Dodge
Cedar Falls
IOWA
Des Moines

Chicago
Joliet
Moline
Bloomington
ILLINOIS
Springfield
Indianapolis
Lafayette
INDIANA
Marion
Columbus
Bowling Green
OHIO
Cincinnati

KANSAS
Kansas City
Topeka
Wichita
Joplin

St. Joseph
Jefferson City
St. Louis
MISSOURI
Springfield
Evansville
Carbondale
New Albany

0 200 400 mi
0 200 400 km

Illinois

Year of Statehood: 1818

Capital: Springfield

Land area: 55,593 sq mi/143,987 sq km

Population: 12,419,293

Largest City: Chicago

Ethnic Groups: 67.8% white; 14.9% African American; 12.3% Hispanic/Latino; 3.4% Asian; 0.1% American Indian/Alaska Native; 1.4% other

Agriculture: corn, soybeans, hogs, cattle, hay, wheat

Industry: mining (coal), electrical and nonelectrical machinery, food products

Indiana

Year of Statehood: 1816

Capital: Indianapolis

Land area: 35,870 sq mi/92,904 sq km

Population: 6,080,485

Largest City: Indianapolis

Ethnic Groups: 85.8% white; 8.3% African American; 3.5% Hispanic/Latino; 1% Asian; 0.2% American Indian/Alaska Native; 1.1% other

Agriculture: corn, wheat, dairy products, soybeans, hay, popcorn, vegetables, fruits

Industry: meatpacking, iron, steel, electrical and transportation equipment

Background Photo: Kansas plains

Iowa

Year of Statehood: 1846

Capital: Des Moines

Land area: 55,875 sq mi/144,716 sq km

Population: 2,926,324

Largest City: Des Moines

Ethnic Groups: 92.6% white, 2.8% Hispanic/Latino; 2.1% African American; 1.2% Asian; 0.3% American Indian/Alaska Native; 1% other

Agriculture: corn, soybeans, hogs, pigs, and cattle, hay, oats

Industry: food processing, nonelectrical machinery, farm machinery, tires

Michigan

Year of Statehood: 1837

Capital: Lansing

Area: 56,809 sq mi/147,135 sq km

Population: 9,938,444

Largest City: Detroit

Ethnic Groups: 78.6% white; 14.1% African American; 3.3% Hispanic/Latino; 1.8% Asian; 0.5% American Indian/Alaska Native; 1.7% other

Agriculture: dairy products, corn, greenhouse products, soybeans, apples

Industry: automobile industry, nonelectrical machinery, metal products, chemicals

Kansas

Year of Statehood: 1861

Capital: Topeka

Land area: 81,823 sq mi/211,922 sq km

Population: 2,688,418

Largest City: Wichita

Ethnic Groups: 83.1% white; 7% Hispanic/Latino; 5.6% African American; 1.7% Asian; 0.8% American Indian/Alaska Native; 1.7% other

Agriculture: wheat, corn, hay, soybeans, sunflowers, cattle, dairy products

Industry: transportation equipment, industrial and computer machinery, aircraft manufacturing, petroleum, coal products

Minnesota

Year of Statehood: 1858

Capital: St. Paul

Land area: 79,617 sq mi/206,207 sq km

Population: 4,919,479

Largest City: Minneapolis

Ethnic Groups: 88.2% white; 3.4% African American; 2.9% Hispanic/Latino; 2.9% Asian; 1.1% American Indian/Alaska Native; 1.5% other

Agriculture: wheat, corn, soybeans, livestock, dairy products, sweet corn

Industry: food processing, electronic equipment, machinery, paper products

Columbus, Ohio

Missouri

Year of Statehood: 1821

Capital: Jefferson City

Land area: 68,898 sq mi/178,446 sq km

Population: 5,595,211

Largest City: Kansas City

Ethnic Groups: 83.8% white; 11.2% African American; 2.1% Hispanic/Latino; 1.1% Asian; 0.4% American Indian/Alaska Native; 1.4% other

Agriculture: soybeans, corn, cattle, hogs, wheat, dairy products

Industry: aerospace and transportation equipment, food products, chemicals

Nebraska

Year of Statehood: 1867

Capital: Lincoln

Land area: 76,878 sq mi/99,113 sq km

Population: 1,711,263

Largest City: Omaha

Ethnic Groups: 87.3% white; 3.9% African American; 5.5% Hispanic/Latino; 1.3% Asian; 0.8% American Indian/Alaska Native; 1.1% other

Agriculture: cattle, corn, hogs, soybeans, wheat, dry beans, oats, potatoes

Industry: food processing, electrical machinery, primary metals, transportation equipment, oil

North Dakota

Year of Statehood: 1889

Capital: Bismarck

Land area: 70,704 sq mi/183,123 sq km

Population: 642,200

Largest City: Fargo

Ethnic Groups: 91.7% white; 4.8% American Indian/Alaska Native; 1.2% Hispanic/Latino; 0.6% African American; 0.6% Asian; 1.1% other

Agriculture: grain, meat, dairy products, wheat, barley, flaxseed, oats, potatoes

Industry: petroleum, sand, gravel, lime, salt, natural-gas, construction and pottery materials, farm equipment

Ohio

Year of Statehood: 1803

Capital: Columbus

Area: 40,953 sq mi/106,067 sq km

Population: 11,353,140

Largest City: Columbus

Ethnic Groups: 84% white; 11.4% African American; 1.9% Hispanic/Latino; 1.2% Asian; 0.2% American Indian/Alaska Native; 1.4% other

Agriculture: corn, soybeans, hay, wheat, cattle, hogs, dairy products

Industry: transportation equipment, primary and fabricated metals, machinery, sand

Wisconsin

Year of Statehood: 1848

Capital: Madison

Area: 54,314 sq mi/140,673 sq km

Population: 5,363,675

Largest City: Milwaukee

Ethnic Groups: 87.3% white; 5.6% African American; 3.6% Hispanic/Latino; 1.6% Asian; 0.8% American Indian/Alaska Native; 1.1% other

Agriculture: dairy products, cattle, corn, soybeans, hay, oats, potatoes, alfalfa, fruits

Industry: food processing, machinery, vehicles and transportation equipment

South Dakota

Year of Statehood: 1889

Capital: Pierre

Area: 75,898 sq mi/196,575 sq km

Population: 754,844

Largest City: Sioux Rapids

Ethnic Groups: 88% white; 8.1% American Indian/Alaska Native; 1.4% Hispanic/Latino; 0.6% African American; 0.6% Asian; 1.3% other

Agriculture: cattle, sheep, soybeans, wheat, corn, oats, sunflowers, flaxseed, barley

Industry: electronics manufacturing, meat-packing, food processing, mining (gold), tourism

Wisconsin

REGIONAL · DATABASE

West

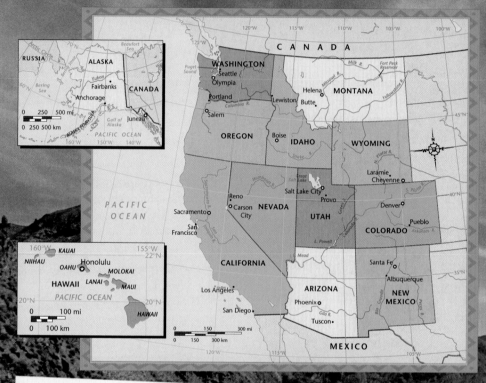

Alaska

Year of Statehood: 1959

Capital: Juneau

Land area: 570,374 sq mi/ 1,477,267 sq km

Population: 626,932

Largest City: Anchorage

Ethnic Groups: 67.6% white; 15.4% American Indian/Alaska Native; 4.1% Hispanic/Latino; 3.9% Asian; 3.4% African American; 5.6% other

Agriculture: greenhouse and dairy products, potatoes, barley, oats, hay

Industry: commercial fishing, lumbering, mining, petroleum, natural gas

Arizona

Year of Statehood: 1912

Capital: Phoenix

Land area: 113,642 sq mi/296,400 sq km

Population: 5,130,632

Largest City: Phoenix

Ethnic Groups: 63.8% white; 25.3% Hispanic/Latino; 4.5% American Indian/Alaska Native; 2.9% African American; 1.7% Asian 1.7% other

Agriculture: cotton, lettuce, cauliflower, broccoli, sorghum, cattle, dairy goods

Industry: electronics, printing and publishing, processed foods, aerospace and transportation

Background Photo: Death Valley, California

California

Year of Statehood: 1850

Capital: Sacramento

Land area: 155,973 sq mi/403,970 sq km

Population: 33,871,648

Largest City: Los Angeles

Ethnic Groups: 46.7% white; 32.4% Hispanic/Latino; 10.8% Asian; 6.4% African American; 0.5% American Indian/Alaska Native; 3.2% other

Agriculture: fruits, vegetables, cotton, flowers, dairy products, grapes, fishing

Industry: petroleum, natural gas, lumber, electronic equipment, computers

Hawaii

Year of Statehood: 1959

Capital: Honolulu

Land area: 6,423 sq mi/16,637 sq km

Population: 1,211,537

Largest City: Honolulu

Ethnic Groups: 40.8% Asian; 22.9% white; 9% Hawaiian Native/Other Pacific Islanders; 7.2% Hispanic/Latino; 1.7% African American; 0.2% American Indian/Alaska Native; 18.2% other

Agriculture: sugarcane, pineapples, macadamia nuts, papayas, greenhouse vegetables, coffee, cattle, dairy products, fishing

Industry: food processing, tourism, defense installations

Colorado

Year of Statehood: 1876

Capital: Denver

Land area: 103,730 sq mi/268,660 sq km

Population: 4,301,261

Largest City: Denver

Ethnic Groups: 74.5% white; 17.1% Hispanic/Latino, 3.7% African American; 2.2% Asian, 0.7% American Indian/Alaska Native; 1.9% other

Agriculture: cattle, sheep, dairy products, wheat, hay, corn, sugar beets

Industry: food processing, computer equipment, aerospace products, electronic equipment, tourism

Idaho

Year of Statehood: 1890

Capital: Boise

Land area: 82,751 sq mi/214,325 sq km

Population: 1,293,953

Largest City: Boise

Ethnic Groups: 88% white; 7.9% Latino/Hispanic; 1.2% American Indian/Alaska Native; 0.9% Asian; 0.4% African American; 1.6% other

Agriculture: cattle, dairy products, potatoes, hay, wheat, peas, beans, sugar beets

Industry: electronic and computer equipment, processed foods, lumber

Montana

Year of Statehood: 1889

Capital: Helena

Land area: 145,556 sq mi/376,991 sq km

Population: 902,195

Largest City: Billings

Ethnic Groups: 89.5% white; 6% American Indian/Alaska Native; 2% Hispanic/Latino; 0.5% Asian; 0.3% African American; 1.6% other

Agriculture: wheat, cattle, sheep, barley, sugar beets, hay

Industry: mining (copper, gold, silver, platinum, zinc), petroleum, natural gas, coal, forest products, processed foods

New Mexico

Year of Statehood: 1912

Capital: Santa Fe

Land area: 121,365 sq mi/314,334 sq km

Population: 1,819,046

Largest City: Albuquerque

Ethnic Groups: 44.7% white; 42.1% Hispanic/Latino; 8.9% American Indian/Alaska Native; 1.7% African American; 1% Asian; 1.6% other

Agriculture: cattle, sheep, hay, sorghum grains, onions, potatoes, dairy products

Industry: mining, defense, food and mineral processing, chemicals, electrical equipment, high-technology manufacturing

Nevada

Year of Statehood: 1864

Capital: Carson City

Land area: 109,806 sq mi/284,397 sq km

Population: 1,998,257

Largest City: Las Vegas

Ethnic Groups: 65.2% white; 19.7% Hispanic/Latino; 6.6% African American; 4.4% Asian; 1.1% American Indian/Alaska Native; 3% other

Agriculture: cattle, sheep, hay, potatoes, onions

Industry: gaming, tourism, mining (gold, silver, and mercury), aerospace equipment, garden irrigation devices

Oregon

Year of Statehood: 1859

Capital: Salem

Area: 96,003 sq mi/248,647 sq km

Population: 3,421,399

Largest City: Portland

Ethnic Groups: 83.5% white; 8% Hispanic/Latino; 2.9% Asian; 1.6% African American; 1.2% American Indian/Alaska Native; 2.8% other

Agriculture: greenhouse products, wheat, cattle, dairy products, hay, onions, pears

Industry: lumber, paper and paper items, machinery, printing and publishing

Utah

Year of Statehood: 1896

Capital: Salt Lake City

Land area: 82,168 sq mi/212,816 sq km

Population: 2,233,169

Largest City: Salt Lake City

Ethnic Groups: 85.3% white; 9% Hispanic/Latino; 1.6% Asian; 1.2% American Indian/Alaskan Native; 0.7% African American; 2.2% other

Agriculture: cattle, dairy products, poultry, hay, corn, barley, wheat, fruit

Industry: mining (copper, gold), aerospace research, missiles, spacecraft, computer hardware and software, electronic systems

Washington

Year of Statehood: 1889

Capital: Olympia

Land area: 66,582 sq mi/172,447 sq km

Population: 5,894,121

Largest City: Seattle

Ethnic Groups: 78.9% white; 7.5% Hispanic/Latino; 5.4% Asian; 3.1% African American; 1.4% American Indian/Alaska Native; 3.6% other

Agriculture: grapes, fruit, wheat, corn, potatoes, nuts, vegetables, cattle, sheep

Industry: computer software, electronics, biotechnology, food processing, commercial fishing, lumber and wood-products

Marine Corps War Memorial, Washington

Wyoming

Year of Statehood: 1890

Capital: Cheyenne

Land area: 97,105 sq mi/251,501 sq km

Population: 493,782

Largest City: Cheyenne

Ethnic Groups: 88.9% white; 6.4% Hispanic/Latino; 2.1% American Indian/Alaska Native; 0.7% African American; 0.5% Asian; 1.4% other

Agriculture: cattle, hay, sugar beets, wheat, sheep, horses

Industry: mining (coal, uranium, gold), petroleum, natural gas, processed foods

Canada

KEY

——— National boundary

⊛ National capital

✪ Provincial capital

• Other city

Lambert Azimuthal Equal-Area Projection

ARCTIC OCEAN

GREENLAND (DEN.)

Beaufort Sea

Baffin Bay

ALASKA (U.S.)

YUKON

NORTHWEST TERRITORIES

NUNAVUT

Arctic Circle

Mackenzie

Great Bear L.

Whitehorse

Yellowknife

• Iqaluit

Great Slave L.

Dubawnt L.

C A N A D A

NEWFOUNDLAND

Liard R.

Williston L.

Peace R.

Athabasca R.

Athabasca L.

Reindeer L.

Hudson Bay

Labrador

Smallwood Res.

BRITISH COLUMBIA

SASKATCHEWAN

MANITOBA

N. Saskatchewan R.

L. Mistassini

ALBERTA

Fraser R.

Edmonton

Saskatoon

S. Sas katchewan

Lake Winnipeg

Manicouagan

St. John's

QUEBEC

PRINCE EDWARD ISLAND

Vancouver

Calgary

Bow R.

Regina

Lake Manitoba

Winnipeg

ONTARIO

NEW BRUNSWICK

Charlottetown

Victoria

Lake of the Woods

L. Nipigon

Quebec

Fredericton

Halifax

0   300   600 mi

0   300   600 km

UNITED STATES

Great Lakes

St. Lawrence R.

Hull

Ottawa

Montreal

NOVA SCOTIA

• Toronto

ATLANTIC OCEAN

Vancouver, British Columbia

Lake Louise, Alberta

GEOFACTS

Canada

Capital: Ottawa

Area: 3,560,217 sq mi/9,220,970 sq km

Population: 30,750,087

Most Populated City: Toronto (4,263,757)

Largest Province or Territory: Nunavut (772,260 sq mi/2,000,671 sq km)

Smallest Province or Territory: Prince Edward Island (2,184 sq mi/5,657 sq km)

Highest Point: Mount Logan (19,850 ft/6,050 m)

Lowest Point: Atlantic Ocean (0 ft/0 m)

Longest River: Mackenzie River (2,635 mi/4,241 km)

Quebec City, Quebec

Background Photo: Ontario, Canada

Alberta

Capital: Edmonton

Area: 248,802 sq mi/644,394 sq km

Population: 2,997,236

Largest City: Calgary

Languages: 91.9% English;
0.1% French; 6.7% bilingual;
1.3% neither English nor French

Agriculture: wheat, beef and dairy
cattle, hogs, poultry, barley,
sugar beets

Industry: mining, refining, petrochemical
industries, meatpacking, flour milling

Manitoba

Capital: Winnipeg

Land Area: 211,719 sq mi/549,350 sq km

Population: 1,147,880

Largest City: Winnipeg

Languages: 89.4% English;
0.1% French; 9.4% bilingual;
1.1% neither English nor French

Agriculture: wheat, barley, oats, rye, flax,
dairy, poultry

Industry: printed materials, clothing,
electrical items, chemicals, furniture,
leather, transportation equipment,
mining

British Columbia

Capital: Victoria

Area: 358,970 sq mi/929,732 sq km

Population: 4,063,760

Largest City: Vancouver

Languages: 90.6% English;
6.7% bilingual; 2.6% neither English
nor French

Agriculture: apples, cherries, plums,
raspberries, cranberries, dairy products

Industry: lumbering, pulp, paper, chemical
products, natural gas, petroleum, mining
(coal, gold, copper, zinc), fishing, tourism

New Brunswick

Capital: Fredericton

Land Area: 27,836 sq mi/
72,088 sq km

Population: 756,598

Largest City: Saint John

Languages: 57.3% English;
10.1% French; 32.6% bilingual

Agriculture: dairy products, potatoes,
hay, clover, oats, fruit, commercial
fishing

Industry: lumber, pulp, paper, food and
beverages, ships, chemicals, refined oil,
mining, natural gas

Nova Scotia

Newfoundland and Labrador

Capital: St. John's

Land Area: 156,185 sq mi/ 404,519 sq km

Population: 538,823

Largest City: St. John's

Languages: 96% English; 3.9% bilingual

Agriculture: livestock, dairy products, poultry, eggs, potatoes, turnips, carrots

Industry: mining (iron, zinc, copper) oil, natural gas, timber, pulp, paper, commercial fishing

Nova Scotia

Capital: Halifax

Land Area: 21,425 sq mi/ 55,491 sq km

Population: 940,996

Largest City: Halifax

Languages: 90.4% English; 0.2% French; 9.3% bilingual

Agriculture: dairy products, apples, hay, grain, vegetables, livestock, blueberries

Industry: iron, steel, processed fish, automobiles, construction materials, tourism

Northwest Territories

Capital: Yellowknife

Land Area: 532,643 sq mi/ 1,379,028 sq km

Population: 42,083

Largest City: Yellowknife

Languages: 87.1% English; 6.3% bilingual; 6.5% neither English nor French

Agriculture: limited; small vegetable gardens

Industry: mining (lead, zinc), oil, trapping, commercial fishing

Nunavut

Capital: Iqaluit

Land Area: 772,260 sq mi/ 2,000,671 sq km

Population: 27,692

Largest City: Iqaluit

Languages: 71.4% Inukitut; 23.6% English; 1.6% French

Agriculture: fish

Industry: mining, hunting, fishing, fur trapping, sealing, arts and crafts

Ontario

Capital: Toronto

Land Area: 344,090 sq mi/891,190 sq km.

Population: 11,669,344

Largest City: Toronto

Languages: 85.7% English; 0.4% French; 11.6% bilingual

Agriculture: cattle, dairy products, hogs, corn, wheat, potatoes, soybeans, orchards, tobacco

Industry: motor vehicles and parts, iron, steel, foods, beverages, electrical goods, machinery, chemicals, petroleum and coal products

Prince Edward Island

Capital: Charlottetown

Land Area: 2,184 sq mi/5,657 sq km

Population: 138,928

Largest City: Charlottetown

Languages: 88.9% English; 0.1% French; 11% bilingual

Agriculture: fruit, vegetables, potatoes, dairy products, hogs, tobacco, eggs, poultry

Industry: food processing, tourism, fur farming, fish products, dairy items, fertilizer, boats, wood products

Georgian Bay, Ontario

Quebec

Capital: Quebec

Land Area: 594,860 sq mi/
1,553,637 sq km

Population: 7,372,448

Largest City: Montreal

Languages: 56.1% French;
5.1% English; 37.8% bilingual

Agriculture: dairy products, sugar beets,
tobacco

Industry: refined petroleum, food
products, beverages, motor vehicles,
aircraft, clothing, furniture, iron, steel

Saskatchewan

Capital: Regina

Land Area: 220,348 sq mi/
570,700 sq km

Population: 1,023,636

Largest City: Saskatoon

Languages: 94.3% English;
5.2% bilingual; 0.5% neither English
nor French

Agriculture: wheat, oats, barley, rye,
rapeseed, flax, dairy products

Industry: mining (uranium, copper, zinc,
gold, coal), oil, natural gas, potash,
processing raw minerals

Yukon Territory

Capital: Whitehorse

Land Area: 184,931 sq mi/
478,970 sq km

Population: 30,663

Largest City: Whitehorse

Languages: 89.2% English; 0.2% French;
10.5% bilingual; 0.2% neither English
nor French

Agriculture: potatoes, animal feed crops,
cattle, horses, pigs

Industry: mining, mineral refining,
furniture, clothing, handicrafts,
fur production

Quebec

Atlas

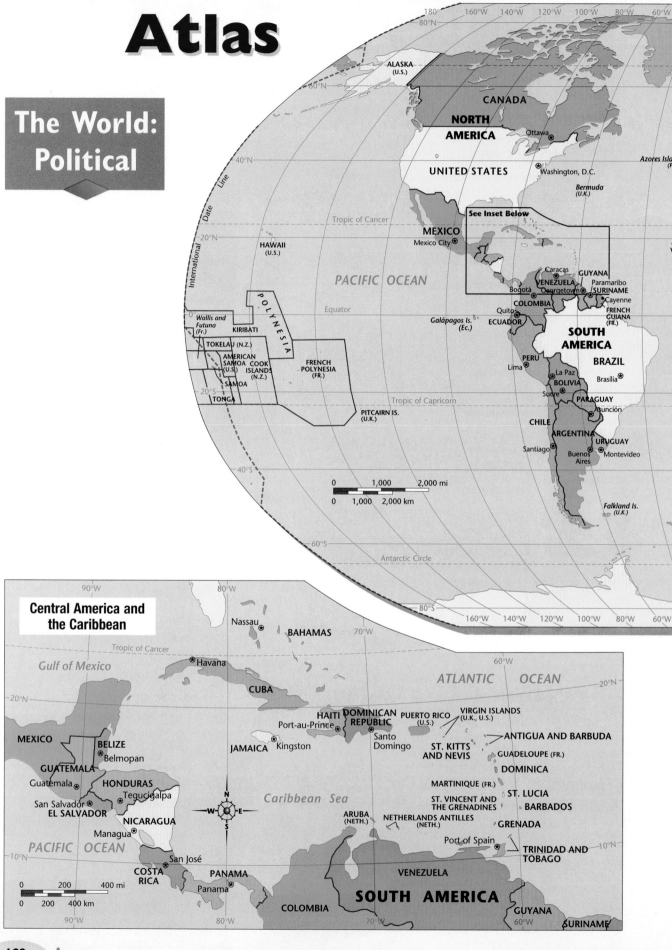

The World: Political

ALASKA (U.S.)

CANADA

NORTH AMERICA

Ottawa ⊛

UNITED STATES

Washington, D.C. ⊛

Azores Islands (Port.)

Bermuda (U.K.)

Tropic of Cancer

MEXICO
Mexico City ⊛

CAPE VERDE

HAWAII (U.S.)

PACIFIC OCEAN

Caracas ⊛
VENEZUELA
Bogotá ⊛
COLOMBIA
Quito ⊛
ECUADOR

GUYANA
Georgetown ⊛
Paramaribo ⊛ SURINAME
Cayenne
FRENCH GUIANA (FR.)

See Inset Below

Equator

Galápagos Is. (Ec.)

International Date Line

P O L Y N E S I A

Wallis and Futuna (Fr.)
KIRIBATI
TOKELAU (N.Z.)
AMERICAN SAMOA (U.S.)
COOK ISLANDS (N.Z.)
FRENCH POLYNESIA (FR.)
SAMOA
TONGA

PITCAIRN IS. (U.K.)

Tropic of Capricorn

SOUTH AMERICA

PERU
Lima ⊛
La Paz ⊛
BOLIVIA
Sucre ⊛

BRAZIL
Brasília ⊛

PARAGUAY
Asunción ⊛

CHILE
ARGENTINA
Santiago ⊛
Buenos Aires ⊛

URUGUAY
Montevideo ⊛

| 0 | 1,000 | 2,000 mi |
| 0 | 1,000 | 2,000 km |

Falkland Is. (U.K.)

Antarctic Circle

Central America and the Caribbean

Nassau ⊛
BAHAMAS

Tropic of Cancer

Gulf of Mexico

Havana ⊛
CUBA

ATLANTIC OCEAN

HAITI
Port-au-Prince ⊛
DOMINICAN REPUBLIC
Santo Domingo ⊛

PUERTO RICO (U.S.)
VIRGIN ISLANDS (U.K., U.S.)

ANTIGUA AND BARBUDA

MEXICO
BELIZE
Belmopan ⊛

JAMAICA
Kingston ⊛

ST. KITTS AND NEVIS
GUADELOUPE (FR.)
DOMINICA

GUATEMALA
Guatemala ⊛

HONDURAS
Tegucigalpa ⊛

MARTINIQUE (FR.)
ST. VINCENT AND THE GRENADINES
ST. LUCIA
BARBADOS

San Salvador ⊛
EL SALVADOR

NICARAGUA
Managua ⊛

Caribbean Sea

ARUBA (NETH.)
NETHERLANDS ANTILLES (NETH.)

GRENADA

PACIFIC OCEAN

San José ⊛
COSTA RICA

PANAMA
Panama ⊛

VENEZUELA

Port of Spain ⊛
TRINIDAD AND TOBAGO

| 0 | 200 | 400 mi |
| 0 | 200 | 400 km |

SOUTH AMERICA

COLOMBIA

GUYANA
SURINAME

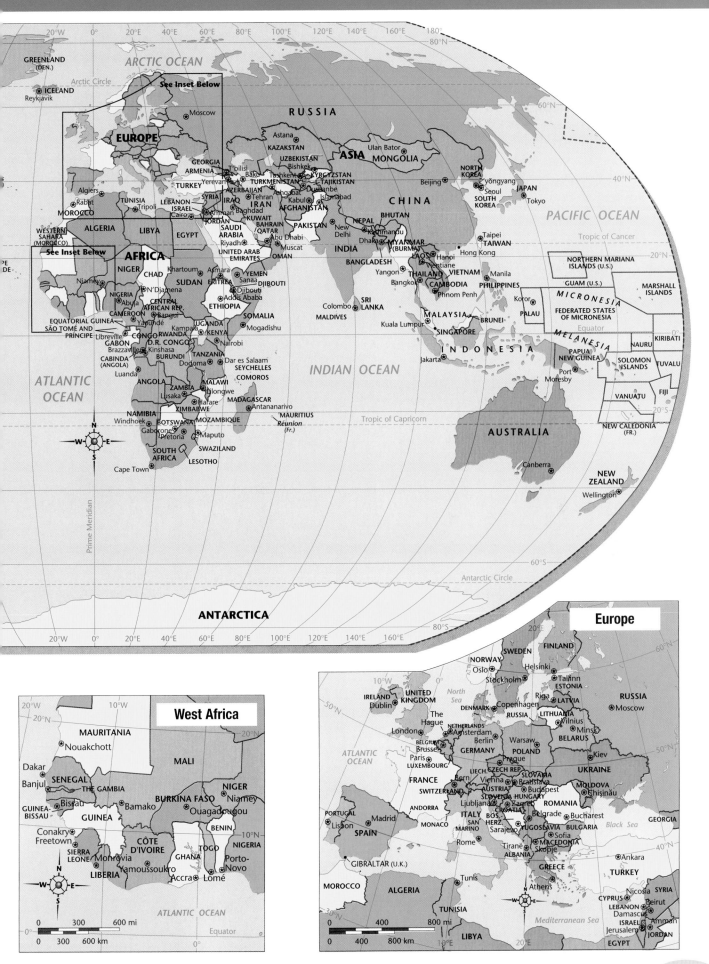

20°W 0° 20°E 40°E 60°E 80°E 100°E 120°E 140°E 160°E 180°
80°N

GREENLAND
(DEN.)

ARCTIC OCEAN

Arctic Circle

ICELAND
Reykjavik

See Inset Below

Moscow

60°N

RUSSIA

EUROPE

Astana

KAZAKSTAN

ASIA

MONGOLIA

Ulan Bator

GEORGIA

ARMENIA

T'bilisi

Baku

Tashkent

UZBEKISTAN

Bishkek

KYRGYZSTAN

NORTH
KOREA

P'yŏngyang

40°N

TURKEY

Yerevan

AZERBAIJAN

Ashgabat

Dushanbe

TAJIKISTAN

Beijing

Seoul

JAPAN

Algiers

Rabat

TUNISIA

Tripoli

LEBANON

ISRAEL

SYRIA

Tehran

Baghdad

IRAQ

IRAN

Kabul

TURKMENISTAN

AFGHANISTAN

Islamabad

CHINA

SOUTH
KOREA

Tokyo

PACIFIC OCEAN

MOROCCO

Cairo

JORDAN

Amman

KUWAIT

BAHRAIN

QATAR

PAKISTAN

New
Delhi

NEPAL

Kathmandu

BHUTAN

MYANMAR
(BURMA)

Taipei

TAIWAN

Tropic of Cancer

WESTERN
SAHARA
(MOROCCO)

ALGERIA

LIBYA

EGYPT

SAUDI
ARABIA

Riyadh

Abu Dhabi

UNITED ARAB
EMIRATES

Muscat

OMAN

INDIA

Dhaka

BANGLADESH

Hanoi

LAOS

Vientiane

Hong Kong

NORTHERN MARIANA
ISLANDS (U.S.)

20°N

See Inset Below

AFRICA

NIGER

CHAD

Khartoum

SUDAN

Asmara

ERITREA

N'Djamena

Sanaa

YEMEN

Djibouti

DJIBOUTI

Yangon

THAILAND

Bangkok

VIETNAM

CAMBODIA

Phnom Penh

Manila

PHILIPPINES

GUAM (U.S.)

MICRONESIA

MARSHALL
ISLANDS

NIGERIA

Abuja

CENTRAL
AFRICAN REP.

Bangui

CAMEROON

Yaoundé

ETHIOPIA

Addis Ababa

SOMALIA

Colombo

SRI
LANKA

MALDIVES

MALAYSIA

Kuala Lumpur

BRUNEI

SINGAPORE

Koror

PALAU

FEDERATED STATES
OF MICRONESIA

Equator

KIRIBATI

0°

EQUATORIAL GUINEA

SÃO TOMÉ AND
PRÍNCIPE

Libreville

GABON

CONGO

Brazzaville

Kinshasa

D.R. CONGO

RWANDA

BURUNDI

UGANDA

Kampala

KENYA

Nairobi

TANZANIA

Mogadishu

Jakarta

INDONESIA

PAPUA
NEW GUINEA

SOLOMON
ISLANDS

NAURU

MELANESIA

TUVALU

ATLANTIC
OCEAN

CABINDA
(ANGOLA)

Luanda

ANGOLA

Dodoma

Dar es Salaam

SEYCHELLES

COMOROS

INDIAN OCEAN

Port
Moresby

VANUATU

FIJI

ZAMBIA

MALAWI

Lilongwe

20°S

Lusaka

Harare

MADAGASCAR

Antananarivo

NEW CALEDONIA
(FR.)

NAMIBIA

Windhoek

BOTSWANA

ZIMBABWE

MOZAMBIQUE

MAURITIUS

Réunion
(Fr.)

Tropic of Capricorn

N

W   E

S

Gaborone

Pretoria

Maputo

SWAZILAND

AUSTRALIA

SOUTH
AFRICA

LESOTHO

Cape Town

Canberra

NEW
ZEALAND

Wellington

60°S

Antarctic Circle

Prime Meridian

ANTARCTICA

80°S

20°W 0° 20°E 40°E 60°E 80°E 100°E 120°E 140°E 160°E

West Africa

20°W 10°W

20°N

MAURITANIA

Nouakchott

MALI

Dakar

SENEGAL

Banjul

THE GAMBIA

NIGER

Niamey

GUINEA-
BISSAU

Bissau

Bamako

BURKINA FASO

Ouagadougou

GUINEA

Conakry

Freetown

SIERRA
LEONE

Monrovia

CÔTE
D'IVOIRE

Yamoussoukro

BENIN

TOGO

GHANA

Accra

Lomé

NIGERIA

Porto-
Novo

10°N

LIBERIA

N

W   E

S

ATLANTIC OCEAN

0° 300 600 mi

0° 300 600 km

Equator

0°

Europe

FINLAND

SWEDEN

NORWAY

Oslo

Helsinki

10°W

0°

IRELAND

Dublin

UNITED
KINGDOM

Stockholm

Tallinn

ESTONIA

RUSSIA

Moscow

60°N

North
Sea

DENMARK

Copenhagen

Riga

LATVIA

50°N

The
Hague

London

NETHERLANDS

Amsterdam

RUSSIA

LITHUANIA

Vilnius

Minsk

BELARUS

ATLANTIC
OCEAN

BELGIUM

Brussels

Berlin

GERMANY

Warsaw

POLAND

Kiev

Paris

LUXEMBOURG

Prague

CZECH REP.

SLOVAKIA

UKRAINE

FRANCE

Bern

Vienna

Bratislava

LIECH.

AUSTRIA

HUNGARY

Budapest

MOLDOVA

Chişinău

SWITZERLAND

SLOVENIA

Ljubljana

Zagreb

CROATIA

ROMANIA

GEORGIA

ANDORRA

PORTUGAL

Lisbon

Madrid

MONACO

ITALY

SAN
MARINO

BOS.
HERZ.

Sarajevo

YUGOSLAVIA

Belgrade

Bucharest

BULGARIA

Sofia

Black Sea

40°N

SPAIN

Rome

Tiranë

MACEDONIA

Skopje

ALBANIA

GREECE

Ankara

TURKEY

GIBRALTAR (U.K.)

Tunis

Athens

CYPRUS

Nicosia

SYRIA

Beirut

MOROCCO

ALGERIA

Mediterranean Sea

LEBANON

Damascus

ISRAEL

Jerusalem

Amman

JORDAN

TUNISIA

LIBYA

EGYPT

0° 400 800 mi

0° 400 800 km

ATLAS   193

The World: Physical

KEY

Elevation

Feet	Meters
14,000	4,270
7,000	2,135
1,500	457
700	213
(sea level) 0	0 (sea level)

Ice pack

Ice shelf

Orthographic Projection

ARCTIC OCEAN

Greenland

Beaufort Sea

Yukon R.

Baffin Island

Bering Sea

Hudson Bay

NORTH AMERICA

CANADIAN SHIELD

St. Lawrence R.

Aleutian Islands

ROCKY MOUNTAINS

GREAT PLAINS

Missouri R.

Great Lakes

APPALACHIAN MTS.

ATLANTIC OCEAN

Mississippi R.

Hawaiian Islands

Tropic of Cancer

SIERRA MADRE OCCIDENTAL

Colorado R.

Rio Grande

Gulf of Mexico

West Indies

Caribbean Sea

PACIFIC OCEAN

Equator

POLYNESIA

Orinoco R.

GUIANA HIGHLANDS

AMAZON

Amazon R.

BASIN

SOUTH AMERICA

BRAZILIAN HIGHLANDS

ANDES MOUNTAINS

Tropic of Capricorn

PAMPAS

Rio de la Plata

PATAGONIA

Cape Horn

Drake Passage

Antarctic Circle

ANTARCTIC PENINSULA

South Pole

SOUTHERN OCEAN

QUEEN MAUD LAND

COATS LAND

ENDERBY LAND

Antarctic Peninsula

Weddell Sea

Amery Ice Shelf

Prime Meridian

Ronne Ice Shelf

TRANSANTARCTIC MTS.

ANTARCTICA

South Pole

0 ——— 800 mi

QUEEN MAUD MTS.

0 ——— 800 km

WILKES LAND

Roosevelt I.

Ross Ice Shelf

Ross Sea

VICTORIA LAND

South Magnetic Pole

International Date Line

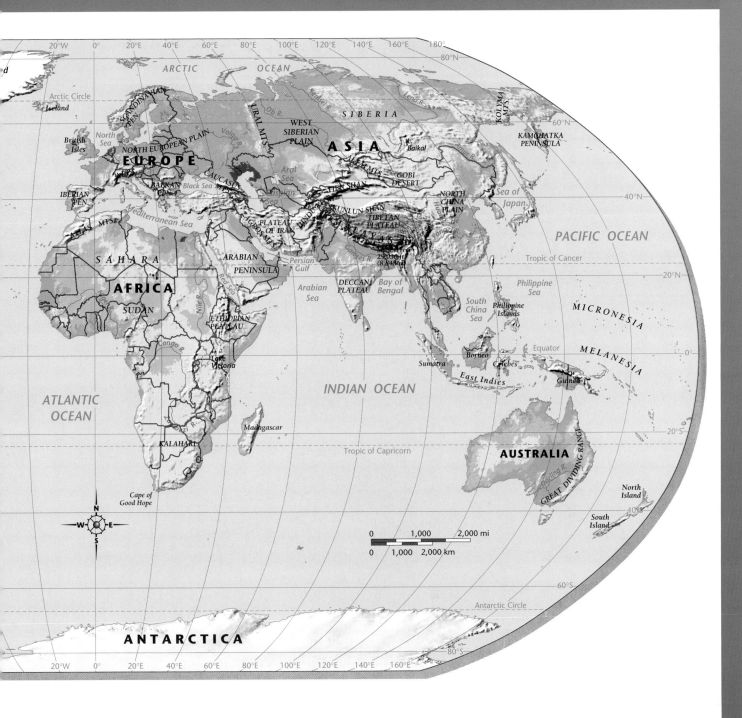

ARCTIC   OCEAN

20°W   0°   20°E   40°E   60°E   80°E   100°E   120°E   140°E   160°E   180°
                                                                              80°N

Arctic Circle
Iceland

British
Isles   *North*   *SIBERIA*   60°N
              Sea   NORTH EUROPEAN PLAIN   *Ob R.*   *KAMCHATKA*
EUROPE   *Volga R.*   A S I A   *Baikal*   *PENINSULA*

IBERIAN   CAUCASUS   *Aral*   *NORTH*   *Sea of*   40°N
PEN.   *BALKAN* *Black Sea* *Caspian* *Sea*   *TIEN SHAN*   *CHINA*   *Japan*
         PEN.   *Sea*   *PLAIN*   PACIFIC OCEAN
ATLAS MTS.   Mediterranean Sea   *PLATEAU* *KUNLUN SHAN* *TIBETAN*
                                     OF IRAN   *PLATEAU*
         S A H A R A   ARABIAN   *HIMALAYAS*   Tropic of Cancer   20°N
                                 PENINSULA   *Ganges R.* Mt. Everest
AFRICA   *Persian*   29,035 ft   *Philippine*
         SUDAN   *Gulf*   *Arabian* DECCAN   (8,848 m)   *Sea*
                                          Sea   PLATEAU *Bay of*   M I C R O N E S I A
              ETHIOPIAN   *Red*   *Bengal* *Philippine*
              PLATEAU   *Sea*   *Islands*
         Congo R.   *South*   M E L A N E S I A   0°
                   Lake   *China*
                   Victoria   *Sea* *Borneo* *Celebes*   *New*
ATLANTIC   INDIAN OCEAN   *Sumatra* *East Indies* *Guinea*
OCEAN   *New*
                        Madagascar   20°S
                                                    AUSTRALIA
              KALAHARI   Tropic of Capricorn

         Cape of   *North*
         Good Hope   *Island*
                                                                        GREAT DIVIDING RANGE
                    N   *South*   40°S
              W   E   0   1,000   2,000 mi   *Island*
                    S   0   1,000   2,000 km   60°S

                                                              Antarctic Circle

A N T A R C T I C A
20°W   0°   20°E   40°E   60°E   80°E   100°E   120°E   140°E   160°E   80°S

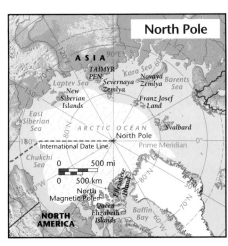

North Pole

A S I A
TAIMYR
PEN.   *Kara Sea*
Laptev Sea *Severnaya* *Novaya* *Barents*
New   *Zemlya*   *Zemlya*   *Sea*
Siberian
Islands   *Franz Josef*
East   *Land*
Siberian   ARCTIC OCEAN   *Svalbard*
Sea
              North Pole
International Date Line   Prime Meridian
Chukchi   0   500 mi
Sea   0   500 km
              North
              Magnetic Pole *Ellesmere*
                             Island *Baffin*
NORTH   *Queen*   *Bay*
AMERICA   *Elizabeth*
             Islands

United States: Political

ARCTIC OCEAN

RUSSIA

ALASKA

CANADA

Arctic Circle

Bering Strait

Yukon River

70°N

70°N

60°N

60°N

Anchorage

Bering Sea

Gulf of Alaska

Juneau

N
W E
S

0   250   500 mi
0   250   500 km

160°W   140°W

50°N   120°W   110°W

Seattle
Olympia   WASHINGTON   Spokane

River

Missouri River

MONTANA

Minc

Bismarc

Columbia   Portland
Salem

OREGON

IDAHO
Boise   Helena

Billings

Sheridan

Pi
Rapid C

Klamath Falls

Snake River

Jackson

WYOMING

40°N   Eureka

Winnemucca

Twin Falls

Great
Salt Lake

Cheyenne

NEBRAS

Sacramento

Carson City

NEVADA   UTAH

Salt Lake City

Denver

Grand
Junction   COLORADO

San Francisco

CALIFORNIA

Cedar
City

Colorado River

Pueblo

Ark

PACIFIC

OCEAN

Las Vegas

Los Angeles

Santa Fe

Albuquerque

ARIZONA

Phoenix   NEW MEXICO

Roswell

San Diego

Tucson

Rio Grande

El Paso

160°W   155°W

Honolulu

N
W E
S

PACIFIC OCEAN

HAWAII

20°N   20°N

Hilo

0   50   100 mi
0   50   100 km   155°W

MEXICO

Tropic of Cancer

120°W   110°W

CANADA

Lake Superior

NORTH DAKOTA

Duluth

Sault Ste. Marie

MICHIGAN

MINNESOTA

Lake Huron

Minneapolis • St. Paul

WISCONSIN

SOUTH DAKOTA

Milwaukee

Lake Michigan

Madison

Lansing

Detroit

Presque Isle

MAINE

• Augusta

Montpelier

VERMONT

Portland

NEW HAMPSHIRE

Concord

• Boston

NEW YORK

MASSACHUSETTS

Albany

Providence

Hartford

RHODE ISLAND

40°N

New Haven

CONNECTICUT

IOWA

Cedar Rapids

Omaha

Des Moines

Chicago

ILLINOIS

INDIANA

OHIO

Columbus

Cincinnati

Cleveland

Lake Erie

PENNSYLVANIA

Harrisburg

Pittsburgh

New York City

Trenton

NEW JERSEY

Philadelphia

Dover

Lincoln

Springfield

Indianapolis

WEST VIRGINIA

Baltimore

Washington, D.C.

Annapolis

DELAWARE

Topeka

Kansas City

St. Louis

Louisville

Frankfort

Charleston

Richmond

MARYLAND

KANSAS

Jefferson City

VIRGINIA

Norfolk

Wichita

MISSOURI

Ohio River

KENTUCKY

Tennessee River

Raleigh

NORTH CAROLINA

Tulsa

Nashville

Charlotte

OKLAHOMA

ARKANSAS

TENNESSEE

Memphis

Columbia

Oklahoma City

Little Rock

Atlanta

SOUTH CAROLINA

Red River

Pine Bluff

Birmingham

Charleston

GEORGIA

Dallas

MISSISSIPPI

ALABAMA

Columbus

Savannah

Shreveport

Jackson

Montgomery

TEXAS

Hattiesburg

Jacksonville

Baton Rouge

Tallahassee

Austin

LOUISIANA

New Orleans

FLORIDA

San Antonio

Houston

Gulf of Mexico

Tampa

Lake Okeechobee

Miami

ATLANTIC OCEAN

30°N

Missouri River

Mississippi River

Rio Grande

Lake Ontario

Buffalo

0   150   300 mi
0   150   300 km

90°W   80°W   70°W

KEY

—— National boundary
—— State boundary
⊕ National capital
✪ State capital
• Other city

Transverse Mercator Projection

North and South America: Political

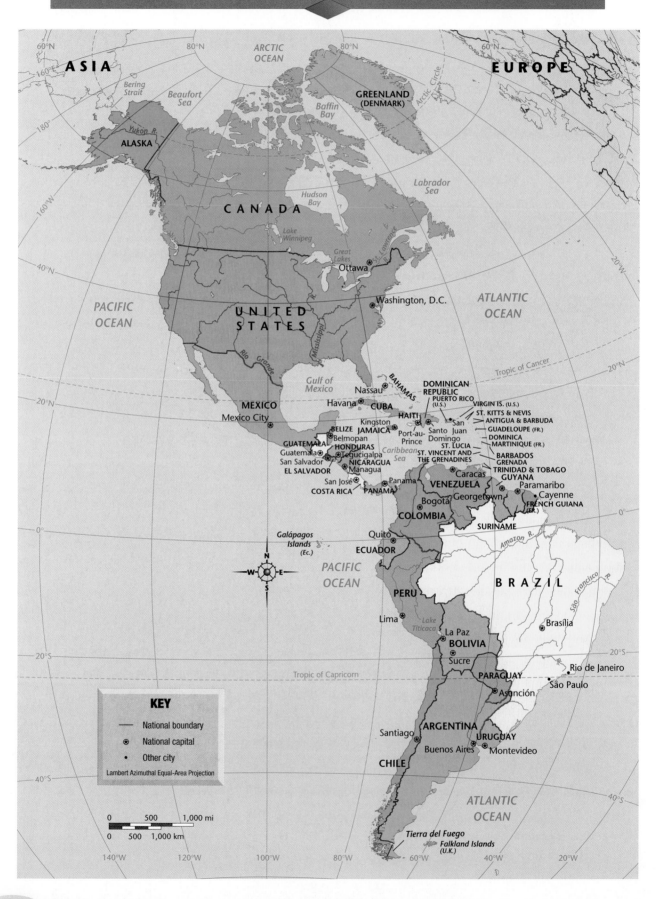

ASIA

EUROPE

ARCTIC OCEAN

60°N   80°N   80°N   60°N

160°E

180°

Bering Strait

Beaufort Sea

160°W

ALASKA

Yukon R.

Baffin Bay

GREENLAND (DENMARK)

Arctic Circle

0°

20°W

40°N

Hudson Bay

Labrador Sea

CANADA

Lake Winnipeg

St. Lawrence R.

Great Lakes

Ottawa

PACIFIC OCEAN

UNITED STATES

Washington, D.C.

ATLANTIC OCEAN

20°W

Rio Grande

Mississippi R.

Tropic of Cancer

20°N

MEXICO

Gulf of Mexico

Nassau

BAHAMAS

Havana

CUBA

DOMINICAN REPUBLIC

PUERTO RICO (U.S.)

VIRGIN IS. (U.S.)

ST. KITTS & NEVIS

20°N

Mexico City

Kingston

HAITI

San Juan

ANTIGUA & BARBUDA

Port-au-Prince

Santo Domingo

GUADELOUPE (FR.)

DOMINICA

BELIZE

JAMAICA

Belmopan

GUATEMALA

HONDURAS

Guatemala

Tegucigalpa

San Salvador

NICARAGUA

EL SALVADOR

Managua

Caribbean Sea

ST. LUCIA

ST. VINCENT AND THE GRENADINES

MARTINIQUE (FR.)

BARBADOS

GRENADA

TRINIDAD & TOBAGO

GUYANA

San José

COSTA RICA

Panama

PANAMA

Caracas

VENEZUELA

Georgetown

Paramaribo

Cayenne

FRENCH GUIANA (FR.)

Bogotá

COLOMBIA

SURINAME

0°

Galápagos Islands (Ec.)

Quito

ECUADOR

Amazon R.

0°

PACIFIC OCEAN

N
W   E
S

PERU

B R A Z I L

São Francisco R.

Lima

Lake Titicaca

La Paz

BOLIVIA

Sucre

Brasília

20°S

Tropic of Capricorn

Rio de Janeiro

PARAGUAY

São Paulo

20°S

Asunción

KEY

ARGENTINA

URUGUAY

Santiago

Buenos Aires

Montevideo

— National boundary

⊗ National capital

• Other city

Lambert Azimuthal Equal-Area Projection

CHILE

40°S

ATLANTIC OCEAN

40°S

0   500   1,000 mi

0   500   1,000 km

Tierra del Fuego

Falkland Islands (U.K.)

140°W   120°W   100°W   80°W   60°W   40°W   20°W

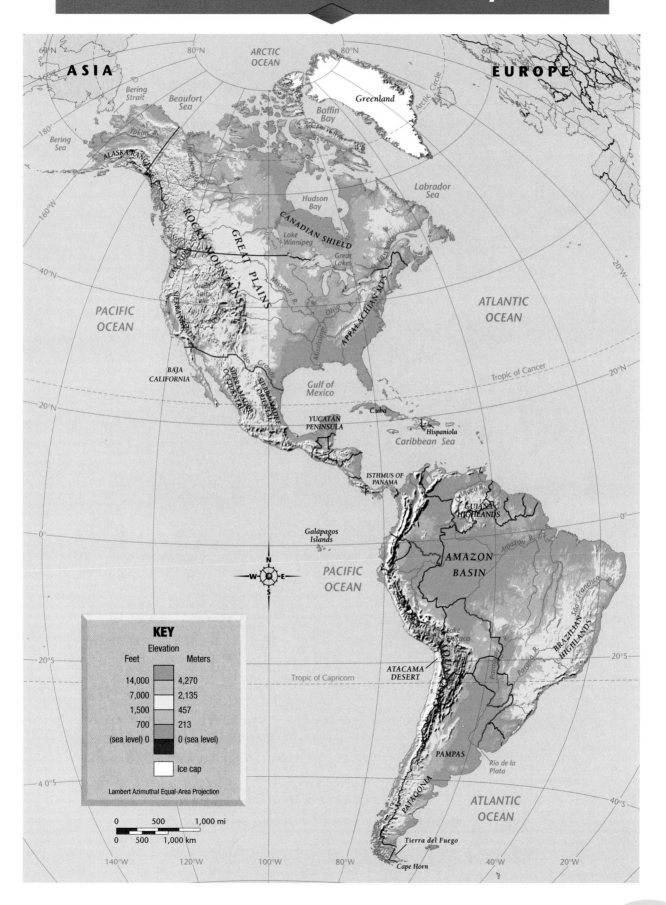

ASIA

ARCTIC OCEAN

EUROPE

60°N

80°N

80°N

Bering Strait

Beaufort Sea

Greenland

Arctic Circle

Baffin Bay

180°

Bering Sea

Yukon R.

ALASKA RANGE

Labrador Sea

160°W

Hudson Bay

CANADIAN SHIELD

20°W

ROCKY MOUNTAINS

40°N

Lake Winnipeg

Great Lakes

CASCADES

GREAT PLAINS

Great Salt Lake

Missouri R.

Ohio

APPALACHIAN MTS.

PACIFIC OCEAN

SIERRA NEVADA

ATLANTIC OCEAN

20°W

Rio Grande

Mississippi R.

BAJA CALIFORNIA

SIERRA MADRE OCCIDENTAL

SIERRA MADRE ORIENTAL

Tropic of Cancer

20°N

20°N

Gulf of Mexico

Cuba

YUCATÁN PENINSULA

Hispaniola

Caribbean Sea

ISTHMUS OF PANAMA

Orinoco R.

GUIANA HIGHLANDS

Galápagos Islands

0°

AMAZON BASIN

Amazon R.

0°

São Francisco R.

PACIFIC OCEAN

BRAZILIAN HIGHLANDS

Lake Titicaca

KEY

Elevation

ATACAMA DESERT

20°S

Feet

Meters

Tropic of Capricorn

Paraná R.

Paraguay R.

20°S

14,000 — 4,270

7,000 — 2,135

1,500 — 457

PAMPAS

700 — 213

Rio de la Plata

(sea level) 0 — 0 (sea level)

Ice cap

PATAGONIA

ATLANTIC OCEAN

40°S

40°S

Lambert Azimuthal Equal-Area Projection

0   500   1,000 mi

0   500   1,000 km

Tierra del Fuego

Cape Horn

140°W

120°W

100°W

80°W

40°W

20°W

Europe: Political

KEY

— National boundary
⊗ National capital
• Other city

Lambert Azimuthal Equal-Area Projection

ARCTIC OCEAN

ATLANTIC OCEAN

ICELAND
Reykjavik

Faeroe Is. (Den.)

Shetland Is. (U.K.)

FINLAND

SWEDEN

NORWAY
Lillehammer
Oslo
Stockholm
Göteborg

Turku
Helsinki
St. Petersburg
Tallinn
ESTONIA

Riga
LATVIA

LITHUANIA
Vilnius
RUSSIA
Gdańsk

RUSSIA
Moscow

BELARUS
Minsk

North Sea

Baltic Sea

DENMARK
Copenhagen

IRELAND
Dublin

UNITED KINGDOM
Manchester
London

Amsterdam
The Hague
NETHERLANDS
Brussels
BELGIUM

Berlin

GERMANY

Cologne
Bonn
Frankfurt

POLAND
Warsaw
Łódź

Katowice
Kraków

UKRAINE
Kiev

English Channel

LUXEMBOURG
Luxembourg

Prague
CZECH REPUBLIC
Brno
SLOVAKIA

Paris

MOLDOVA
Chişinău

FRANCE

Munich
Vienna
Bratislava

Budapest
HUNGARY

Cluj-Napoca
ROMANIA

Bern
SWITZERLAND
LIECHTENSTEIN

AUSTRIA

Ljubljana
SLOVENIA
Zagreb

Bucharest

Black Sea

Bay of Biscay

Milan

CROATIA

BOSNIA-HERZEGOVINA
Sarajevo

Belgrade
YUGOSLAVIA

BULGARIA

SAN MARINO

Marseille
MONACO

ITALY

Podgorica
Sofia

PORTUGAL

ANDORRA

Corsica

VATICAN CITY
Rome

Skopje
ALBANIA
MACEDONIA
Tiranë

Adriatic Sea

Madrid
Barcelona

Naples

GREECE

Aegean Sea

Lisbon

SPAIN

Sardinia

Tyrrhenian Sea

Ionian Sea

Athens

Balearic Is.

Strait of Gibraltar

GIBRALTAR (U.K.)

Mediterranean Sea

Sicily

Crete

MALTA

AFRICA

0   250   500 mi
0   250   500 km

N
W   E
S

Europe: Physical

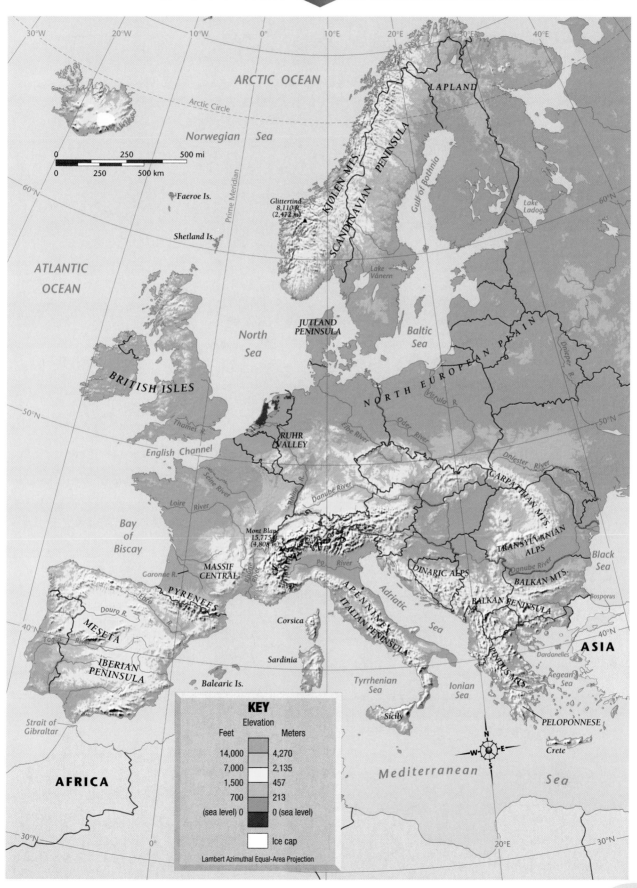

ARCTIC OCEAN

LAPLAND

Arctic Circle

Norwegian Sea

0 250 500 mi
0 250 500 km

Faeroe Is.

Prime Meridian

Glittertind
8,110 ft
(2,472 m)

Gulf of Bothnia

Lake Ladoga

60°N

Shetland Is.

ATLANTIC OCEAN

KJÖLEN MTS.

SCANDINAVIAN PENINSULA

Lake Vänern

JUTLAND PENINSULA

North Sea

Baltic Sea

BRITISH ISLES

NORTH EUROPEAN PLAIN

Dnieper R.

50°N

Thames R.

RUHR VALLEY

Elbe River

Oder River

Vistula R.

English Channel

Seine River

Danube River

Dniester River

CARPATHIAN MTS.

Loire River

Rhine

Bay of Biscay

Mont Blanc
15,775 ft
(4,808 m)

Po River

TRANSYLVANIAN ALPS

Black Sea

MASSIF CENTRAL

Garonne R.

DINARIC ALPS

Danube River

BALKAN MTS.

Bosporus

PYRENEES

Rhône River

Ebro

Corsica

APENNINES

Adriatic Sea

BALKAN PENINSULA

ASIA

Douro R.

MESETA

ITALIAN PENINSULA

Dardanelles

40°N

Tagus River

Sardinia

PINDUS MTS.

Aegean Sea

IBERIAN PENINSULA

Balearic Is.

Tyrrhenian Sea

Ionian Sea

PELOPONNESE

Crete

Strait of Gibraltar

Sicily

Mediterranean Sea

AFRICA

30°N

KEY

Elevation

Feet		Meters
14,000		4,270
7,000		2,135
1,500		457
700		213
(sea level) 0		0 (sea level)

Ice cap

Lambert Azimuthal Equal-Area Projection

N W E S

Africa: Political

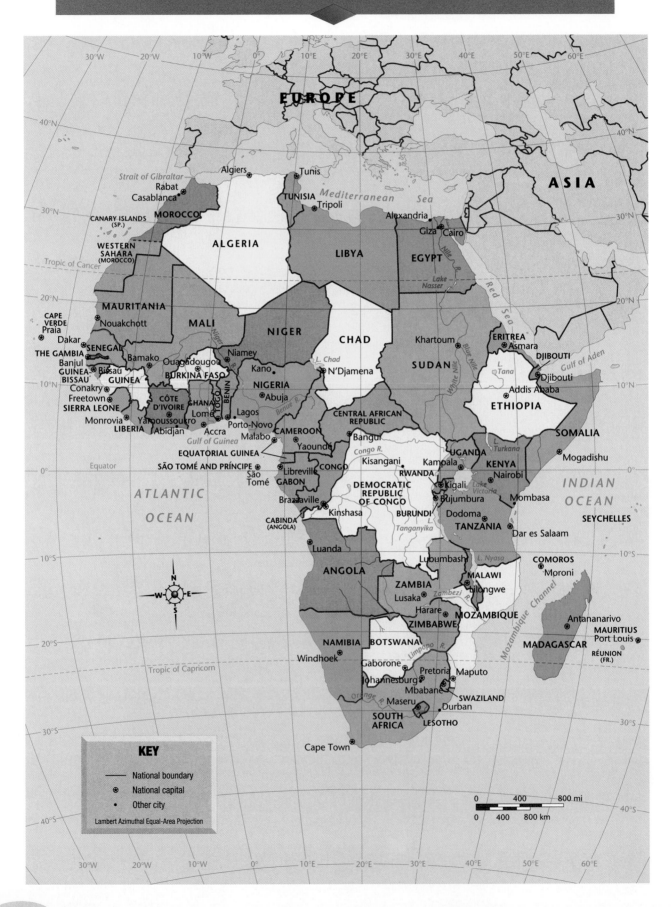

EUROPE

ASIA

Strait of Gibraltar
Algiers
Tunis
TUNISIA
Mediterranean Sea
Rabat
Casablanca
Tripoli
CANARY ISLANDS (SP.)
MOROCCO
Alexandria
Giza Cairo
WESTERN SAHARA (MOROCCO)
ALGERIA
LIBYA
EGYPT
Nile R.
Tropic of Cancer
Lake Nasser
CAPE VERDE
Praia
MAURITANIA
Nouakchott
MALI
NIGER
CHAD
Khartoum
ERITREA
Asmara
Red Sea
Dakar
Niamey
SENEGAL
Bamako
L. Chad
SUDAN
DJIBOUTI
L. Tana
Gulf of Aden
THE GAMBIA
Banjul
Ouagadougou
Kano
N'Djamena
Blue Nile R.
Bissau
GUINEA-BISSAU
BURKINA FASO
Djibouti
GUINEA
NIGERIA
White Nile R.
Addis Ababa
Conakry
Abuja
CÔTE D'IVOIRE
GHANA
TOGO
BENIN
CENTRAL AFRICAN REPUBLIC
ETHIOPIA
Freetown
SIERRA LEONE
Lomé
Lagos
Monrovia
Yamoussoukro
Porto-Novo
SOMALIA
LIBERIA
Abidjan
Accra
CAMEROON
Bangui
UGANDA
L. Turkana
Malabo
Gulf of Guinea
Yaoundé
Congo R.
Kisangani
Kampala
KENYA
Mogadishu
EQUATORIAL GUINEA
SÃO TOMÉ AND PRÍNCIPE
Libreville
CONGO
RWANDA
Nairobi
Equator
São Tomé
GABON
Kigali
Lake Victoria
INDIAN OCEAN
ATLANTIC OCEAN
Brazzaville
DEMOCRATIC REPUBLIC OF CONGO
Bujumbura
Mombasa
CABINDA (ANGOLA)
Kinshasa
BURUNDI
Dodoma
SEYCHELLES
L. Tanganyika
TANZANIA
Dar es Salaam
Luanda
Lubumbashi
L. Nyasa
COMOROS
Moroni
ANGOLA
ZAMBIA
MALAWI
Lilongwe
Lusaka
Zambezi R.
MOZAMBIQUE
Antananarivo
Harare
MAURITIUS
Port Louis
NAMIBIA
BOTSWANA
ZIMBABWE
MADAGASCAR
RÉUNION (FR.)
Windhoek
Limpopo R.
Mozambique Channel
Gaborone
Pretoria
Maputo
Johannesburg
Mbabane
Orange R.
SWAZILAND
Maseru
Durban
SOUTH AFRICA
LESOTHO
Cape Town

KEY
— National boundary
⊛ National capital
• Other city

Lambert Azimuthal Equal-Area Projection

0   400   800 mi
0   400   800 km

Africa: Physical

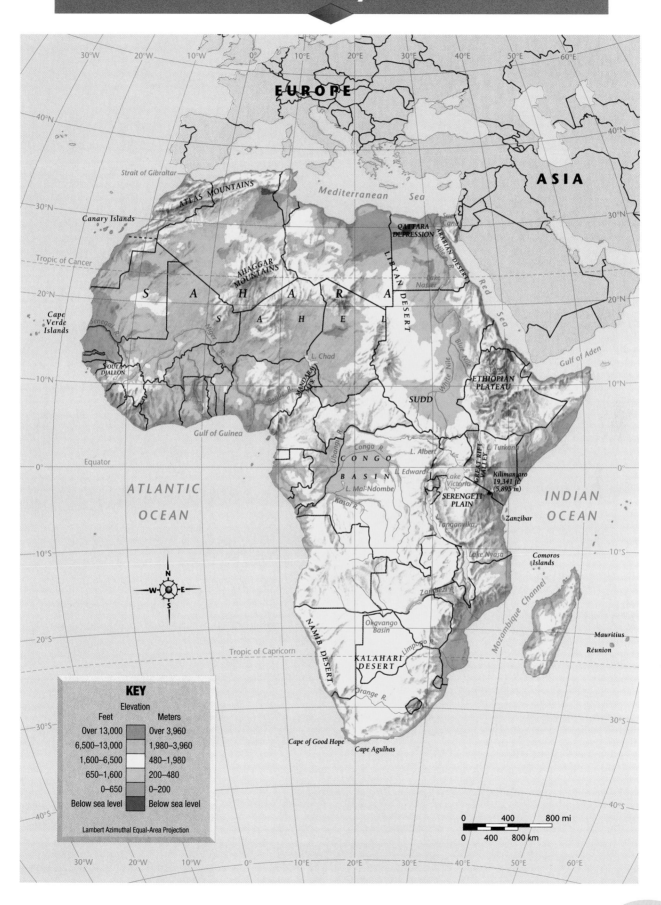

EUROPE

ASIA

Strait of Gibraltar

Mediterranean Sea

ATLAS MOUNTAINS

Canary Islands

Tropic of Cancer

QATTARA DEPRESSION

Suez Canal

Cape Verde Islands

AHAGGAR MOUNTAINS

S   A   H   A   R   A

LIBYAN DESERT

ARABIAN DESERT

Nile R.

Lake Nasser

Red Sea

Senegal R.

S   A   H   E   L

Niger R.

FOUTA DJALLON

L. Chad

Benue R.

MANDARA MTS.

Blue Nile

White Nile

Gulf of Aden

Tana

ETHIOPIAN PLATEAU

SUDD

Gulf of Guinea

Ubangi R.

Congo R.

L. Albert

L. Edward

GREAT RIFT VALLEY

L. Turkana

Equator

ATLANTIC OCEAN

CONGO BASIN

L. Mai-Ndombe

Lake Victoria

Kilimanjaro 19,341 ft (5,895 m)

INDIAN OCEAN

Kasai R.

SERENGETI PLAIN

Zanzibar

Tanganyika

Lake Nyasa

Comoros Islands

Zambezi R.

Mozambique Channel

Mauritius

Réunion

NAMIB DESERT

Okavango Basin

Limpopo R.

Tropic of Capricorn

KALAHARI DESERT

Orange R.

Cape of Good Hope

Cape Agulhas

KEY

Elevation

Feet	Meters
Over 13,000	Over 3,960
6,500–13,000	1,980–3,960
1,600–6,500	480–1,980
650–1,600	200–480
0–650	0–200
Below sea level	Below sea level

Lambert Azimuthal Equal-Area Projection

0   400   800 mi

0   400   800 km

Asia: Political

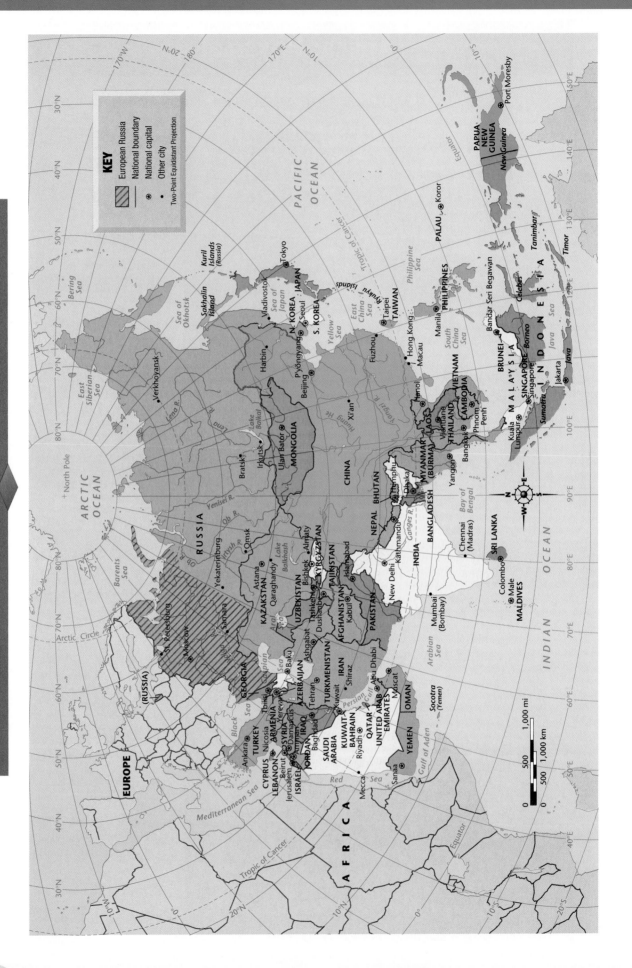

KEY
- European Russia
- National boundary
- ⊛ National capital
- • Other city

Two-Point Equidistant Projection

ARCTIC OCEAN

+ North Pole

Bering Sea

East Siberian Sea

Barents Sea

Kuril Islands (Russia)

• Verkhoyansk

Sakhalin Island

Sea of Okhotsk

• Tokyo

JAPAN

Sea of Japan

• Vladivostok

N. KOREA
P'yŏngyang ⊛

S. KOREA
⊛ Seoul

Yellow Sea

East China Sea

Ryukyu Islands

PACIFIC OCEAN

⊛ Taipei
TAIWAN

Philippine Sea

⊛ Manila
PHILIPPINES

Tropic of Cancer

PALAU ⊛ Koror

Equator

PAPUA NEW GUINEA
New Guinea
Port Moresby ⊛

• Harbin

Beijing ⊛

Huang He

• Xian

Yangtze R.

Fuzhou •

• Hong Kong

• Macau

South China Sea

VIETNAM
Hanoi ⊛

Bandar Seri Begawan ⊛
BRUNEI

Borneo

Celebes

I N D O N E S I A

Tanimbar

Timor

• Bratsk

Irkutsk •

Lake Baikal

Ulan Bator ⊛

MONGOLIA

CHINA

LAOS
Vientiane ⊛

THAILAND
Bangkok ⊛

CAMBODIA
Phnom Penh ⊛

MALAYSIA

Kuala Lumpur ⊛

SINGAPORE ⊛
Singapore

Sumatra

Java
Jakarta

Java Sea

MYANMAR (BURMA)
Yangon •

BHUTAN
Thimphu ⊛

BANGLADESH
Dhaka ⊛

Bay of Bengal

RUSSIA

Lena R.

Yenisei R.

Ob R.

Irtysh R.

• Omsk

• Yekaterinburg

Astana •

• Qaraghandy

KAZAKHSTAN

Lake Balkhash

• Almaty

Bishkek ⊛
KYRGYZSTAN

UZBEKISTAN
Tashkent ⊛

Dushanbe ⊛
TAJIKISTAN

Islamabad ⊛

NEPAL
Kathmandu ⊛

Ganges R.

INDIA
New Delhi ⊛

SRI LANKA
Colombo ⊛

Male •
MALDIVES

INDIAN OCEAN

Arctic Circle

St. Petersburg •
Moscow ⊛

Samara •

(RUSSIA)

EUROPE

Black Sea

Aral Sea

Caspian Sea

Baku ⊛

GEORGIA
Tbilisi ⊛
ARMENIA
Yerevan ⊛
AZERBAIJAN

Ashgabat ⊛
TURKMENISTAN

AFGHANISTAN
Kabul ⊛

PAKISTAN

Mumbai (Bombay) •

Chennai (Madras) •

TURKEY
Ankara ⊛

CYPRUS
Nicosia ⊛

LEBANON
Beirut ⊛
Damascus ⊛
SYRIA
Amman ⊛
ISRAEL
Jerusalem ⊛
JORDAN

Baghdad ⊛
IRAQ

Tehran ⊛
IRAN

Shiraz •

Kuwait ⊛
KUWAIT

BAHRAIN
QATAR
Abu Dhabi ⊛
UNITED ARAB EMIRATES

Muscat ⊛
OMAN

Socotra (Yemen)

Arabian Sea

Persian Gulf

Gulf of Oman

SAUDI ARABIA
Riyadh ⊛

YEMEN
Sanaa ⊛

Gulf of Aden

Red Sea

Mecca •

Mediterranean Sea

A F R I C A

Tropic of Cancer

Equator

1,000 mi

1,000 km

500

0

500

0

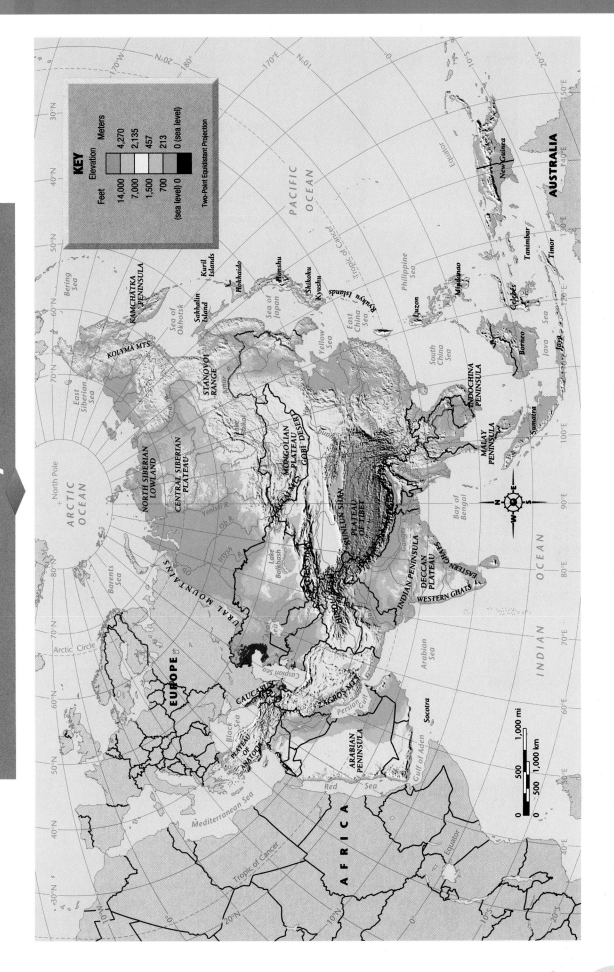

Asia: Physical

KEY

Feet	Meters
14,000	4,270
7,000	2,135
1,500	457
700	213
(sea level) 0	0 (sea level)

Elevation

Two-Point Equidistant Projection

EUROPE

AFRICA

AUSTRALIA

ARCTIC OCEAN

North Pole

PACIFIC OCEAN

INDIAN OCEAN

Bering Sea

Sea of Okhotsk

Sea of Japan

Yellow Sea

East China Sea

South China Sea

Philippine Sea

Java Sea

Bay of Bengal

Arabian Sea

Caspian Sea

Black Sea

Mediterranean Sea

Red Sea

Gulf of Aden

Persian Gulf

Barents Sea

East Siberian Sea

Lake Balkhash

Lake Baikal

KAMCHATKA PENINSULA

KOLYMA MTS.

STANOVOY RANGE

NORTH SIBERIAN LOWLAND

CENTRAL SIBERIAN PLATEAU

URAL MOUNTAINS

Sakhalin Island

Kuril Islands

Hokkaido

Honshu

Shikoku

Kyushu

Ryukyu Islands

Luzon

Mindanao

Celebes

Borneo

Sumatra

Java

Timor

Tanimbar

New Guinea

INDOCHINA PENINSULA

MALAY PENINSULA

MONGOLIAN PLATEAU

GOBI DESERT

KUNLUN SHAN

PLATEAU OF TIBET

INDIAN PENINSULA

DECCAN PLATEAU

WESTERN GHATS

EASTERN GHATS

Ganges

CAUCASUS MTS.

ZAGROS MTS.

PLATEAU OF ANATOLIA

ARABIAN PENINSULA

Socotra

Yenisei R.

Ob R.

Irtysh

Amur

Arctic Circle

Tropic of Cancer

Equator

1,000 mi

1,000 km

500

500

0

0

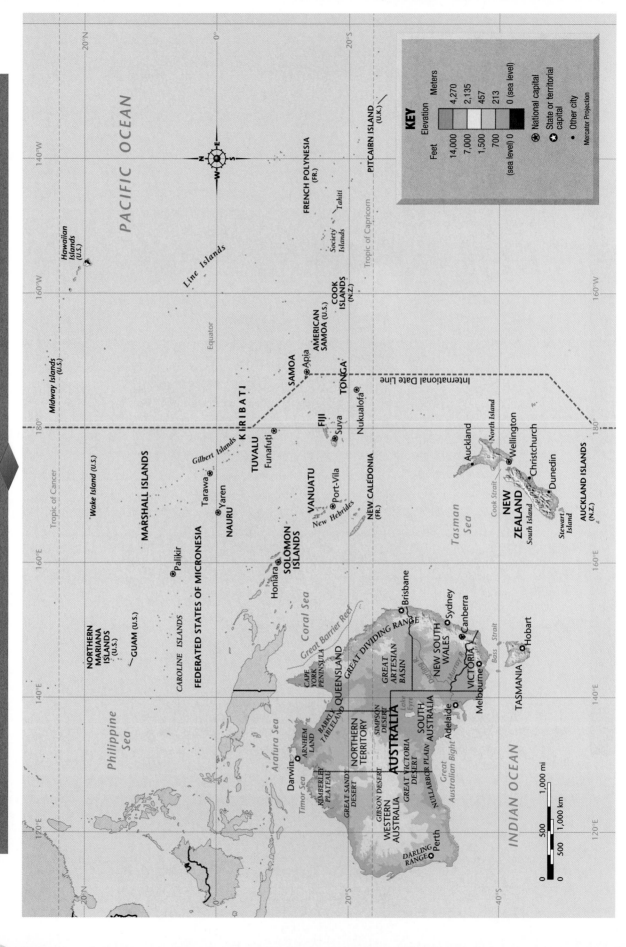

KEY

Elevation	Meters
	4,270
	2,135
	457
	213
	0 (sea level)

Feet	
14,000	
7,000	
1,500	
700	
(sea level) 0	

⊛ National capital
⊛ State or territorial capital
• Other city

Mercator Projection

PACIFIC OCEAN

Hawaiian Islands (U.S.)

Line Islands

FRENCH POLYNESIA (FR.)

Society Islands Tahiti

Tropic of Capricorn

PITCAIRN ISLAND (U.K.)

Midway Islands (U.S.)

Equator

COOK ISLANDS (N.Z.)

AMERICAN SAMOA (U.S.)

SAMOA ⊛Apia

TONGA

Nukualofa

International Date Line

Wake Island (U.S.)

MARSHALL ISLANDS

KIRIBATI

FIJI
⊛Suva

TUVALU
Funafuti

Gilbert Islands

Tarawa ⊛
⊛Yaren
NAURU

VANUATU
⊛Port-Vila
New Hebrides

NEW CALEDONIA (FR.)

Auckland

North Island

Wellington
Christchurch

Cook Strait

NEW ZEALAND
South Island Dunedin

Stewart Island

AUCKLAND ISLANDS (N.Z.)

Tropic of Cancer

NORTHERN MARIANA ISLANDS (U.S.)

GUAM (U.S.)

CAROLINE ISLANDS

FEDERATED STATES OF MICRONESIA

⊛Palikir

SOLOMON ISLANDS

Honiara ⊛

Coral Sea

Great Barrier Reef

Tasman Sea

Philippine Sea

Arafura Sea

Timor Sea

Darwin

ARNHEM LAND

KIMBERLEY PLATEAU

GREAT SANDY DESERT

WESTERN AUSTRALIA

GIBSON DESERT

GREAT VICTORIA DESERT

Perth
DARLING RANGE

NORTHERN TERRITORY

BARKLY TABLELAND

SIMPSON DESERT

Lake Eyre

SOUTH AUSTRALIA

NULLARBOR PLAIN

Great Australian Bight

AUSTRALIA

CAPE YORK PENINSULA

QUEENSLAND

GREAT DIVIDING RANGE

GREAT ARTESIAN BASIN

Brisbane

NEW SOUTH WALES

Darling R.

Murray R.

Sydney
⊛Canberra

VICTORIA
Melbourne ⊛

Adelaide ⊛

Bass Strait

TASMANIA
Hobart ⊛

INDIAN OCEAN

1,000 mi
1,000 km
500
500
0
0

The Arctic

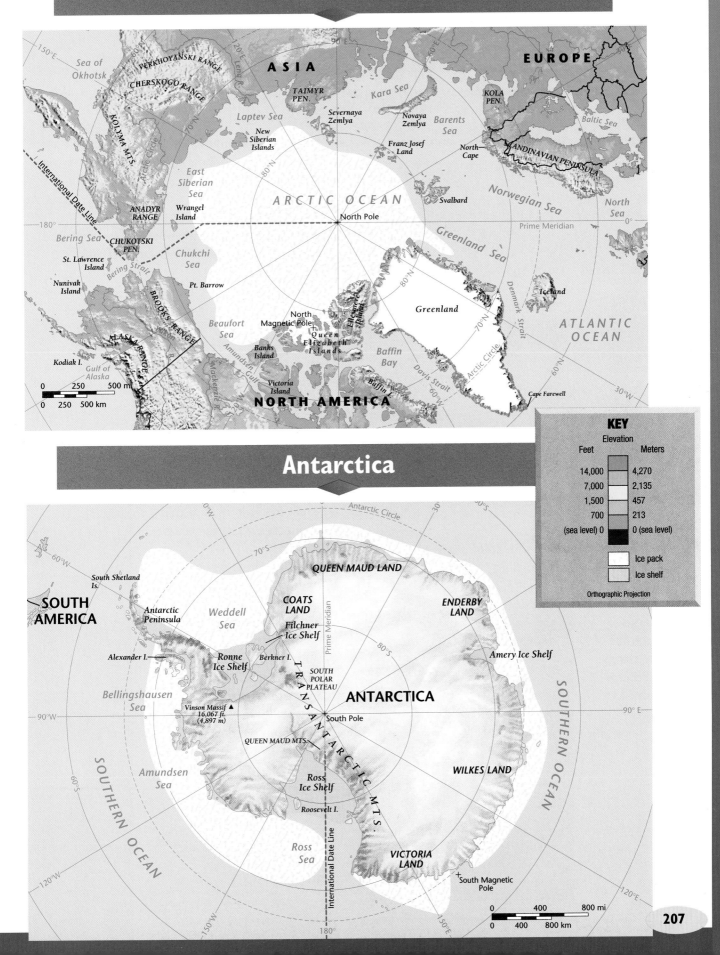

150°E
Sea of Okhotsk
VERKHOYÄNSKI RANGE
CHERSKOGO RANGE
KOLYMA MTS.
ASIA
90° E
EUROPE
TAIMYR PEN.
Kara Sea
Laptev Sea
Severnaya Zemlya
New Siberian Islands
Novaya Zemlya
Barents Sea
KOLA PEN.
Baltic Sea
Franz Josef Land
North Cape
SCANDINAVIAN PENINSULA
Arctic Circle
80° N
ARCTIC OCEAN
Svalbard
Norwegian Sea
North Sea
East Siberian Sea
ANADYR RANGE
Wrangel Island
North Pole
Prime Meridian
0°
180°
International Date Line
Bering Sea
CHUKOTSKI PEN.
Chukchi Sea
Greenland Sea
St. Lawrence Island
Bering Strait
80° N
Denmark Strait
Iceland
Nunivak Island
Pt. Barrow
70° N
ATLANTIC OCEAN
BROOKS RANGE
Beaufort Sea
North Magnetic Pole
Greenland
Kodiak I.
ALASKA RANGE
Banks Island
Queen Elizabeth Islands
Ellesmere Island
Baffin Bay
Gulf of Alaska
Amundsen Gulf
Mackenzie R.
Arctic Circle
60° N
0   250   500 mi
0   250   500 km
Victoria Island
Baffin I.
Davis Strait
30° W
Cape Farewell
NORTH AMERICA

Antarctica

Antarctic Circle
0° W
30°
30°
South Shetland Is.
QUEEN MAUD LAND
70° S
ENDERBY LAND
SOUTH AMERICA
Antarctic Peninsula
Weddell Sea
COATS LAND
Filchner Ice Shelf
Prime Meridian
Amery Ice Shelf
Alexander I.
Ronne Ice Shelf
Berkner I.
80° S
SOUTH POLAR PLATEAU
SOUTHERN OCEAN
Bellingshausen Sea
TRANSANTARCTIC MTS.
ANTARCTICA
90° W
Vinson Massif ▲ 16,067 ft. (4,897 m)
South Pole
90° E
QUEEN MAUD MTS.
Amundsen Sea
60° S
Ross Ice Shelf
WILKES LAND
Roosevelt I.
Ross Sea
VICTORIA LAND
SOUTHERN OCEAN
South Magnetic Pole
International Date Line
120° W
120° E
150° W
180°
150° E
0   400   800 mi
0   400   800 km

KEY

Elevation

Feet		Meters
14,000		4,270
7,000		2,135
1,500		457
700		213
(sea level) 0		0 (sea level)

Ice pack

Ice shelf

Orthographic Projection

Glossary of Geographic Terms

basin
a depression in the surface of the land; some basins are filled with water

bay
a part of a sea or lake that extends into the land

butte
a small raised area of land with steep sides

▲ butte

canyon
a deep, narrow valley with steep sides; often has a stream flowing through it

cataract
a large waterfall; any strong flood or rush of water

◀ cataract

delta
a triangular-shaped plain at the mouth of a river, formed when sediment is deposited by flowing water

flood plain
a broad plain on either side of a river, formed when sediment settles on the riverbanks

glacier
a huge, slow-moving mass of snow and ice

hill
an area that rises above surrounding land and has a rounded top; lower and usually less steep than a mountain

island
an area of land completely surrounded by water

isthmus
a narrow strip of land that connects two larger areas of land

mesa
a high, flat-topped landform with cliff-like sides; larger than a butte

mountain
an area that rises steeply at least 2,000 feet (610 m) above surrounding land; usually wide at the bottom and rising to a narrow peak or ridge

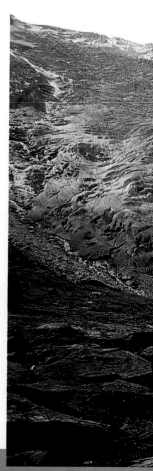

▶ glacier

◄ delta

mountain pass
a gap between mountains

peninsula
an area of land almost completely surrounded by water and connected to the mainland by an isthmus

plain
a large area of flat or gently rolling land

plateau
a large, flat area that rises above the surrounding land; at least one side has a steep slope

river mouth
the point where a river enters a lake or sea

strait
a narrow stretch of water that connects two larger bodies of water

tributary
a river or stream that flows into a larger river

volcano
an opening in the Earth's surface through which molten rock, ashes, and gasses from the Earth's interior escape

▶ volcano

Gazetteer

A

Acadia the first permanent French settlement in North America, p. 140

Appalachian Mountains a mountain system in eastern North America, p. 11

Atlanta (33°N, 84°W) the capital of the state of Georgia, p. 93

B

Boston (42°N, 71°W) the capital of the state of Massachusetts, p. 87

C

Calgary (51°N, 114°W) a city in southern Alberta, Canada, p. 131

Canadian Shield a region of rocky, rugged land that covers about half of Canada, p. 120

Cariboo Mountains a mountain range in eastern British Columbia, Canada; a place where miners struck gold in the 1800s, p. 134

Chicago (41°N, 87°W) a major city in the state of Illinois, on Lake Michigan, p. 102

Cuyahoga River a river in northeastern Ohio, p. 57

D

Dawson (64°N, 139°W) a city located in western Yukon Territory, Canada, p. 144

Death Valley (36°N, 117°W) the hottest, driest region of North America, located in southeastern California, p. 11

Detroit (42°N, 83°W) a city in the state of Michigan, p. 103

F

Fraser River a major river of western North America, along the border between British Columbia and Alberta, p. 134

G

Grand Coulee Dam (47°N, 119°W) a dam on the Columbia River in the state of Washington, p. 23

Great Lakes a group of five large lakes in central North America: Lakes Superior, Michigan, Huron, Erie, and Ontario, p. 13

I

Imperial Valley a valley in the Colorado Desert, extending from southeastern California to Mexico, p. 22

Iqaluit (64°N, 69°W) the capital of Nunavut, Canada, p. 145

J

Jamestown the first permanent British settlement in North America, located in present-day Virginia; now a site of historic preservation, p. 36

L

Lake Erie the fourth largest of the five Great Lakes; forms part of the boundary between Canada and the United States, p. 57

L'Anse aux Meadows location of the earliest known North American Viking settlement, located in Newfoundland, p. 138

M

Minneapolis–St. Paul (44°N, 93°W) two cities in Minnesota; also called the Twin Cities, p. 104

Mississippi River a large river in the central United States flowing south from Minnesota to the Gulf of Mexico, p. 14

Montreal (45°N, 73°W) the largest city in the province of Quebec, Canada, p. 119

N

New York City (40°N, 73°W) a large city and port at the mouth of the Hudson River in the state of New York, p. 87

Niagara Falls (43°N, 79°W) a waterfall on the Niagara River between Ontario, Canada, and New York state; one of North America's most famous spectacles, p. 60

Nunavut a Canadian territory in the northeastern part of Canada; home to a large Inuit population, p. 78

O

Ontario (50°N, 88°W) the second-largest province in Canada, p. 52

Ottawa (45°N, 76°W) the capital city of Canada, located in Ontario, p. 119

P

Pacific Northwest the region in the northwestern United States that includes Oregon, Washington, and part of Idaho, p. 107

Pacific Rim the countries bordering on the Pacific Ocean, p. 136

Pennsylvania Colony a colony in America founded in 1682 by William Penn, who purchased land from the Native Americans, p. 36

Philadelphia (40°N, 75°W) a city and port in Pennsylvania, on the Delaware River, p. 87

Portland (45°N, 122°W) the largest city in the state of Oregon, p. 108

Q

Quebec (51°N, 70°W) a province in southeastern Canada, p. 51

R

Regina (50°N, 104°W) the capital of the province of Saskatchewan, Canada, p. 129

Rocky Mountains the major mountain range in western North America, extending south from Alberta, Canada, through the western United States to Mexico, p. 10

S

St. Lawrence Lowlands a major agricultural region in eastern Canada, p. 12

St. Lawrence River a river in eastern North America; the third-longest river in Canada, p. 12

St. Lawrence Seaway a navigable seaway from the Atlantic Ocean to the western end of the Great Lakes, maintained jointly by the United States and Canada, p. 13

St. Louis (38°N, 90°W) a major city in Missouri, on the Mississippi River, p. 103

San Jose (37°N, 121°W) a city in western California, p. 109

Sierra Nevada Mountains a mountain range in California in the western United States, p. 11

T

Toronto (44°N, 79°W) the largest city in the province of Ontario, Canada, p. 119

V

Vancouver (49°N, 123°W) a city in southwestern British Columbia, Canada, p. 16

Victoria (48°N, 123°W) the capital of British Columbia, Canada, p. 134

W

Washington, D.C. (38°N, 77°W) the capital city of the United States, located between Maryland and Virginia on the Potomac River, pp. 87, 98

Winnipeg (49°N, 97°W) the capital city of Manitoba, Canada, p. 16

Y

Yukon (63°N, 135°W) a territory in northwestern Canada, p. 12

Glossary

This glossary lists key terms and other useful terms from the book.

A

abolitionist a person who believed that enslaving people was wrong and who wanted to end the practice, p. 42

acid rain a rain containing acid that is harmful to plants and trees, formed when pollutants from cars and factories combine with moisture in the air, p. 58

agribusiness a large company that runs huge farms to produce, process, and distribute agricultural products, p. 22

alliance formal agreement to do business together, sometimes formed between governments, p. 38

alluvial deposited by water, relating to the fertile topsoil left by rivers after a flood, p. 22

amid in the middle of; within, p. 73

aquaculture the cultivation of fish and water plants, p. 141

aurora borealis colorful bands of light that can be seen in northern skies, p. 142

autonomous self-governing, p. 121

B

bilingual speaking two languages; having two official languages, p. 55

bison buffalo; a large animal something like an ox, p. 33

boomtown a settlement that springs up quickly, often to serve the needs of miners, p. 134

boycott a refusal to buy or use goods and services, p. 37

C

civil rights movement a large group of people who worked together in the United States beginning in the 1960s to end the segregation of African Americans and support equal rights for all minorities, p. 48

Civil War the war between the northern and southern states in the United States, which began in 1861 and ended in 1865, p. 42

clear-cutting a type of logging in which all the trees in an area are cut down, p. 59

Cold War a period of great tension between the United States and the former Soviet Union, which lasted for more than 40 years after World War II, p. 48

communism a theory of government in which property such as farms and factories is owned by the government for the benefit of all citizens; a political system in which the central government controls all aspects of citizens' lives, p. 48

commute to travel regularly to and from a place, particularly to and from a job, p. 87

complex complicated; not simple, p. 130

conservation preserving and protecting from loss, p. 105

Continental Divide the boundary that separates rivers flowing toward opposite sides of a continent; in North America, in the Rocky Mountains, p. 14

corporate farm a large farm run by a corporation; may consist of many smaller farms once owned by families, p. 101

counter to act in defense, p. 109

crucial extremely important, p. 52

cultural diversity a wide variety of cultures, p. 69

cultural exchange a process in which different cultures share ideas and ways of doing things, p. 70

D

debate argument; disagreement expressed in words, p. 41

dense thick and crowded, p. 133

descendant child, grandchild, great-grandchild (and so on) of an ancestor, p. 123

descent ancestry, p. 129

dictator a person who rules a country completely and independently, p. 47

distinct clearly different; separate, p. 35

diverse varied, p. 35

dominion a self-governing area subject to Great Britain, for example, Canada prior to 1939, p. 53

drought a long period of weather with no rain, p. 127

dwindle to become fewer in number, p. 100

E

economy a system for producing, distributing, consuming, and owning goods, services, and wealth, p. 8

enslave to force someone to become a slave, p. 35

ethnic group a group of people who share the same ancestors, culture, language, or religion, p. 71

exile force to leave an area, p. 140

expanse a wide open space or area, p. 22

F

federation a union of states, groups, provinces, or nations, p. 120

fertile containing substances that plants need in order to grow well; productive, p. 11

forty-niner one of the first miners of the California Gold Rush of 1849, p. 107

fossil fuel a fuel formed over millions of years from animal and plant remains, includes coal, petroleum, and natural gas, p. 58

Francophone a person who speaks French as his or her first language, p. 123

free trade trade with no tariffs, or taxes on imported goods, p. 61

freshwater consisting of water that has no salt in it, p. 13

fugitive a runaway; someone who runs from danger, p. 41

fundamental basic; being the foundation on which something is built, p. 105

G

gangplank a movable bridge or walkway people cross to get on or off a ship, p. 92

geographic diversity a variety of landforms, climates, and vegetation, p. 70

gunny sack a bag or sack made of burlap or other coarse materials, p. 99

H

habitat the area in which a plant or an animal naturally grows or lives, p. 108

haze foglike air, often caused by pollution, p. 58

Homestead Act a law passed in 1862 giving 160 acres (65 hectares) of land on the Midwestern plains to any adult willing to live on and farm it for five years, p. 45

hydroelectricity electric power produced by moving water, usually generated by releasing water from a dam across a river, p. 23

I

immigrant a person who moves to a new country in order to settle there, p. 40

immunity a natural resistance to disease, p. 130

indentured servant a person who, in exchange for benefits received, must work for a period of years to gain freedom, p. 35

indigenous belonging to a certain place, p. 35

industrialization the process of building new industries in an area dominated by farming; the development of large industries, p. 96

Industrial Revolution the change from making goods by hand to making them by machine, p. 40

interdependent dependent upon each other, p. 60

L

labor force the supply of workers, p. 45

lacrosse ballgame played by two teams with long rackets, p. 79

land bridge a bridge formed by a narrow strip of land connecting one landmass to another, p. 33

landmass a large area of land, p. 10

lock an enclosed section of a canal used to raise or lower a ship to another level, p. 13

Louisiana Purchase the sale of land in 1803 by France to the United States; all the land between the Mississippi River and the eastern slope of the Rocky Mountains, p. 38

lowlands lands that are lower than the surrounding land, p. 11

M

mammoth a huge animal something like an elephant, now extinct, p. 33

Manifest Destiny a belief that the United States had a right to own all the land from the Atlantic Ocean to the Pacific Ocean, p. 40

maritime related to navigation or commerce on the sea, p. 140

mass transit a system of subways, buses, and commuter trains used to transport large numbers of people, p. 109

megalopolis a number of cities and suburbs that blend into one very large urban area, p. 87

migration movement of people from one country or region to another in order to make a new home, p. 33

missionary a person who tries to convert others to his or her religion, p. 35

mixed-crop farm a farm that grows several different kinds of crops, p. 100

N

NAFTA North American Free Trade Agreement, signed in 1994 by Canada, the United States, and Mexico to establish mutual free trade, p. 61

navigate to plot or direct the course of a ship or aircraft, p. 13

nomadic moving from one place to another frequently in search of food or pastureland, p. 78

O

obstacle something that is in the way, p. 135

Oceania the region of the world that includes Australia and the Pacific islands, p. 7

ore rock that contains valuable metal or minerals, p. 25

P

pastime recreation; activity that makes time pass pleasantly, p. 73

permafrost permanently frozen layer of ground below the top layer of soil, p. 19

petrochemical a substance, such as plastic, paint, or asphalt, that is made from petroleum, p. 95

plantation a large, one-crop farm with many workers, common in the Southern United States before the Civil War, p. 36

population density the average number of people per square mile or square kilometer, p. 88

prairie a region of flat or rolling land covered with tall grasses, p. 19

prosperity continued success or good fortune, especially concerning wealth, p. 39

province a political division of land in Canada, similar to a state in the United States, p. 19

Q

Quiet Revolution a peaceful change in the government of Quebec, Canada, in which the Parti Québécois won control of the legislature and made French the official language, p. 124

R

rain shadow an area on the side of a mountain away from the wind that receives little rainfall, p. 17

recession a downturn in business activity and economic prosperity, not as severe as a depression, p. 101

Reconstruction United States plan for rebuilding the nation after the Civil War, included a period when the South was governed by the United States Army, p. 43

referendum a ballot or vote in which voters decide for or against a particular issue, p. 125

represent to speak for someone else and guard their interests, p. 37

reserve land set aside for a specific purpose, as by the Canadian government for indigenous peoples, p. 77

Revolutionary War the war in which the American colonies won their independence from Britain, fought from 1775 to 1781, p. 37

rural of or like the countryside, p. 96

S

segregate to set apart and force to use separate schools, housing, parks, and so on because of race or religion, p. 43

separatist in Canada, someone who wants the province of Quebec to break away from the rest of the country, p. 125

settlement house a community center for poor immigrants to the United States, p. 45

shield a lowland area of exposed bedrock, p. 12

slum a usually crowded area of a city, often with poverty and poor housing, p. 44

sod top layer of soil containing grass plants and their roots, p. 127

sparsely thinly; in a scattered, uncrowded way, p. 120

subway commuter train that travels underground, p. 87

Sun Belt area of the United States stretching from the southern Atlantic Coast to the coast of California; known for its warm weather, p. 97

T

tariff a fee charged on imported goods, p. 61

tenement an apartment house that is poorly built and crowded, p. 44

totem pole a tall, carved wooden pole containing symbols, found among Native Americans of the Pacific Northwest, p. 132

tropics the area on the Earth between the $23\frac{1}{2}°$N and $23\frac{1}{2}°$S lines of latitude, where the climate is almost always hot, p. 17

tundra a cold, dry region covered with snow for more than half the year; a vast, treeless plain where the subsoil is always frozen, p. 19

U

unique having no equal; the only one of its kind, p. 11

V

vast huge; enormous in size, p. 10

Index

The *italicized* page numbers refer to illustrations. The *m, c,* or *p* preceding the number refers to maps (*m*), charts, tables, or graphs (*c*) or pictures (*p*).

A

abolitionists, 42, 212
Acadia, 51, 139–140, 210
acid rain, 58, 212
Activity Shop
    interdisciplinary, 66–67
    lab, 30–31
Adams, Samuel, 37
Addams, Jane, 45
Africa, *m 202–203*
    immigrants from, *c 7*
African Americans
    American civil rights movement and, 48–49
    participation of, in the Civil War, 43, *p 43*
    slavery and, 36, 41–43
    voting rights of, 39
agribusiness, 22, 212
agriculture. *See* farming
air pollution, 58, *m 58,* 109
    See also environmental issues
Alabama, 174
    aerospace industry in, 97
    farming in, 94
    mining in, 95
Alaska, 9, 10, 33, 46, 182
    climate of, 17
    glaciers in, 12
    natural resources of, 23
    U.S. acquisition of, 46
Alberta, 127–131, 188
    grain industry in, *p 61*
Ali, Muhammad, *p 93*
alliance, 38, 212
Allied Powers, 46
alluvial soil, 22, 212
American Constitution.
    See Constitution, American
American Revolution, 37, *p 52,* 89
"America's breadbasket." *See* Midwest (U.S.)
Anaheim Mighty Ducks, *p 79*

ancestry, most common U.S. and Canadian sources of, 7, *c 7*
Andereasen, Joseph, *p 74*
Anne of Green Gables, 78
Appalachian Mountains, 10, 29, 210
    coniferous forests in, 20
aquaculture, 141, 212
Arizona, 9, 182
    climate of, 17
    Native Americans in, *p 34*
    tourism in, *p 107*
Arkansas, 95, 174
art, 54
    in Canada, *p 77,* 78–79
    Inuit, *p 78*
    in New York City, 91
    in the United States, 73–74
Asia, 33, 137, *m 204–205*
    physical, *m 205*
    political, *m 204*
Atlanta, Georgia, 210
    cable television and, 97
    and the 1996 Summer Olympic Games, 93, *p 93*
Atlantic Ocean, 18, 29, 56, 60
Atlantic Provinces, 138–141
    economy of, 139, 140–141
    ethnic groups of, 139
    fishing in, 140–141
    Regional Profile of, *m 139, c 139*
atomic bomb, 48
Atwood, Margaret, 78
aurora borealis, 142, *p 142,* 212
Austin, Texas, 97
Australia
    physical-political, *m 206*
Austria-Hungary, 46
authors
    American, 35, 41–42, 74, 89
    Canadian, 78
automobile industry, in Detroit, Michigan, 103
autonomous, 121, 212
Azimuthal projection, 161

B

Baptiste, Jean, 126
Barton, Clara, 42
baseball, *p 74*

basin, 208
Battle of Quebec, 51, *p 51*
bauxite, *m 23,* 95
bay, 208
Bay of Fundy, 140
bears, black, *p 108*
beavers
    importance of, to French fur traders, 51
    importance of, to native peoples of Canada, 50, *p 50*
Benét, Stephen Vincent, 84–85
Benjamin, Florence, 72
Bicentennial, U.S., *p 49*
bilingualism, 212
    in Canada, 55, 76
    See also Quebec
Billy the Kid, 73
bird watching. *See* forests, bird watching and
bison, 33, 212
Black River Falls, Wisconsin, 99
bluegrass, 73
boll weevil, 95
Bond, Rebecca, 54
boomtowns, 134, 212. *See also* Gold Rush, Canadian
border, Canadian and U.S., *p 56,* 59
Boston, Massachusetts, 89, 210
boycott, 212
    American, of British goods, 37
    by Mexican-American farm workers, 109
Bressette, Thomas M., 77–78
British Columbia, 12, 59, 118, *m 118,* 132–137, 188
    Canadian Pacific Railway and, 135
    Gold Rush in, 136, *p 136*
    indigenous people of, 132, 134
    Provincial Profile of, *m 133, c 133*
    timber industry and, 25
British North American Act, 53
Broadway. *See* New York City, art in
Brooklyn Bridge, *p 90*
buffalo, *p 129*
    European slaughter of, in Canada, 129
    on the plains, *p 129*
Burgess Shale, 12
burrowing owls, 129
butte, 208, *p 208*

C

Cajuns, 51, 140
   music of, 73
Calgary, 131, 210
   Stampede, 131, *p 131*
California, *p 1*, 11, 183
   admitted to the Union, 41
   climate of, 17
   Gold Rush in, 107
   natural resources of, 21 *p 21*
Cambridge, Massachusetts, 89
Canada
   British control of, 51–52
   climate of, *m 6*, 15–17, *p 16*
   culture of, 78–79, *p 79*
   environmental issues of, 57–59
   ethnic groups of, 76–78, *c 76*
   France and, 51–53, 123
   government of, 120
   and Great Britain, 51–53
   immigrants in, *c 7*, 54, 76, *c 76*
   independence of, 54
   land use, *m 5*
   location of, *m 2*, 10
   natural resources of, 24–25, *p 25*
   physical map, *m 4*
   political map, *m 3, m 186*
   population distribution, *m 27*
   provinces and territories
      established in, *m 55*
   Regional Database, 186–191
   relative size of, *m 2*
   vegetation zones, 18–20, *m 18*
   World Wars I and II and, 54
"Canada's breadbasket." *See*
   Canadian Plains, Prairie Provinces
Canadian Mounted Police, *p 75*, 135
Canadian Pacific Railway, *p 53*, 135
Canadian Plains, 127–131
Canadian Shield, 12, 25, 29, 120, 210
cancer research, "Marathon of
   Hope" and, 79
canyon, 208
Cape Canaveral, Florida, 97
Caribbean Sea, 35
Cariboo Mountains, 134, 210
Carlotta, California, 21
Cartier, Jacques, 123
Cascade Mountains, 11
cataract, 208, *p 208*
Cathedral-Basilica of Mary, Queen
   of the World, 126
Catholics, French, 51

cattle, and the Great Plains, 19, *p 19*
Central America, *m 198–199*
Central Plains, 11, 14
Central Powers, 46
Chamberland, Paul, 76
Charleston, South Carolina, 98
Chavez, Cesar, 109
Chemainus, British Columbia, *p 77*
Cherokee nation
   Supreme Court case and, *m 39*
   See also Native Americans;
      Sequoyah
Chesapeake Bay, 96
Cheyenne, *m 70. See also* Native
   Americans
Chicago, Illinois, 102–103, *p 102,*
   p 154, 210
child labor, 45, 49
Chilkoot Pass, 144
China, *c 7*, 10
Chinatown. *See* New York City, ethnic
   groups in
Chinese Americans, *p 72*
Chinese New Year, *p 72*
Chippewas, 77. *See also* Native
   Americans
Chukchees, 71. *See also* indigenous
   peoples
circle graphs, 110–111
cities, U.S., 87–91, *p 87, m 88, m 89,*
   p 91, 96–97, 102–104, *p 102,*
   p 104, 108–109, *p 109*
civil rights movement, 48–49, 212
   and Mexican American farmworkers,
      48
Civil War, 212
   African American soldiers in, *p 43*
   causes of, 40–42
   Reconstruction and, 43
Clark, William, 38, *p 38*
Clayoquot Sound, 59
clear-cutting, 59, *p 59*, 212. *See also*
   logging industry
Cleveland, Ohio, *m 58*
   and pollution of the Cuyahoga
      River, 57
climate
   in Florida, 17
   of the Midwest, 71
   of the U. S. and Canada, 6, *m 6*
   zones, 15–18
   See also climate regions; Provincial
      Profiles; Regional Database;
      Regional Profiles

climate regions, 167, 168, *c 168*
CN Tower, *p 54*
coal, *m 23, m 106*
Coast Mountains, 12
cod fishing, 141, *p 141*
Cold War, 48, 212
colonies, early American, 36–37, *p 37*
Colorado, *p 34*, 183
Colorado River, 14
Columbia River, 14, 23, 108
   Grand Coulee Dam and, 23
Columbus, Christopher, 35
Comanches, *m 70. See also* Native
   Americans
combine harvester, *p 45*
Commonwealth of Nations, 55
communism, 48, 212
commuters, 87, 212
compass, European explorers and, *p 35*
computer industry
   in the South (U.S.), 97
   in the West, 109
concentration camps, 47
concept map, 80–81
Confederacy, 42
Confederate States of America.
   See Confederacy
Congressional Medal of Honor, *p 43*
coniferous forest, *m 18, c 169*
   in mountain regions, 20
Connecticut, 172
conservation, 59, 212
Constitution, American, 37, 89
constitutional monarchy, 55
Continental Divide, 14, 212
Cook, James, 133
Copland, Aaron, 73
copper, *m 23*, 24, *m 106*
corn, importance of, to European
   trade, 35
corporate farms, 101–102, 212
cotton
   importance of, to South's economy,
      94–95, *p 95*
   slaves and, 40–41
cotton gin, 40
Cree, 129
Crown of Columbus, The, 35
cultural diversity, 69, 212
cultural exchange, 70–71, 213
culture
   Canadian, 78–79
   U.S., 73–74
Cuyahoga River, 57, *p 57*, 210

D

Dallas, Texas, *p 96*
dams, 108
Dawson, 144, 210
Death Valley, 11, 17, 210
debate, 213
deciduous forest, *m 18*, 20, *c 169*
Declaration of Independence, 37, 89
Delaware, 96, 175
Delaware River, 89
democracy
 parliamentary, 55
 U.S. system of, 39
delta, 208, *p 208*
Dene, 143
dentalia, p 135
descent, 129, 213
desert scrub, 18, *m 18*, 20
Detroit, Michigan, 103, 210
diagrams
 interpreting, 62–63
 of how a locomotive works, 63
dictator, 47, 213
diorama, instructions for making a, 151
disabled Americans, 48
disease, spread of, by European
 settlers, 130
distribution maps, 26–27
District of Columbia. *See*
 Washington, D.C.
Dixieland. *See* jazz
dominion, 53, 213
Drake, Edwin L., *p 24*
drought, 127, 213
Duluth, Minnesota, 60
Durham, Earl of. *See* Earl of Durham

E

Earl of Durham, 53
Earth
 maps and globes of, 157, *m 157*
 movements of, 156, *c 156*
Eaton Centre, *p 15*
economy, 213
 free trade and the, 61
 Great Depression, 47
 interdependence and the, 60
 recession, 101
Ellis Island, 92
Emancipation Proclamation, 42
endangered species. *See* Grasslands
 National Park

energy resources. *See* natural
 resources
England
 colonies of, 35–36
environmental issues
 acid rain, 58, 200
 air pollution, 58, *p 58*, 109
 forest conservation and renewal, 59
 water pollution, 57
equal-area projection, 161
equal rights
 African Americans and, 39, 48–49
 indigenous peoples and, 77
 women and, 39, 47, 48
Equator, 16
Erdrich, Louise, 35
Ericsson, Leif, 138
ethnic groups, 213
 in British Columbia, 132–134
 in Canada, 76–78, *c 76*, *p 76*
 Chinese Americans, *p 72*
 defined, 71
 Mexican Americans, 48
 in New York City, 91–92
 in the United States, 70–73
 in World War II, 47
 See also Native Americans;
  indigenous peoples
Europe, *m 200–201*
 immigrants from, *c 7*
 physical, *m 201*
 political, *m 200*
European settlers, 36–37
 and Canada, 76
 diseases brought to the New
  World by, 130
 and Native Americans, *m 70*
 and the United States, 70–71
exile, 140, 213

F

factories, 54, 55, 57
farming
 in Canada, *p 12*, 24, 53, 130, *p 130*
 corporate, 101–102
 equipment, 45, 102
 irrigation systems, *p 22*
 in the Midwest (U.S.), 99–102
 mixed-crop, 100
 in Saskatchewan, *p 130*
 in the South (U.S.), 94–95, *c 101*
 technology, 99–100
farmworkers, civil rights of Mexican

American, 48–49, 109
"Father of Waters." *See* Mississippi
 River
federation, 120, 213
Festival du Voyageur, 131
Fête des Neiges, 126
fishing industry
 in the South (U.S.), 96
 in the Atlantic Provinces, 140–141
flood plain, 208
Florida, 9, 175
 aerospace industry in, 97
 climate in, 17
 farming in, 95
foreign trade, 60
forests
 bird watching and, *p 20*
 in Canada, 24, *p 24*
 clear-cutting of, 59
 coniferous, *m 18*, 20
 conservation of, 59
 deciduous, *m 18*, 20
 rain, *m 18*
 renewal of, 59
 of the South (U.S.), 96
 in the United States, 24
 use of in the Atlantic
  Provinces, 140
 See also national parks and forests
Fort Lincoln, *p 43*
Fort York, *p 52*
forty-niners, 107, 213
fossil fuels, 58, 213
Fourth of July, *p 49*, *p 73*
Fox, Terry, 79
France
 Canada and, 51–53, 123
 exploration by, 35, *m 36*
Francophones, 123–124, 213
Fraser River, 14, 134, 210
free trade, 213. *See also* North
 American Free Trade Agreement
 (NAFTA)
French, 35, 50, 51
French and Indian War, 36–37, 51,
 123
French Canadians, *p 12*, 52, 55,
 123–126
 cultural preservation of, 76, 126
freshwater, 13, 213
fruits, *m 106*
fugitive, 41, 213
Fugitive Slave Act, 41
fur trappers, 134

G

Gadsden Purchase, *m 41*
gangplank, 92, 213
"Gateway to the West." *See St. Louis, Missouri*
geographic diversity, 213
geography, five themes of, 154–155
Georgia, 93, 95, 96–97, 175
Germany, 46–47
    in World War I, 46
    in World War II, 47–48
glaciers, 12, 208, *p 208*
    and formation of the Great Lakes, 13
    Kahiltna, *p 9*
gold, *m 23*, 24, *m 106*
    early discovery of, in the Yukon, 53
    production in the West, *c 106*
Gold Hill, 144
Gold Rush
    American, 107
    Canadian, 134, *p 134*
grain industry, in Alberta, *p 61*
Grand Canyon National Park, *p 107*
Grand Coulee Dam, 23, 210
granite, 24
Grapes of Wrath, The, 74
graphs, circle, 110–111
grassland, *m 18*
Grasslands National Park, 129
Great Basin, 11, 20, 29
    sheep and, 20
Great Britain
    American Revolution and, 37
    Canada and, 51–53
    taxes and, *p 37*
Great Depression
    Canada and, 54
    United States and, 47, 48, 117
Great Lakes, 3, 13, *p 13*, 20, 29, 56, 57, 58, 59, *c 60*, 210
    Chicago and, 102
Great Lakes Fishery Commission, 56
Great Plains, 11, 19, 29, 49
    cattle and, 19
    climate of, 17
Great Salt Lake, 11
"Group of Seven." *See art, in Canada*
Guam, U.S. control of, 46
Gulf Coast. *See Gulf of Mexico*
Gulf of Mexico, 10, 14, 93, 98
    hurricanes and, 19
gunny sack, 99, 213

H

habitat, 108, 213
Haida, 50. *See also* indigenous peoples
Harlem Renaissance. *See Langston Hughes*
Harvard University, 89
Hawaii, 10, 46, 155, 183
    climate of, 17
    Loihi, 11
    physical map of, *m 165*
    U.S. acquisition of, 46
    volcanoes in, *p 11*
headwaters, of the Mississippi, 14
heartland. *See* Midwest (U.S.)
hectare, 45
hemispheres, 158, *m 158*
Henry, Patrick, 37
heritage, cultural, 72–73
Highlands, *c 169*
high technology, 97
    and farming in the Midwest (U.S.), 99–100
    See also Silicon Valley
hills, defined, 167, 208
Hitler, Adolf, 47
hockey, 79, *p 79*
Holocaust, 47
homelessness, in the United States, 49
Homestead Act, 45, 213
horses, importance of, to Native American culture, 70
Houston, Texas, 97
How the Other Half Lives, 44
Hudson Bay, 3, *m 3*, 51, 127
Hughes, Langston, 74
hunger, in the United States, 49
Huntsville, Alabama, 97, *p 98*
hunters and gatherers, 33
hurricanes, 18, 19
    and the Gulf of Mexico, 19
hydroelectricity, 23, *m 23*, *m 106*, 107, 213

I

Idaho, 183
Illinois, 178
ice age, migration of hunters during, 33
ice cap, *m 18*, *c 169*
ice hockey. *See* hockey
Immigrant Station. *See* Ellis Island
immigrants, *c 7*, 40, 45, 213
    and Canada, 54, 76, 122, 127

and the United States, 40, 70–73, *c 71*, 92
immunity, 213
    to disease, 130
Imperial Valley, 22, 210
indentured servants, 35, 36, 214. *See also* slavery
independence
    American, 37
    Canadian, 54
India, 10
Indian Removal Act, 39–40, *m 39*
Indian Territory, *m 39*
Indiana, 178
indigenous peoples, 35, 214
    of British Columbia, 132–135
    of Canada, 77, *p 77*, 123, 129, 130
    of the Prairie Provinces, 127–130
    and reserves, 77, 129
    See also Native Americans
industrialization, 54–55, 96, 214
Industrial Revolution, 40, 45, 48, 214
interdependent, 60, 214
Interior Plains, 11, 12, 16
Inuits, 19, 143, 145
    art of, 78, *p 78*
Iowa, 179
Iqaluit, 145, 210
iron, *m 23*, 24
irrigation, 22, *p 22*
island, 208
isthmus, 208

J

Jackson, Andrew, 39
Jamestown, Virginia, 36, 210
jazz, 97
Jefferson, Thomas, 37
    and the Lewis and Clark expedition, 38
Johnson, Andrew, 43
Jones, Mary Harris, 45
Jones, Pattie Frances Ridley, 114

K

Kahiltna Glacier, *p 9*
Kansas, 101, 179
Kariya, Paul, *p 79*
Kennedy, John F., 59
Kentucky, 95, 175

King, Martin Luther, Jr., 48
"King Cotton." See cotton,
importance of to South's economy
Klondike Gold Rush, 144
Kocour, Ruth, 9
Korean War, 48
Kuralt, Charles, 30

L

L'Anse aux Meadows, 138, p 138,
210
labor force, 45, 214
lacrosse, 79, 214
Lake Erie, p 13, 57, 60, 210
Lake Huron, 13
Lake Michigan, 13, p 102
Lake Ontario, p 13, p 55, 60
Lake Superior, 13, 60, 79
lake trout, 56, 57
land bridge, 214
between Siberia and Alaska, 33
landforms, 10–12, 167
diversity of North American, 70
landmass, 10, 214
land use, in the United States and
Canada, 5, m 5
languages, of Canada, 51, 55, 75,
123–124
latitude, 159. See also maps and
globes
Laurentian Highlands, 10
lead, m 23, 24, 95, m 106
LeFevre, Camille, 99, 102, 104
Lesage, Jean, 124
Lewis and Clark expedition, 38, 106
Lewis, Meriwether, 38, p 38. See also
Lewis and Clark expedition
Lightfoot, Gordon, 79
Lincoln, Abraham, 42
assassination of, 43
See also Civil War
Lindbergh, Charles, 47, p 47
literature, 84–85, 114–117
Little, Lessie Blanche Jones, 114,
115
Little Italy. See New York City, ethnic
groups in
locks, 214
of the St. Lawrence Seaway, 13, c 60
logging industry
in British Columbia, 25
clear-cutting, 59, p 59
in Quebec, 25

in the West (U.S.), 107
Loihi, 11
Lone Star Republic, 40
longitude, 159. See also maps and
globes
Louisiana, 51, 175
Cajun music in, 73
drilling in, 95
farming in, 95, p 115
fishing in, 96
Louisiana Purchase, 38–39, 214
Louisiana Territory, 106
Lower Canada, 52, 121
lowlands, 11, 214
Loyalists, British, 52

M

Macdonald-Cartier bridge, 119
Mackenzie River, 13
as shipping route, 22
Mackenzie, William, 52
Maine, 172
Malcolm, Andrew H., 75
mammoth, 33, 214
Manifest Destiny, 40, 214
Manitoba, 127–131, 188
maple sugar, in French-Canadian
cooking, 126
maps
using distribution, 26–27
of Indian removal during the
1830s, m 39
of land use in the United States
and Canada, m 5
of Native Americans and
Europeans in 1753, m 70
of North America in 1783, m 36
physical, of Africa, m 203
physical, of Asia, m 205
physical, of Hawaii, m 165
physical, of North and South
America, m 199
physical, of the United States and
Canada, m 4
physical, of the world, m 194–195
political, of Africa, m 202
political, of Asia, m 204
political, of North and South
America, m 198
political, of Russia, m 164
political, of the United States and
Canada, m 3, m 196–197

political, of the world, m 192–193
of the Underground Railroad, m 42
of vegetation in the United States
and Canada, m 18
See also Regional Database;
Regional Profiles; Provincial
Profiles
maps and globes, 153–167
hemispheres, 158, m 158
parts of, 162
physical, 165
political, 164
projections, 160–161
scale of, 163
special purpose, 166
"Marathon of Hope," 79
maritime, 140, 214
Maryland, 96, 175
Massachusetts, 89, 172
early settlement of, 36
Pilgrims in, 36
mass transit, 109, 214
McElroy, Kim, 59
meat-packing. See Chicago, Illinois
megalopolis, 87, 214
Mercator projection, 160
meridians of longitude, 159
mesa, 208
métis, 53
Mexican Americans, 48
Mexico
free trade and, 61
immigrants from, c 7
Texas and, 40
Miami Beach, Florida, 15, 97
Michigan, 103, 179
Midwest (U.S.), 19, 71, 45 m 86,
99–104, 178–181, m 178
cities in, 102–104
farming in, 99–102
Regional Profile of, m 100, c 100
migrant farmworkers, 109
migration, 33, 214
military takeover, of Chippewa land,
77–78
millionaire, origin of the term, 91
mineral resources
of the South (U.S.), 95
of the United States, 23–24
See also natural resources
Minneapolis–St. Paul, Minnesota,
104, p 104, 210
Minnesota, 14, 60, 101, 179
missile silos, 48

missionaries, 35, 214
Mississippi, 94, 95, 176
Mississippi River, 14, *p 14,* 22, 36, 38, 97, *p 97,* 210
Missouri, 180
Missouri River, 22, 38
mixed-crop farming, 100, 214
monarchy. *See* constitutional monarchy
"money capital." *See* New York Stock Exchange (NYSE)
Montana, 184
Montgomery, Lucy Maud, 78
Montreal, Quebec, 119, 123, 210
Moore, Annie, 92
Mother Jones. *See* Jones, Mary Harris
"Mother of Canada." *See* St. Lawrence River
"Motor City." *See* Detroit, Michigan
Mount Hood National Forest, *p 59*
Mount Logan, 12
Mount McKinley, 9, *p 9*
"Mount Royal." *See* Montreal, Quebec
Mount St. Helens, 11
mountains, 167, 208
    Appalachian, 10, 29
    Cariboo, 134
    Cascade, 11
    Coast, 12
    Laurentian Highlands, 10–11
    Mount Logan, 12
    Mount McKinley, 9, *p 9*
    Mount St. Helens, 11
    Ozark, 98
    Rocky, 8, 10, 14
    Sierra Nevada, 11
Muir Woods National Monument, California, *p 21*
Munro, Alice, 78
music
    of Aaron Copland, 73
    bluegrass, 73
    jazz, 97
    zydeco, 73

N

NAFTA. *See* North American Free Trade Agreement
NASA. *See* National Aeronautics and Space Administration
National Aeronautics and Space Administration (NASA), 97

National Film Board, 78
National Hockey League (NHL), *p 79*
national parks and forests
    Canada's Grasslands National Park, 129
    careers in, 151
    Grand Canyon National Park, *p 107*
    Mount Hood National Forest, *p 59*
    Volcanoes National Park, *p 11*
    Yosemite National Park, *p 105*
Native Americans, 14, 21
    building styles of, *p 34*
    in Canada, 50, 53, 77, *p 77*
    Cherokee nation, *m 39, p 39*
    Chukchee, 71
    farming and, 35
    Indian Removal Act and, 39–40, *m 39*
    Inuits, 19, 78, *p 78,* 143, 145
    number systems of, 71
    population of, in 1753, *m 70*
    pre-European cultures of, 35
    San Gabrielino group, 71
    Saulteaux, 129
    trade and, 38, 70
    villages of, 30
    writing system of, *p 39*
    See also indigenous people
natural gas, 23
natural resources
    of Canada, 23–25, *m 23*
    in the South (U.S.), 94–97
    of the United States, 21–23, *m 23*
    of the West (U.S.), 106–108, *m 106*
    See also farming; forests; mineral resources; Provincial and Regional Profiles
navigate, 13, 214
Nebraska, 180
Nevada, 17, 184
New Brunswick, 51, 53, 138–141, 188
New Deal, 47
"New France." *See* Quebec
Newfoundland, 53, 58, 138–141
Newfoundland and Labrador, 189
New Hampshire, 173
New Jersey, 173
New Mexico, *p 34,* 184
New Orleans Jazz. *See* jazz
New Orleans, Louisiana, 97, 98
New World, 70–71
New York, 173
New York City, *p 68,* 91, *p 91,* 211
    art in, 91

    Brooklyn Bridge, *p 90*
    ethnic groups in, 92
    immigration and, 92
    traffic jams in, 87, *p 87*
New York Stock Exchange (NYSE), 91
NHL. *See* National Hockey League
Niagara Falls, 60, 211
nickel, *m 23, m 106*
nomadic, 78, 214
Nootka, 133. *See also* indigenous peoples
North America, 10, 32, *m 192, m 194*
    European land claims in, in 1682 and 1763, *m 140*
    oil reserves in, 23
    physical, *m 199*
    political, *m 198*
    in 1783, *m 36*
North American Free Trade Agreement (NAFTA), 61, 214
North Carolina, 96, 176
North Dakota, 180
Northeast (U.S.), *m 86, m 88, c 88* 172–173, *m 172*
    cities and, 87–92
Northern Territories, 142–145
    aurora borealis in, 142
    governments of, 144
    indigenous groups of, 143, 145
    Regional Profile of, *m 143, c 143*
Northwest Territories, 78, 142–145, 189
Nova Scotia, 51, 53, 138–141, 189
number systems, Native American, 71
Nunavut, 78, 142–145, 190, 211
    forming a new territory, 145
    legislative building in, *p 145*
NYSE. *See* New York Stock Exchange

O

Ohio, 181
Ohio River, 14, 22
Ohio River Valley, 51
Oklahoma, 176
    drilling in, 95
    Native Americans in, 40
Olympic Games, 1996, 93
Ontario, 52, 58, 119–122, 190, 211
    Canadian government in, 120–121
    Regional Profile, *m 121, c 121*

timber industry and, 25
ore, 25, 214
Oregon, 11, p 59, 184
Ottawa, Ontario, p 16, 119, 120, p 120, 121, 211
Ozark Mountains, 98

P

Pacific Coast, 38
Pacific Northwest, 24, 107, 211
Pacific Ocean, 10, 16, 29
trade routes across, m 136
Pacific Rim, 211
British Columbia and, 136, 137
Paine, Thomas, 37
Pamlico Sound, 116
paper mills, 107
Papineau, Louis, 52
parallels of latitude, 159
Parliament, English, 55
parliamentary democracy, 55
Parmele, North Carolina, 114–117
Peach State. See Georgia
Pearl Harbor, Japanese attack on, 48
peninsula, 209
Penn, William, 36
Pennsylvania, 89, 173
Pennsylvania Colony, 36, 211
permafrost, 19, 214
petrochemicals, 95, 214
petroleum, 23, m 23, m 106
Petronas Twin Towers, 103
Pettigrove, Francis W., 108
Philadelphia, Pennsylvania, 37, 89, 211
Philippines, 46
Phoenix, Arizona, p 109
phosphates, m 23, m 106
physical maps
of Africa, m 208
of Asia, m 205
of Europe, m 201
of Hawaii, m 165
of the United States and Canada, m 4
Pilgrims, 36, 106
Pittsburgh, Pennsylvania, m 58
plains, 167, 209
plantations, 36, 214
cotton, 40–41
plateau, 167, 209
Platte River, 14

Plymouth, Massachusetts, 36
Poland
invasion of, by Germany, 47
political maps
of Africa, m 202
of Europe, m 200
of North America, m 198
of Russia, m 164
of South America, m 198
of the United States, m 196–197
political systems
communism, 48
constitutional monarchy, 55
democracy, 39
parliamentary democracy, 55
pollution, 49
population
immigrant, c 7
of New York City, 91
of the United States, 10
population density, 88, 214
of the Northeast (U.S.), 88
of Ontario, 121
of Quebec, 124
population distribution, 26–27
Portland, Oregon, 108, 211
Potomac River, 98
power looms, 40
Prairie Provinces, 127–131, m 128, c 128
immigration to, 130
wheat and, 130
prairies, 19, 45, 130, 215
prairie schooner, p 40, 84
precipitation, 16–17, c 111
in various climate regions, c 168
Prime Meridian, 158, 159
Prince Edward Island, 139–141, 190
project possibilities, 150–151
provinces, 215
Canadian, 19
dates joined Canada, 55
See also Provincial Profiles;
Regional Profiles
Provincial Profiles
British Columbia, 133
Ontario, 121
Quebec, 124
pueblo, p 34
Puerto Rican Day Parade, p 68
Puerto Rico
immigrants from, p 68
U.S. control of, 46

Punjabi language, 137

Q

Quebec, 118, m 118, 123–126, 191, 211
Battle of, 51, p 51
French influence in, 123–126, p 123
independence of, 76, p 125
logging industry and, 25
Provincial Profile of, m 124, c 124
society of, 123–124
Quebec Act, 51
Quebec Movement, 76
Quiet Revolution, 124, 215

R

railroads, 40, p 63, 114–118
Canadian Pacific, 53, p 53, 135, p 135
Transcontinental, 48
U.S., 45, m 103
rainfall, in various climate regions, c 168
rain forest, m 18
tropical, c 169
rain shadow, 17, 215
Raleigh, North Carolina, 97
ranches, 130
cattle, 19
sheep, 99
recession, 215
U.S., in the 1980s, 101
Reconstruction, 43, 48, 215
Red River Basin, m 41
referendum, 125, 215
Regina, Saskatchewan, 129, 211
Regional Database
of Canada, 186–191, m 186
of the Midwest (U.S.), 178–181, m 178
of the Northeast (U.S.), 172–173, m 172
of the South (U.S.), 174–177, m 174
of the West (U.S.), 182–185, m 182
Regional Profiles
Atlantic Provinces, m 139, c 139
Midwest (U.S.), m 100, c 100
Prairie Provinces, m 128, c 128
Northeast (U.S.), m 88, c 88

Northern Territories, *m 143, c 143*
South (U.S.), *m 94, c 94*
West (U.S.), *m 106, c 106*
regions of the United States. *See* Midwest; Northeast; Regional Database; Regional Profiles; South; West
relative location, of the United States and Canada, 2, *m 2*
Republic of Texas, *m 39*
reserves, 215
 indigenous peoples and, 77, 129
Revolutionary War, 37, 215. *See also* American Revolution
Rhode Island, 37, 173
Riel, Louis, 53
Riis, Jacob, 44, *p 44*
Rindisbacher family, 127, 130
river mouth, 209
rivers
 Colorado, 14
 Columbia, 14, 23, 108
 Cuyahoga, 57, 210
 Fraser, 14, 134, 210
 importance of, to settlement, 30
 Mackenzie, 13, 22
 Mississippi, 14, *p 14*, 22, 36, 38, 97, *p 97*, 210
 Missouri, 14, 22, 28
 Ohio, 14, 22
 Platte, 14
 Potomac, 98
 St. Lawrence, 12, 51, 211
 Willamette, 108
Robinson projection, 161
Rocky Mountains, 8, 10, 14, 29, 57, 211
 coniferous forests in, 20
rodeo
 in Alberta, 131, *p 131*
Roosevelt, Franklin D., 47–48
Roosevelt, Theodore, 105
"Rupert's Land." *See* Saskatchewan
rural, 96, 215

S

St. Lawrence Lowlands, 12, *p 12*, 24, 211
 farming and, 24
St. Lawrence River, 12, 51, 211. *See also* St. Lawrence Seaway
St. Lawrence Seaway, *p 13, c 60,* 211

St. Louis, Missouri, 103, 211
St. Peter's Basilica. *See* Cathedral-Basilica of Mary, Queen of the World
salt, 95
San Antonio, Texas, *p 69*
San Francisco, California, 107
San Gabrielino, 71
San Jose, California, 109, 211
Saskatchewan, 118, *m 118,* 127–131, 191
 indigenous peoples in, 129
 traditions of, 131
Saskatoon, Saskatchewan, 130, *p 130*
Saulteaux, 129. *See also* indigenous peoples
savanna, *c 169*
"Sea of grass." *See* Midwest (U.S.)
Sears Tower, 103. *See also* Chicago, Illinois
segregation, 43, 48
separatists, 125, 215
Sequoya, *p 39*
settlement house, 45, 215
settlers
 in Canada, 127, 129–130
 in the United States, 35–36
Seven Years' War, 51, *p 51*
Seward, William, 46
sheep
 and the Great Basin, 20
 Suffolk, *p 99*
shield, 12, 215
short-horned lizards, 129
Siberia, 33
Sierra Nevada Mountains, 11, 107, 211
Silicon Valley, 109
silver, *m 23, m 106*
skyscraper, 103
slavery
 in Canada, 42
 in the United States, 36, 40–41, 43
 Underground Railroad and, *m 42, p 42*
slum, 44, 215
Social Security, 47
Social Studies Skills Activities
 interpreting diagrams, 62–63
 organizing information, 80–81
 understanding circle graphs, 110–111
 using distribution maps, 26–27

writing for a purpose, 146–147
"soddies," 127
soil
 alluvial, 22
 top-, 22
South (U.S.), *m 86,* 93–98, 174–177, *m 163*
 farming in, 94–95
 mineral resources of, 95
 Regional Profile, *m 94, c 94*
 urban areas of, 96–98
South America, 33, 35
 physical, *m 199*
 political, *m 198*
South Carolina, 96, 176
Soviet Union, communism and, 48
space program, American. *See* National Aeronautics and Space Administration
Spain, 35, *m 36*
Spanish-American War, 46, 48
spinning machines, 40
Spirit of St. Louis, *p 47*
sports, *p 1, p 74,* 79, *p 79*
Stadacona, 123. *See also* indigenous peoples
standard of living, U.S., 23–24
Stanley Cup, 79
Statue of Liberty, 92, *p 92*
steamboats, 40, *p 97*
Steinbeck, John, 74
Stowe, Harriet Beecher, 41–42
strait, 209
student art, 54, 74
"stumptown," 134
subway, 87, 215
Suffolk sheep. *See* sheep, Suffolk
sugar cane, *m 106*
sulfur, 95
Sun Belt, 97, 98, 215. *See also* South (U.S.)

T

tariffs, 61, 215
technology, 97, 99–100
 pollution and, 57–59
tenements, 44, *p 44,* 215
Tennessee, 95, 177
Terre Québec. *See* Quebec Movement
Texas, 177
 aerospace industry in, 97
 drilling in, 95
 farming in, 94

fishing in, 96
independence of, 40
textile industry
effect of Industrial Revolution on, 40
in the South (U.S.), 96–97
in the United States, 40
Thoreau, Henry David, 89
time line
instructions for making a, 151
United States from the 1860s to 1990s, 48
Titusville, Pennsylvania, p 24
topsoil, 22
Tornado Alley, m 17
tornadoes, m 17
Toronto, Ontario, 15, p 15, p 55, 122, p 122, 211
underground tunnels in, 15
totem poles, 132, p 132, 215
tourism, 97–98
trade
among Native Americans, 38
between the United States and Canada, 60–61
See also North American Free Trade Agreement
traditions, prairie, 131
traffic jams, New York City and, 87, p 87
Trail of Tears, 40
trains. See railroads; Transcontinental Railroad
Transcontinental Railroad, 48
transportation, 40, 66–67, 97, p 97
Treaty of Guadalupe Hidalgo, m 41
Treaty of Paris, m 36, 37, 51
Treaty of Versailles, 46
trees
abundance of, in Canada, 25
abundance of, in the United States, 24
See also clear-cutting, forests; national parks and forests
tributary, 14, 209
tropics, the, 17, 215
Truman, Harry S., 48
Tubman, Harriet, p 42, m 42
tundra, m 18, 19, c 169, 215
tungsten, m 23, m 106
Turkey, 46
Twain, Mark, 78
Twin Cities. See Minneapolis–St. Paul, Minnesota

Ukraine, 130
Uncle Tom's Cabin, 41–42
Underground Railroad, m 42
underground tunnels, in Toronto, 15
Union Army, 42
United States
bicentennial of, p 49
cities of, 87–91, m 86, p 87, m 89, p 91, 96–97, p 96, 102–104, p 102, p 104, 108–109, p 109
Civil War in, 40–43, m 42
climate of, m 6, 15, 17–18, m 17
culture of, 73–74, p 73, p 74
environmental issues of, 57–59
government of, 37
growth of, m 41
immigrants in, c 7, 69–74, p 69, m 70, c 71, p 72
land use, m 5
location, m 2, 10
natural resources of, 21–24, p 21, m 23, p 24
physical map of, m 4
political map of, m 3, m 196–197
population of, 10
Regional Database, 170–185
regions of, m 86
relative size of, m 2
time line of, c 48
tornadoes in, m 17
vegetation zones in, 18–20, m 18
in World War I, 46–47, p 46
in World War II, 47–48
Upper Canada, 52, 121
uranium, m 23, m 106
Utah, p 34, 185

"Valley of Heart's Content." See San Jose, California
Vancouver, British Columbia, 59, 132, 133, 211
climate of, 16, p 137
Vancouver Island. See Vancouver, British Columbia
Vatican City, 126
vegetation
in the United States and Canada, 18–20, m 18

world, regions of, 167, 169, c 169
Vermont, 173
Victoria, British Columbia, 211
Vietnam War, 48
Vikings, 138
Virginia, 96, 177
volcanoes, 209, p 209
Hawaii Volcanoes National Park, p 11
Loihi, 11
Mount St. Helens, 11
voting rights
of African Americans, 39
of women, 39, 47

W

wagon trains, 84–85
Walcott, Dr. Charles, 12
Walden, 89
Walden Pond, 89
war bonds, p 46
War of 1812, 39, 52, p 52
wars
Civil War, 40–42, 43, p 43
Korean War, 48
Spanish-American War, 46, 48
Vietnam War, 48
War of 1812, 39, 52, p 52
World War I, 46, p 46, 48
World War II, 47–48, 54, 77
Washington, 185
farming in, p 45
natural resources of, 23
Washington, D.C., 87, 98, 211
Washington, George, 37
water, 22–23
pollution, 57
See also environmental issues
water sources, major, of the United States and Canada, 3, m 3
weather satellites, 19
weather station, instructions for creating a, 151
web. See concept map
Welland Canal, p 13
West (U.S.), m 86, 105–109, 182–185, m 182
natural resources of, 106–108
Regional Profile of, m 106, c 106
urban areas of, 108–109
West Virginia, p 10, 95, 177

Weyburn, 131
wheat, importance of, as Canadian
    export, *p 61,* 130, 131
Willamette River, 108
Wilson, Woodrow, 46
wind, 16
    and air pollution, *m 58*
Winnipeg, 16, 131, 211
Winter Carnival, in Quebec, 126,
    p 126
Wisconsin, *p 73,* 99, 181
women

    in Civil War, 42
    rights of, 39, 47, 48
    in the Underground Railroad, *p 42*
world, *m 192–193, m 194–195*
World Financial Center, 103
World War I, 46, 48
World War II, 47–48, 77
    Canada and, 54
**"Wreck of the Edmund
    Fitzgerald, The,"** 78–79
Wyeth, Andrew, 73
Wyoming, 185

Y

Yosemite Falls. *See* Yosemite
    National Park
Yosemite National Park, *p 105,* 108
Yukon Territory, 12, 142–145, 191,
    211
    gold in, 53, 144, *p 144*

Z

zinc, 95
zydeco, 73

Acknowledgments

Cover Design

Bruce Bond, Suzanne Schineller, and Olena Serbyn

Cover Photo

Jon Chomitz

Maps

MapQuest.com, Inc.
Map information sources: Columbia Encyclopedia, Encyclopaedia Britannica, Microsoft® Encarta®, National Geographic Atlas of the World, Rand McNally Commercial Atlas, The Times Atlas of the World.

Staff Credits

The people who made up the **World Explorer** team—representing editorial, editorial services, design services, on-line services/multimedia development, product marketing, production services, project office, and publishing processes—are listed below. Bold type denotes core team members.

Joyce Barisano, Margaret Broucek, Ed DeLeon, **Paul Gagnon, Mary Hanisco, Dotti Marshall,** Kirsten Reichert, Susan Swan, and Carol Signorino.

Additional Credits

Art and Design: Emily Soltanoff. Editorial: Debra Reardon, Nancy Rogier. Market Research: Marilyn Leitao. Publishing Processes: Wendy Bohannan.

Program Development and Production

Editorial and Project Management: Summer Street Press
Production: Pronk&Associates

Text

35, From *The Crown of Columbus* by Louise Erdrich and Michael Dorris. Copyright © 1991 by Michael Dorris and Louise Erdrich. Reprinted by permission of HarperCollins Publishers, Inc. **44,** From *How the Other Half Lives* by Jacob A. Riis. Copyright © 1971 by Dover Publications, Inc. Reprinted by permission. **69, 72** From *New Kids on the Block: Oral Histories of Immigrant Teens* by Janet Bode. Copyright © 1989 by Janet Bode. Published by Franklin Watts. **75,** From *The Land and People of Canada* by Andrew H. Malcolm. Text copyrighted © 1992 by Andrew H. Malcolm. Reprinted with permission of HarperCollins Publishers, Inc. **78,** From "Chippewas Push Claims for Land in Canada," by Clyde H. Farnsworth, *New York Times,* August 27, 1995. Copyright © 1995 by The New York Times Co. Reprinted by permission. **84,** From *The Book of Americans* by Rosemary and Stephen Vincent Benét. Copyright © 1933 by Rosemary and Stephen Vincent Benét. Copyright © renewed 1961 by Rosemary Carr Benét. Reprinted by permission of Brandt & Brandt Literary Agents, Inc. **85,** "The chief of the world," "Glooscap's wigwam," from *Whirlwind Is a Ghost Dancing* by Natalia Belting. Copyright © 1974 by Natalia Belting. Used by permission of Dutton Children's Books, a division of Penguin Books USA Inc. **95,** From *Fannie Lou Hamer: From Sharecropping to Politics* by David Rubel. Copyright © 1990 by Silver Burdett Press, Simon & Schuster Elementary. Used by permission. **105,** From *History of the United States* by Thomas V. DiBacco, Lorna C. Mason, and Christian G. Appy. Copyright © 1991 by Houghton Mifflin Company. Reprinted by permission. **114,** From *Childtimes: A Three-Generation Memoir* by Eloise Greenfield and Lessie Jones Little. Copyright © 1979 by Eloise Greenfield and Lessie Jones Little. Reprinted by permission of HarperCollins Publishers, Inc. **123,** From *Quebec, I Love You* by Miyuki Tanobe. Copyright © 1976 by Miyuki Tanobe, published by Tundra Books. Reprinted by permission.

Photo Research

Feldman & Associates, Inc.

Photos

v bottom left, © Rosemary Calvert/Tony Stone Images, **v top right,** © Robert Brenner/PhotoEdit, **Cover,** Jon Chomitz, **1 background,** Artbase Inc., **1 top left,** John Edwards/Tony Stone Images, **1 top right,** © The Granger Collection, **1 top center,** © Rob Van Patten/The Image Bank, **1 bottom left,** © Bill Brooks, **1 bottom right,** © Bob Thomason/Tony Stone Images, **4 center right,** © Mark Thayer, Boston, **8 center right,** © John Edwards/Tony Stone Images, **9 bottom right,** © Olaf Soot/Tony Stone Images, **10 bottom,** © Francis Lepine/Valan Photos, **11 top left,** © G. Brad Lewis/Tony Stone Images, **12 bottom right,** © Phillip Norton/ Valan Photos, **13 top,** © Thomas Kitchin/Tom Stack & Associates, **14 top,** © Science VU/Visuals Unlimited, **15 bottom right,** © Donald Nausbaum/Tony Stone Images, **16 bottom left,** © John Eastcott/Yva Momatiuk/Valan Photos, **16 bottom right,** © D.S. Henderson/The Image Bank, **19 top left,** © Stephen Krasemann/Valan Photos, **20 top right,** © M. Julien/Valan Photos, **21 bottom right,** © Harald Sund/The Image Bank, **22 center,** © Bruce Forster/Tony Stone Images, **24 top,** © H. Armstrong Roberts, **25 top left,** © Vince Streano/Tony Stone Images, **30 bottom,** © Ronald E. Partis/Unicorn Stock Photos, **31 top left,** © David Young-Wolff/PhotoEdit, **31 top right,** © David Young-Wolff/ PhotoEdit, **33 bottom right,** © Steve McCutcheon/Visuals Unlimited, **34 top left,** © John Garrett/Tony Stone Images, **35 bottom right,** © Michael Holford/National Maritime Museum, **37 top right,** © The Bostonian Society/Old State House, **38 bottom left,** © The Granger Collection, **39 top right,** © The Granger Collection, **40 bottom left,** © Michael Keller/West Virginia State Museum, **42 bottom left,** © The Granger Collection, **43 top center,** © Corbis-Bettman, **43 center right,** © Seth Goltzer/ William Gladstone/West Point Museum Collections, **44 bottom left,** © The Granger Collection, **45 bottom center,** © The Granger Collection, **45 bottom right,** © The Oakland Museum History Department, **46 bottom right,** National Archives #111-SC-25026, **46 center left,** © CORBIS/MAGMA, **47 top left,** © The Granger Collection, **49 top left,** © UPI/Corbis-Bettman, **50 bottom,** © John D. Cunningham/Visuals Unlimited, **51 top left,** © Library of Congress, **52 top right,** © Winston Fraser/Fraser Photos, **53 bottom,** © Hulton Getty/Tony Stone Images, **54 bottom right,** Toronto and the CN Tower, by Rebecca Bond, age 10, of Ajax, Ontario, Canada, **56 bottom left,** COMSTOCK IMAGES/Grant Heilman, **57 bottom right,** © Cleveland Public Library/ Photograph Collection, **57 bottom left,** © Audrey Gibson/Visuals Unlimited, **59 bottom,** © Rich Iwasaki/Tony Stone Images, **61 top left,** © Glen Allison/Tony Stone Images, **62 center right,** © Michael Newman/PhotoEdit, **66 center left,** © SuperStock International, **66 bottom left,** © The Bettmann Archive/Corbis-Bettmann, **66 center,** © Dennis MacDonald/PhotoEdit, **66 bottom right,** © Ann Trulove/Unicorn Stock Photos, **68 center right,** © Robert Brenner/PhotoEdit, **69 bottom right,** © Michael Newman/ PhotoEdit, **72 top right,** © Lawrence Migdale/Tony Stone Images, **73 bottom,** © Paul Damien/Tony Stone Images, **74 top right,** Here's the Pitch, by Joseph Andereasen, age 11, USA. Courtesy of the International Children's Art Museum, **75 bottom right,** © Back From Abroad/The Image Bank, **77 bottom left,** © Dave G. Houser/Dave Houser Photography, **78 center left,** © J. Eastcott/ Yva Momatiuk/Valan Photos, **79 top left,** © Elsa Hasch/AllSport USA, **85 top left,** © The Granger Collection, **87 bottom,** © Wayne Eastep/Tony Stone Images, **88 center left,** © Dorling Kindersley,